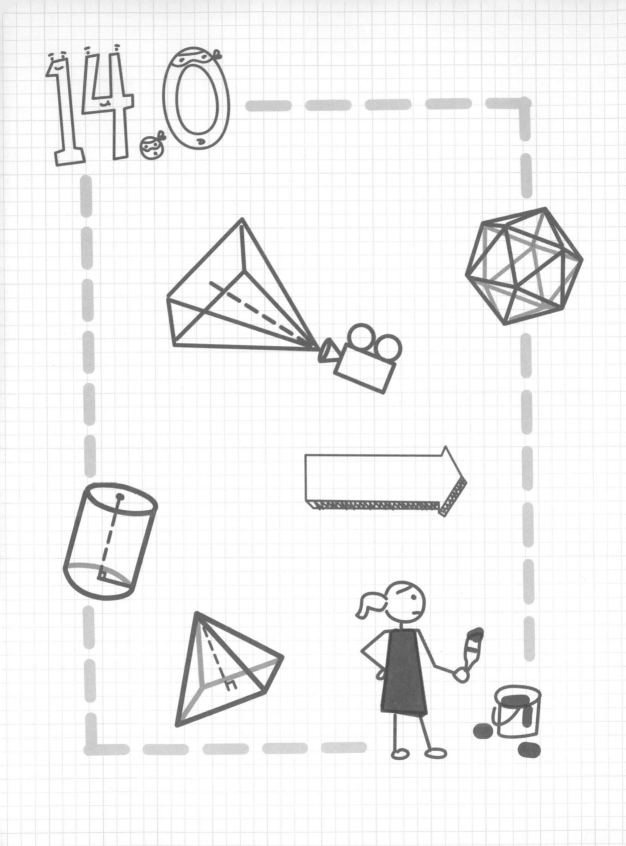

THE
BIG FAT
MIDDLE SCHOOL
MATH
WORKBOOK

WORKMAN PUBLISHING
NEW YORK

Library of Congress Cataloging-in-Publication Data is available.

ISBN: 978-1-5235-1358-1

Designer: John Passineau

Workman books are available at special discounts when purchased in bulk for premiums, sales promotions, fundraising, catalogs, subscription boxes, and more. Workman also offers special discounts for schools and educators purchasing books in bulk. For more information, please email specialmarkets@workman.com.

Workman Publishing Co., Inc.
225 Varick Street
New York, NY 10014-4381
workman.com

WORKMAN, BRAIN QUEST, and BIG FAT NOTE-BOOK are registered trademarks of Workman Publishing Co., Inc.

Printed in Malaysia

First printing July 2021

10 9 8 7 6 5 4 3 2 1

WELCOME TO THE BIG FAT WORKBOOK.

This workbook is designed to support you as you work your way through *Everything You Need to Ace Math In One Big Fat Notebook* or through your math class. Consider the *Notebook* your main source book and this *Workbook* extra practice.

Each chapter in this workbook corresponds to the content of the same chapter number in the *Notebook*. It begins with a brief recap of the key concepts, followed by an example solved step by step. Then there is a series of extra practice problems for you to solve that will help you really master the concept.

The solution process section in the back of the book guides you through each step of finding the solution for every question. No more trying to figure out where you went wrong. The path to the correct answer is clearly laid out.

Whether you're reviewing for a test or need to strengthen your problem-solving skills, look no further than this companion book. You'll encounter the same fun approach to math and easy-to-understand language that you love in *Everything You Need to Ace Math in One Big Fat Notebook*.

Together you'll have everything you need to ace that math class!

CONTENTS

UNIT 3: EXPRESSIONS and EQUATIONS **153**

UNIT 4: GEOMETRY **227**

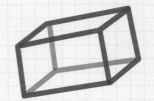

UNIT 5: STATISTICS and PROBABILITY **289**

UNIT 6: THE COORDINATE PLANE and FUNCTIONS **313**

SOLUTIONS:

Unit

1

The Number System

CHAPTER 1

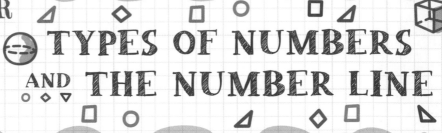

TYPES OF NUMBERS AND THE NUMBER LINE

There are many types of numbers. Here are the types used most often.

> **REAL NUMBERS:**
> All the numbers that can be found on a number line. Real numbers are made up of *Rational Numbers* and *Irrational Numbers*.

Rational Numbers

Any number that *can* be written as a fraction or ratio

EXAMPLES: 1.25 or $1\frac{1}{4}$; 6 or $\frac{6}{1}$; $-\frac{20}{2}$ or -10; $\frac{1}{2}$ or 0.5; $\frac{1}{3}$ or 0.333 . . .

THINK: All integers are rational numbers.

INTEGERS (no fractions or decimals, includes negative numbers):
. . . –4, –3, –2, –1, 0, 1, 2, 3, 4 . . .

WHOLE NUMBERS (no fractions, decimals, or negative numbers):
0, 1, 2, 3, 4 . . .

NATURAL NUMBERS (only whole numbers from 1 and up): 1, 2, 3, 4, 5 . . .

Irrational Numbers

Any number that *cannot* be written as a simple fraction because the decimal goes on forever *without* repeating.

EXAMPLES:

$\sqrt{5} = 2.2360679775\ldots$
$\pi = 3.1415926535\ldots$

Real Numbers

Rational Numbers

Integers

Whole Numbers

Natural Numbers

Irrational Numbers

Rational Numbers and the Number Line

A **NUMBER LINE** is a line that orders and compares rational numbers.

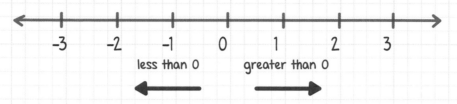

less than 0   greater than 0

EXAMPLES: Classify the numbers in as many categories as possible.

▶ 2.75

2.75 can be written as the fraction $2\frac{75}{100}$ or $2\frac{3}{4}$.

Since it can be written as a fraction, it is rational and real.

▶ 8

8 is an integer. It can also be written as the fraction or ratio $\frac{8}{1}$.

So, 8 is natural, whole, an integer, rational, and real.

▶ Bea says that the number $-\frac{21}{7}$ is greater than 0 and can be classified as irrational and real. Ted says it is less than zero and can be classified as an integer, rational, and real. Who is correct and why?

Since $-\frac{21}{7}$ is a fraction, it must be rational. $-\frac{21}{7} = -3$, which is an integer. $^-3$ is less than zero because it is to the left of zero on the number line.

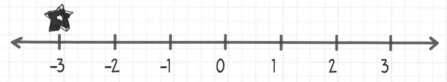

So, Ted is correct. $-\frac{21}{7}$ is classified as an integer, rational, and real.

3

FOR 1 THROUGH 6, CLASSIFY THE NUMBERS IN AS MANY CATEGORIES AS POSSIBLE.

1. 4

$$\frac{4}{1}$$

integer
whole

2. -6.5

$$-\frac{13}{2} \quad -6\frac{1}{2} \quad \text{rational}$$

3. 4.22222...

$$4\frac{22}{100} \quad 4\frac{11}{50} \quad \text{irrational}$$

4. 1.41213562…

irrational

5. 3$\frac{1}{5}$ 3.2 = 3$\frac{2}{10}$ =
         3 1/5 $\frac{2}{5\sqrt{10}}$

6. −9.353535…

FOR 7 THROUGH 9, WRITE TRUE OR FALSE.

7. A repeating decimal is irrational.

8. 4$\frac{1}{2}$ is an integer and a rational number.

9. −3.56 is a rational number but not an integer.

FOR 10 THROUGH 12, USE THE NUMBER LINE TO ANSWER THE FOLLOWING QUESTIONS. WRITE **TRUE** OR **FALSE**.

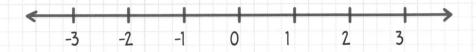

10. −2 is greater than 0 and to the left of 0.

11. 3 is greater than 0 and to the right of 0.

12. −1 is greater than −3.

FOR 13 THROUGH 15, WHICH STUDENT IS CORRECT? EXPLAIN WHY.

13. Kelly says that the number −5.5 is classified as rational and real. Ray says it is also an integer, and he classified it as an integer, rational, and real.

RATIONAL, AND REAL?

INTEGER, RATIONAL, AND REAL?

-5.5

14. Nate says that the number $2\frac{1}{3}$ can be classified as irrational and real. Hailey says it can be classified as rational and real.

15. Gia says $-1.666\ldots$ is a rational number but not an integer. Kyle says all rational numbers are integers.

POSITIVE AND NEGATIVE NUMBERS

This number line shows **POSITIVE** and **NEGATIVE** integers. Numbers to the left of 0 are negative, and numbers to the right of 0 are positive. Zero is neither positive nor negative.

> Arrows on each end of the number line illustrate that numbers keep going all the way to INFINITY (∞) and NEGATIVE INFINITY (−∞).

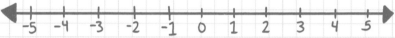

-5 is 5 spaces to the left of 0, and +5 is 5 spaces to the right of 0.

The numbers on the number line determine the distance from 0.

NEGATIVE NUMBERS are *less than* 0. The farther you move to the left of 0, the *lesser the quantity* will be.

-2 is *less than* 0, and -5 is *less than* -2.

POSITIVE NUMBERS are *greater than* 0. The farther you move to the right of 0, the *greater the quantity* will be.

+2 or 2 is *greater than* 0, and +5 is *greater than* +2.

Positive and negative signs are called **OPPOSITES**.

> +3 and −3 are also called opposites!

The **OPPOSITES OF OPPOSITES PROPERTY** says that the opposite of the opposite of a number is the number itself.

> So, the opposite of −11 is 11, and the opposite of the opposite of −11 is −11.

Real-world uses of positive and negative numbers:

Negative	Positive
Below-zero temperatures	*Above*-zero temperatures
Withdrawal from a bank account	*Credit* to a bank account
Loss of revenue	*Gain* in profits
Spend money	*Save* money

EXAMPLES: Write the integer that represents each quantity.

1. A person is swimming 100 feet below sea level.   −100 feet

2. Dean deposits 60 dollars.   + 60 dollars

3. The airplane is flying 1,500 feet above the ground.   +1,500 feet

4. The opposite of losing 123 points.   Gaining 123 points
or +123 points

▶ Draw a number line that extends from −5 to +5. Then use the number line to locate the opposite of the opposite of +4.

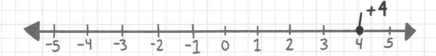

THINK:
The opposite of the opposite of a number is the number itself. So, the opposite of the opposite of +4 is +4!

CHAPTER 2

FOR 1 THROUGH 6, WRITE THE INTEGER THAT REPRESENTS EACH QUANTITY.

1. The temperature was 12 degrees warmer in the afternoon.

2. Darren loses $500 of his earnings in the stock market.

3. The player advances 25 feet.

4. Tara withdraws $950 from her checking account.

5. The submarine is 365 feet below sea level.

6. The scientist monitoring a weather balloon reports the balloon climbed 12,000 feet above the ground.

FOR 7 THROUGH 12, ANSWER THE QUESTIONS BY WRITING THE WORDS THAT EXPRESS EACH NUMERICAL QUANTITY.

7. What is the opposite of 100 feet above sea level?

8. What is the opposite of the opposite of -35 degrees?

9. What is the opposite of gaining 6% of the stock revenue?

10. What is the opposite of the opposite of 75 feet?

11. Use the number line to show the location of the opposite of 3.

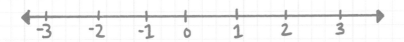

12. Draw a number line that extends from −4 to +4. Then use the number line you drew to show the location of the number that is not positive or negative.

ABSOLUTE VALUE

The **ABSOLUTE VALUE** of a number is its distance from 0 on the number line.

$\lvert-6\rvert$ is read as "the absolute value of -6." -6 is 6 *spaces* from 0 $\lvert-6\rvert = 6$	$\lvert 5\rvert$ is read as "the absolute value of 5." 5 is 5 *spaces* from 0 $\lvert 5\rvert = 5$

6 SPACES   5 SPACES

-7 -6 -5 -4 -3 -2 -1 0 1 2 3 4 5 6 7

Absolute value bars are also grouping symbols. You <u>must</u> evaluate the operations inside them first, then take the absolute value.

$\lvert 8 - 5\rvert = ?$

$\lvert 8 - 5\rvert = \lvert 3\rvert$ ⟵ STEP 1: Perform the operation. Subtract.

$\lvert 3\rvert = 3$

STEP 2: Find the absolute value of 3 (the distance from 0 on the number line).

So, $\lvert 8 - 5\rvert = 3$.

$-\lvert-14\rvert = ?$

$-\lvert-14\rvert = -(14)$ ⟵ STEP 1: Find the absolute value of -14 (the distance from 0 on the number line).

$-(14) = -14$ ⟵

STEP 2: Apply the negative symbol on the outside of the absolute value bars to get your answer.

So, $-\lvert-14\rvert = -14$.

A number in front of the absolute value bars means multiplication (like when we use parentheses).

Evaluate: $-3|-2| = ?$

$-3 \cdot |-2| = ?$ ← This multiplication sentence is read as "-3 times the absolute value of -2."

$-3 \cdot |-2| = -3(2)$ ← STEP 1: Find the absolute value of -2 (the distance from 0 on the number line).

$-3 \cdot 2 = -6$ ← STEP 2: Multiply.

So, $-3|-2| = -6$.

THINK: To find the opposite, first evaluate.

EXAMPLES:

Evaluate: $-|6 \cdot 4| = ?$

$-|6 \cdot 4| = -|24|$

Perform the operation inside the absolute value bars. In this case multiply.

$-|24| = -24$

Apply the negative symbol on the outside of the absolute value bars.

So, $-|6 \cdot 4| = -24$.

What is the opposite of $-|-4|$?

$-|-4| = -(4)$

Find the absolute value of -4.

$-(4) = -4$

Apply the negative symbol.

So, $-|-4| = -4$

The opposite of -4 is $+4$.

So, the opposite of $-|-4|$ is 4.

FOR 1 THROUGH 9, EVALUATE.

1. $|98|$

2. $|-6.35|$

3. $-\left|-7\dfrac{3}{5}\right|$

4. $\left| -1\frac{1}{5} \right|$

5. $\left| 16 - 10 \right|$

6. $\left| 9 + 12 \right|$

7. $\left| 2 \cdot 11 \right|$

8. $-|3 - 2|$

9. $-|18 \div 3|$

SOLVE THE PROBLEMS. USE WHAT YOU KNOW ABOUT ABSOLUTE VALUE.

10. Jonathan writes a check for $45. That transaction leaves his account with a balance of −$22. What is the absolute value of his account's debt?

11. What is the opposite of $|-68|$?

12. An oceanographer is staying in a campground that is 118 feet below sea level. What is the absolute value of the elevation difference between the campground and the sea level? (Hint: Consider sea level 0 on a number line.)

Chapter

FACTORS AND GREATEST COMMON FACTOR

FACTORS are integers you multiply together to get another integer.

Factors of 12: 1, 2, 3, 4, 6, 12.

$1 \cdot 12 = 12$
$2 \cdot 6 = 12$
$3 \cdot 4 = 12$

> To find factors, ask yourself:
> "What numbers can be multiplied together to give me this number?"

Factors of 36: 1, 2, 3, 4, 6, 9, 12, 18, 36.

$1 \cdot 36 = 36$
$2 \cdot 18 = 36$
$3 \cdot 12 = 36$
$4 \cdot 9 = 36$
$6 \cdot 6 = 36$

Use these shortcuts to find an integer's factors.

▶ An integer is divisible by 2 if it ends in an even number. ←—— 0, 2, 4, 6, 8, 10, 12, 14, 16, 18…

▶ An integer is divisible by 3 if the sum of its digits is divisible by 3. ←—— 42 is divisible by 3 because 4 + 2 = 6, and 6 is divisible by 3.

▶ An integer is divisible by 5 if it ends in 0 or 5. ←—— 5, 10, 15, 20, 25, 30, 35…

▶ An integer is divisible by 9 if the sum of its digits is divisible by 9. ←—— 315 is divisible by 9 because 3 + 1 + 5 = 9, and 9 is divisible by 9.

▶ An integer is divisible by 10 if it ends in 0. ←—— 10, 20, 30, 40, 50, 60, 70…

Any factors that are the *same* for two or more numbers are called **COMMON FACTORS**. The *largest* factor that both numbers share is called the **GREATEST COMMON FACTOR**, or **GCF** for short.

Greatest common factors of 24 and 42:

Factors of 24:
1, 2, 3, 4, 6, 8, 12, 24

Factors of 42:
1, 2, 3, 6, 7, 14, 21, 42

GCF: 6

To find the GCF, follow these steps.

1. List the factors of each number.

2. Find the common factors.

3. Select the greatest common factor.

EXAMPLE: Solve this problem using what you know about factors and the greatest common factor.

A lab assistant is putting together experiment kits for science classes. There are 48 eyedroppers and 32 beakers. The assistant's goal is to divide the supplies so that each kit has the same number of eyedroppers and beakers with nothing left over. What is the greatest number of kits the lab assistant can make? How many eyedroppers and how many beakers will be in each experiment kit?

To find the greatest number of kits the lab assistant can make, first find the factors of 48 and 32. Then list the common factors and choose the greatest common factor (GCF).

48 EYEDROPPERS	32 BEAKERS	COMMON FACTORS	GREATEST COMMON FACTOR (GCF)
Factors of 48: 1, 2, 3, 4, 6, 8, 12, 16, 24, 48 $1 \times 48 = 48$ $2 \times 24 = 48$ $3 \times 16 = 48$ $4 \times 12 = 48$ $6 \times 8 = 48$	Factors of 32: 1, 2, 4, 8, 16, 32 $1 \times 32 = 32$ $2 \times 16 = 32$ $4 \times 8 = 32$	1, 2, 4, 8, 16	16

To find how many eyedroppers and how many beakers will be in each experiment kit, look at the **MULTIPLICATION EXPRESSION** containing the GCF, or 16. The factor multiplied by the GCF tells you the number of eyedroppers and beakers in each kit.

$3 \times 16 = 48$; meaning 48 eyedroppers will be divided into 16 groups of 3. (48 eyedroppers with 3 eyedroppers in each kit = 16 kits.)

$2 \times 16 = 32$; meaning 32 beakers will be divided into 16 groups of 2. (32 beakers with 2 beakers in each kit = 16 kits.)

So, the greatest number of experiment kits the lab assistant can make = 16. Each kit will have 3 eyedroppers and 2 beakers.

ANSWER THE QUESTIONS. USE WHAT YOU KNOW ABOUT FACTORS AND THE GREATEST COMMON FACTOR.

1. What are the factors of 64?

2. What are the factors of 49?

3. What are the factors of 55?

4. A grocer is arranging a display of 60 containers of homemade soup for an in-store promotion. What are the different ways the grocer can arrange the rows of containers of homemade soup so that each row has the same number of containers?

5. Which numbers are not prime numbers? How do you know?

11, 17, 21, 31, 36, 47, 54

PRIME NUMBER
a number with only two factors: 1 and itself

6. Is 528 divisible by 2? How do you know?

7. Is 105 divisible by 3? How do you know?

8. Is 693 divisible by 9? How do you know?

9. Is 260 divisible by 5 and 10? How do you know?

10. Find the greatest common factor of 45 and 75.

11. Find the greatest common factor of 56 and 96.

12. Find the greatest common factor of 39 and 104.

SOLVE THE PROBLEMS.

13. A florist wants to create identical bouquets of flowers. She has 90 yellow roses and 72 white orchids. What is the greatest number of bouquets the florist can create dividing up all the flowers equally with none left over? How many yellow roses and white orchids will be in each bouquet?

14. Todd and Charles are making emergency kits to share with their neighbors. The boys have 54 water bottles and 42 boxes of adhesive bandages, which they would like to distribute equally among the bags, with nothing left over. What is the greatest number of emergency kits Todd and Charles can make? How many water bottles and boxes of bandages will be in each kit?

EMERGENCY

Chapter

MULTIPLES AND LEAST COMMON MULTIPLE

Every number has an infinite list of **MULTIPLES**. A multiple is the result or product of one number being multiplied by another number. It is helpful to always list the multiples for a number in order from least to greatest.

Multiples of 12: 12, 24, 36, 48, 60, 72...

$1 \cdot 12 = 12$
$2 \cdot 12 = 24$
$3 \cdot 12 = 36$
$4 \cdot 12 = 48$
$5 \cdot 12 = 60$
$6 \cdot 12 = 72$

and so on ... forever!

Multiples of 8: 8, 16, 24, 32, 40, 48...

$1 \cdot 8 = 8$
$2 \cdot 8 = 16$
$3 \cdot 8 = 24$
$4 \cdot 8 = 32$
$5 \cdot 8 = 40$
$6 \cdot 8 = 48$

and so on ... forever!

> Any multiples that are the same for two (or more) numbers are called Common Multiples.

Up to this point: 12 and 8 have the multiples 24 and 48 in common.

What is the smallest multiple 12 and 8 have in common? The smallest multiple is 24. We call this the **LEAST COMMON MULTIPLE**, or **LCM**.

To find the LCM of two or more numbers, follow these steps.

1. List the multiples of each number from least to greatest. Get at least five multiples.

2. Identify the *first* multiple both numbers have in common. That is the least common multiple!

Find the least common multiple, or LCM, of 6 and 9.

▶ The multiples of 6 are 6, 12, 18, 24, 30, 36...

▶ The multiples of 9 are 9, 18, 27, 36, 45...

18 is the first multiple 6 and 9 have in common.

So, the LCM of 6 and 9 is 18.

EXAMPLE: Solve this problem using what you know about multiples and the least common multiple.

▶ A caterer can only purchase dinner plates in packages of 8 and soup bowls in packages of 10. How many packages of plates and bowls will the caterer need to purchase to have the same number of each type of dinnerware?

To find how many packages of plates and bowls the caterer will need to purchase, first list the multiples of 8 and 10. Then list the common multiples and choose the least common multiple (LCM).

PACKAGE OF 8 DINNER PLATES	PACKAGE OF 10 SOUP BOWLS	COMMON MULTIPLES	LEAST COMMON MULTIPLE (LCM)
Multiples of 8:	Multiples of 10:	40 and 80	40
$1 \cdot 8 = 8$	$1 \cdot 10 = 10$		
$2 \cdot 8 = 16$	$2 \cdot 10 = 20$		
$3 \cdot 8 = 24$	$3 \cdot 10 = 30$		
$4 \cdot 8 = 32$	$4 \cdot 10 = 40$		
$5 \cdot 8 = 40$	$5 \cdot 10 = 50$		
$6 \cdot 8 = 48$	$6 \cdot 10 = 60$		
$7 \cdot 8 = 56$	$7 \cdot 10 = 70$		
$8 \cdot 8 = 64$	$8 \cdot 10 = 80$		
$9 \cdot 8 = 72$			
$10 \cdot 8 = 80$			

So, the least number of plates and bowls the caterer can purchase is 40.

To find how many packages the caterer needs to purchase for each type of dinnerware, look at the **MULTIPLICATION EXPRESSION** containing the LCM, or 40. What numbers did we multiply 8 and 10 by to get 40?

$5 \times 8 = 40$ (5 packages of 8 dinner plates)
$4 \times 10 = 40$ (4 packages of 10 soup bowls)

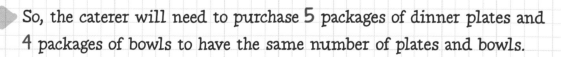

So, the caterer will need to purchase 5 packages of dinner plates and 4 packages of bowls to have the same number of plates and bowls.

ANSWER THE QUESTIONS. USE WHAT YOU KNOW ABOUT MULTIPLES AND THE LEAST COMMON MULTIPLE.

1. List the first five multiples of 7.

2. List the first five multiples of 15.

3. Find the LCM of 3 and 11.

4. Find the LCM of 12 and 18.

5. Find the LCM of 4 and 13.

6. Find the LCM of 2, 5, and 12.

SOLVE THE PROBLEMS.

7. Brad teaches piano lessons every fifth day and guitar lessons every fourth day. If he had both piano lessons and guitar lessons on June 1, what will be the next date that Brad has both piano and guitar lessons?

8. A train to Great Mountain leaves the station every 8 minutes. Another train traveling to Overlook Mountain leaves the station every 6 minutes. If it is 6:00 a.m. and both trains leave the station, when is the next time these trains will leave the station together?

9. Martin can save $12 every week. Patricia can save $18 every week. Who will save $36 first? After how long?

10. Explain the difference between determining the greatest common factor (GCF) and the least common multiple (LCM). Use the integers 6 and 8 to illustrate your answer.

Chapter 6

FRACTION BASICS:
TYPES OF FRACTIONS, AND ADDING AND SUBTRACTING FRACTIONS

Fractions are real numbers that represent a *part of a whole*.

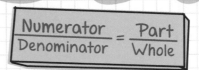

$$\frac{\text{Numerator}}{\text{Denominator}} = \frac{\text{Part}}{\text{Whole}}$$

A whole apple pie has 8 slices. A family eats 5 slices.

Therefore, a family ate $\frac{5}{8}$ of the apple pie.
Only 3 slices remain!
The leftover slices are the **remainder**.

There are three types of fractions.

Proper Fractions

The numerator is *less than* the denominator.

EXAMPLE: $\frac{2}{4}$

You can *simplify* some proper fractions by finding the GCF of the numerator and denominator and then dividing the numerator and the denominator by that number.

The GCF of 2 and 4 is 2.

$$\frac{2}{4} = \frac{2 \div 2}{4 \div 2} = \frac{1}{2}$$

$$\frac{2}{4} = \frac{1}{2}$$

Improper Fractions

The numerator is *greater than, or equal to,* the denominator.

EXAMPLE: $\frac{13}{6}$

You can convert an improper fraction to a mixed number by dividing. Note: The fraction bar is another way to show division.

$13 \div 6 = 2$ R 1 ("R" stands for remainder.)

$\frac{13}{6} = 2\frac{1}{6}$ ⟵

Mixed Numbers

There is a whole number and a fraction.

EXAMPLE: $2\frac{4}{5}$

You can convert a mixed number to an improper fraction by multiplying the denominator and the whole number, and then adding the numerator.

ADD
MULTIPLY
$2\frac{4}{5}$

$(2 \times 5) + 4 = 14$

$2\frac{4}{5} = \frac{14}{5}$

You can **ADD** and **SUBTRACT FRACTIONS** with the same or different denominators.

TO ADD OR SUBTRACT FRACTIONS:

ADD OR SUBTRACT FRACTIONS: *same* denominator

Add or subtract the numerators. Denominator stays the same.

$$\frac{4}{6} + \frac{1}{6} = \frac{5}{6}$$

$$\frac{5}{8} - \frac{3}{8} = \frac{2}{8} = \frac{1}{4}$$

THINK:
You can simplify the difference. Divide the numerator and denominator by the GCF. The GCF of 2 and 8 is 2.

$$\frac{2 \div 2}{8 \div 2} = \frac{1}{4}$$

ADD FRACTIONS: *different denominators*

$$\frac{1}{6} + \frac{3}{8} = ?$$

1. Find the LCM of the denominators 6 and 8:

6, 12, 18, 24 . . .
8, 16, 24 . . .

2. Rewrite as equivalent fractions.

$$\frac{1 \times 4}{6 \times 4} + \frac{3 \times 3}{8 \times 3} =$$

$$\frac{4}{24} + \frac{9}{24}$$

3. Add the numerators.

$$\frac{4}{24} + \frac{9}{24} = \frac{13}{24}$$

So, $\frac{1}{6} + \frac{3}{8} = \frac{13}{24}$

SUBTRACT FRACTIONS: *different denominators*

$$\frac{4}{5} - \frac{2}{7} = ?$$

1. Find the LCM of the denominators 5 and 7:

5, 10, 15, 20, 25, 30, 35 . . .
7, 14, 21, 28, 35 . . .

2. Rewrite as equivalent fractions.

$$\frac{4 \times 7}{5 \times 7} - \frac{2 \times 5}{7 \times 5} =$$

$$\frac{28}{35} - \frac{10}{35}$$

3. Subtract the numerators.

$$\frac{28}{35} - \frac{10}{35} = \frac{18}{35}$$

So, $\frac{4}{5} - \frac{2}{7} = \frac{18}{35}$

EXAMPLE: Solve the problem. Use what you know about adding and subtracting fractions.

▶ Gerard ran $\frac{9}{10}$ of a mile to get to the athletic center. Jose ran $\frac{3}{4}$ of a mile. How much farther did Gerard run than Jose?

To find how much farther Gerard ran than Jose, *subtract* the number of miles Jose ran from the number of miles Gerard ran.

Subtract:

$\frac{9}{10} - \frac{3}{4} = ?$

Find the LCM of 10 and 4. It is 20.

Rewrite the fractions.

$\frac{9 \times 2}{10 \times 2} - \frac{3 \times 5}{4 \times 5} = \frac{18}{20} - \frac{15}{20}$

Subtract the numerators.

$\frac{18}{20} - \frac{15}{20} = \frac{3}{20}$

So, Gerard ran $\frac{3}{20}$ of a mile more than Jose.

FIND THE SUM OR DIFFERENCE. SIMPLIFY THE SUM OR DIFFERENCE IF NECESSARY.

1. $\frac{1}{4} + \frac{1}{6} = ?$

2. $\frac{1}{3} + \frac{5}{7} = ?$

3. $\frac{5}{16} + \frac{13}{16} = ?$

4. $\frac{5}{12} + \frac{7}{10} = ?$

5. $\dfrac{11}{12} - \dfrac{5}{12} = ?$

6. $\dfrac{14}{15} - \dfrac{2}{3} = ?$

7. $\dfrac{7}{9} - \dfrac{5}{6} = ?$

8. $\dfrac{13}{12} - \dfrac{13}{16} = ?$

SOLVE THE PROBLEMS. USE WHAT YOU KNOW ABOUT ADDING AND SUBTRACTING FRACTIONS.

9. Stephanie worked on her science project poster board for $\frac{4}{5}$ of an hour. She then wrote the lab report for $\frac{9}{10}$ of an hour. How much time did Stephanie spend working on her science project?

10. Jack purchased 3 yards of material to make a coat. He used $\frac{5}{8}$ of a yard. How many yards of material does Jack have left? (Hint: You can rewrite 3 as $\frac{3}{1}$.)

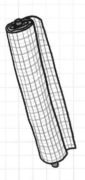

Chapter 7 MULTIPLYING AND DIVIDING FRACTIONS

The denominators do *not* have to be the same when multiplying or dividing fractions.

To **MULTIPLY** fractions follow these steps:

1. Multiply the numerators.

2. Multiply the denominators.

3. Simplify your answer (the product) if necessary.

CALCULATE: $\frac{6}{12} \cdot \frac{8}{24} = ?$

TIP: You can sometimes simplify the fractions using the GCF of a numerator and denominator *before* you follow the steps. This is called **CROSS-REDUCING** or **CANCELING**.

First, cross-reduce.

$\frac{6}{12} \frac{1}{2} \cdot \frac{8}{24} \frac{1}{3} = ?$

The GCF of 8 and 24 is 8.
(8 ÷ 8 = 1 and 24 ÷ 8 = 3)

The GCF of 6 and 12 is 6.
(6 ÷ 6 = 1 and 12 ÷ 6 = 2)

CANCELING is not necessary to solve a problem, but it does make multiplying a whole lot simpler.

Next, multiply the numerators, then the denominators.

$\frac{1}{2} \cdot \frac{1}{3} = \frac{1 \times 1}{2 \times 3} = \frac{1}{6}$

So, $\frac{6}{12} \cdot \frac{8}{24} = \frac{1}{6}$.

To **DIVIDE** fractions follow these steps:

1. Flip the second fraction to make its **RECIPROCAL**.

2. Change the division symbol to multiplication.

3. Multiply. Follow the steps for multiplying fractions.

A RECIPROCAL is a number in a mathematical set that, when multiplied together, has a product of 1. Reciprocal of $\frac{2}{4}$ is $\frac{4}{2}$.

$$\frac{2}{4} \cdot \frac{4}{2} = \frac{8}{8} = 1$$

CALCULATE: $\frac{9}{15} \div \frac{33}{45} = ?$

To divide, first "flip" the second fraction to make its reciprocal. Then change the division symbol to multiplication.

$$\frac{9}{15} \div \frac{33}{45} = \frac{9}{15} \cdot \frac{45}{33} = ? \longleftarrow$$

The GCF of 9 and 33 is 3. (9 ÷ 3 = 3 and 33 ÷ 3 = 11)

The GCF of 15 and 45 is 15. (15 ÷ 15 = 1 and 45 ÷ 15 = 3)

Now, follow the steps for multiplying fractions.

Cross-reduce:

$$\frac{\cancel{9}}{\cancel{15}}\frac{3}{1} \cdot \frac{\cancel{45}}{\cancel{33}}\frac{3}{11} = ?$$

Next, multiply the numerators, then the denominators.

$$\frac{3}{1} \cdot \frac{3}{11} = \frac{3 \times 3}{1 \times 11} = \frac{9}{11}$$

So, $\frac{9}{15} \div \frac{33}{45} = \frac{9}{11}$.

Sometimes it makes sense to only cross-reduce one numerator and one denominator. Like the problem below:

$$\frac{7}{8} \div \frac{1}{4} = \frac{7}{\underset{2}{\cancel{8}}} \cdot \frac{\cancel{4}^{1}}{1}$$

$$\frac{7}{2} \cdot \frac{1}{1} = \frac{7}{2} \text{ or } 3\frac{1}{2}$$

SOLVE THE PROBLEMS. SIMPLIFY THE FRACTIONS USING THE GCF WHEN POSSIBLE.

1. $\dfrac{5}{6} \div \dfrac{3}{4} = ?$

2. $\dfrac{15}{28} \cdot \dfrac{14}{9} = ?$

3. $\dfrac{7}{10} \cdot \dfrac{5}{42} = ?$

4. $1\dfrac{1}{7} \div 1\dfrac{13}{22} = ?$

5. $2\frac{1}{3} \cdot \frac{6}{8} = ?$

6. $8\frac{2}{3} \div \frac{4}{3} = ?$

7. $6\frac{1}{2} \cdot 4\frac{4}{7} = ?$

SOLVE THE PROBLEMS. USE WHAT YOU KNOW ABOUT FRACTION MULTIPLICATION AND DIVISION.

8. Four bakers share $1\frac{1}{2}$ cups of flour. How much flour does each baker get?

9. How many $\frac{1}{3}$-ounce spoonfuls of salt are in a filled $4\frac{3}{4}$-ounce saltshaker?

10. A recipe calls for $\frac{5}{8}$ of a cup of milk, but Jason wants to double the recipe. How much milk does he need?

11. A sprinkler system uses $5\frac{9}{12}$ gallons of water every hour. How many gallons of water will the system use in $3\frac{3}{5}$ hours?

12. Tasha can run $7\frac{7}{10}$ miles in 2 hours. How many miles can she run in $1\frac{1}{4}$ hours, assuming her running pace stays the same?

Chapter 8

ADDING AND SUBTRACTING DECIMALS

To add or subtract decimals, follow these steps:

1. Line up the decimal points. You can use a decimal place-value chart to help.

2. Add or subtract the same way you do with whole numbers.

3. Write the decimal point in the sum or difference.

Find the sum of 89 and 12.356.

Decimal Place Value Chart

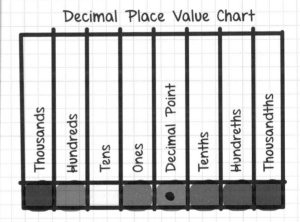

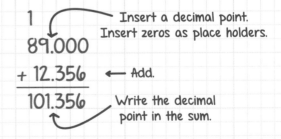

Insert a decimal point. Insert zeros as place holders.

$$
\begin{array}{r}
1 \\
89.000 \\
+\ 12.356 \\
\hline
101.356
\end{array}
$$

← Add.

Write the decimal point in the sum.

So, the sum of 89 and 12.356 is 101.356.

IMPORTANT!

▶ Any time you add a whole number and a decimal, include the "invisible" decimal point to the right of the whole number.

▶ When adding money in dollars, everything to the left of the decimal point represents *whole dollars*, and everything to the right represents *cents*, or parts of a dollar.

EXAMPLE: Solve the problem. Use what you know about adding and subtracting decimals.

A chemist creates a mixture using two solutions that weigh a total of 912.65 grams. Solution A weighs 468.72 grams. How many grams does Solution B weigh?

To find how many grams Solution B weighs, subtract the weight of Solution A (468.72 grams) from the total weight of the mixture (912.65 grams).

912.65 – 468.72

$$
\begin{array}{r}
\overset{\scriptstyle 8\ 10\ 11\ \ 1}{9\cancel{1}\,2.65} \\
-\ 4\,6\,8.7\,2 \\
\hline
4\,4\,3.9\,3
\end{array}
$$

Write the subtraction sentence vertically. Line up the decimal points.

Subtract the same way you do whole numbers.

Write the decimal point in the answer.

So, the weight of Solution B is 443.93 grams.

FIND THE SUM OR DIFFERENCE.

1. 6.29 + 3.48

2. $43.26 + $98.06

3. 15 + 0.074

4. 6,789.02 + 456.235 + 1,406.91

5. 71.23 - 0.98

6. 1,975.23 - 88.52

7. 300 - 65.11

FOR 8 THROUGH 10, SOLVE THE PROBLEMS. USE WHAT YOU KNOW ABOUT ADDING AND SUBTRACTING DECIMALS.

8. Allen cycles 7.25 miles on Thursday, 5.8 miles on Friday, and 10.65 miles on Sunday. How many miles did Allen cycle from Thursday through Sunday?

9. If a wooden board is 14.5 feet in length and it is cut down to 6.8 feet, how many feet of the wooden board are left?

10. The school band members raised $500 for new band equipment. They purchased a new keyboard for $119.99 and a saxophone for $349.99. How much money does the band have remaining after these purchases?

Chapter 9

MULTIPLYING DECIMALS

To multiply decimals, follow these steps:

1. Multiply the decimal numbers as though they were whole numbers. (Ignore the decimal points.)

2. Count the total number of decimal places in each factor.

3. Locate the same number of decimal places in the answer.

4. Write the decimal point in the product.

Gilda's Catering purchases 42.8 pounds of produce at $4.79 per pound. What is the total cost of the produce?

To find the total cost of the produce, multiply:

42.8 pounds • $4.79 = ?

$$
\begin{array}{r}
42.8 \\
\times\ 4.79 \\
\hline
3852 \\
2996 \\
+1712 \\
\hline
205.012
\end{array}
$$

Ignore the decimal points. Multiply as you do whole numbers.

The total number of decimal places in 42.8 and 4.79 is 3. Place the decimal point 3 places from the end of the product, between 5 and 0.

So, the total cost of the produce is $205.01.

Since the product represents a dollar and cent amount, the answer was rounded to the nearest hundredths.

FOR 1 THROUGH 6, FIND THE PRODUCT.

1. $8.7 \cdot 6.2$

2. $53.526 \cdot 7.41$

3. $(9.96)(3.74)$

4. $0.35 \cdot 0.88$

5. 750 • 0.0003

6. (3.44) (9.6102)

FOR 7 THROUGH 10, SOLVE THE PROBLEMS. USE WHAT YOU KNOW ABOUT MULTIPLYING DECIMALS.

7. A hardware store sells 32.25 yards of fencing at $16.20 per yard. What is the total sale of the fencing?

8. Ms. Jessa bought theater tickets for herself and 23 students in her class. She got a great bargain! She paid $25.75 for each ticket. How much did Ms. Jessa pay for all the tickets?

9. Mia owns 2,700 shares of stock. The stock is valued at $31.56 per share. What is the total value of Mia's shares of stock?

10. Daren can run 8.55 kilometers in one hour. Umberto can run 9.5 kilometers in one hour. If Daren plans to run for 3.5 hours and Umberto plans to run for 3 hours, who will run more kilometers, assuming their running pace stays the same for the entire time? How do you know?

DIVIDING DECIMALS

To divide decimals, follow these steps:

1. Rewrite the division sentence so that each decimal is a whole number. To do this, you must multiply *both* the divisor and dividend by the same power of ten.

For example: $3.75 \div 0.25$

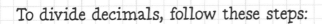

$$\frac{3.75 \times 100}{0.25 \times 100} = \frac{375}{25} \quad \text{power of 10}$$

$$0.25\overline{)3.75} =$$

$$25\overline{)375}$$

> **quotient**
> $\text{divisor}\overline{)\text{dividend}}$ or $\dfrac{\text{dividend}}{\text{divisor}} = \text{quotient}$

THINK:
To change the divisor, 0.25 to 25, you must move the decimal point *two places to the right* or multiply by 100. Do the same to the dividend.

2. Divide.
$$375 \div 25 = 15$$
$$25\overline{)375}^{\,15}$$

3. Place the decimal point in the quotient.
$$25\overline{)375}^{\,15.0}$$

EXAMPLE: Solve the problem. Use what you know about dividing decimals.

Carol's Cafe receives 25.60 pounds of trail mix. The manager wants to fill each container with 0.8 of a pound. How many containers of trail mix can the manager fill?

To find how many containers of trail mix the manager can fill, divide: 25.60 ÷ 0.8

$$
\begin{array}{r}
3\,2.0 \\
0.8\,\overline{)\,25.6.0} \\
-\ 24 \\
\hline
16 \\
-\ 16 \\
\hline
0
\end{array}
$$

Move the decimal point in the divisor (0.8) *one place* to the right. That will make the divisor a whole number. 0.8 • 10 = 8

Move the decimal point in the dividend (25.60) the *same number of places* to the right. 25.60 • 10 = 256.0

Divide.

Place the decimal point in the quotient.

So, the manager can fill 32 containers with trail mix.

FOR 1 THROUGH 7, FIND THE QUOTIENT.

1. 6.24 ÷ 2.4

2. 52.17 ÷ 14.1

3. 254.01 ÷ 0.2

4. $3{,}250 \div 0.0005$

5. $\dfrac{7.5}{0.24}$

6. $\dfrac{2.6}{0.4}$

7. $\dfrac{1.066}{0.02}$

FOR 8 THROUGH 10, SOLVE THE PROBLEMS. USE WHAT YOU KNOW ABOUT DIVIDING DECIMALS.

8. Stephen can bike 27.3 miles every 3.5 hours. Assuming the pace of his cycling is constant, how many miles can Stephen bike in one hour?

9. Felicia earns $175.50 a week answering phones at the community library. If she works 18.75 hours a week, how much money does Felicia earn per hour?

10. A uniform company purchases 14.25 yards of material. If the item being sewn requires 0.75 yards of material, how many items can they make?

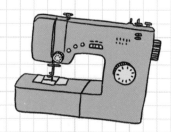

Chapter 11

ADDING POSITIVE AND NEGATIVE NUMBERS

To add positive and negative numbers, you can use a number line or use absolute value.

Technique #1: Use a Number Line

Draw a number line and begin at ZERO. Wherever you end up is the answer!

$-9 + 4 = ?$

For a negative (-) number, move that many spaces to the left.

For a positive (+) number, move that many spaces to the right.

Where did you end up? -5 is correct!

Technique #2: Use Absolute Value

You can use the absolute value technique.

If the signs of the numbers you are adding are the same, add and keep the sign.

$-150 + (-35) = -185$ Add 150 and 35, then keep the negative sign.

If the signs of the numbers you are adding are *different*, subtract the absolute value of each of the two numbers and use the sign of the number with the greater absolute value for the sum.

$-256 + 56 = -200$ ← Subtract 56 from 256. $|-256| = 256$; $|56| = 56$
Greater absolute value is 256.
Use the negative sign in the answer.

EXAMPLE: A zoologist reported a tiger lost 15 pounds from an illness. After getting nursed back to health, the tiger gained back 22 pounds. What was the tiger's total weight gain or loss? Use integers to solve the problem.

Tiger *lost* 15 pounds: -15

Tiger *gained back* 22 pounds: +22

Since these numbers make using a number line challenging, it is best to use the absolute value technique to solve this problem.

$-15 + (+22)$ Write the addition expression that represents the problem.

$|-15| - |+22|$ -15 and +22 have different signs, so subtract the absolute value of each of the two numbers.

$22 - 15 = 7$ Subtract 15 from 22.

Since 22 had the greater absolute value, the answer is also positive or +7.

So, the tiger had a weight gain of 7 pounds.

ADD THE INTEGERS USING A NUMBER LINE.

1. −4 + 6

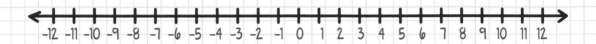

2. −7 + (−1)

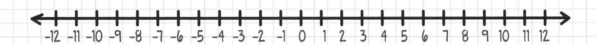

3. 8 + (−5)

ADD THE INTEGERS USING ABSOLUTE VALUE.

4. −62 + (−108)

5. −245 + 691

6. 48 + (−79)

7. −1252 + 864

SOLVE THE PROBLEMS USING INTEGERS AND THE TECHNIQUE YOU THINK IS BEST.

8. Jake borrows $35 from his sister. He pays her back $16. How much money does Jake still owe?

9. The temperature in Alaska is -4 degrees Fahrenheit in the morning. At 2 p.m. the temperature has risen by 30 degrees Fahrenheit. What was the temperature at 2 p.m.?

10. Tammy has $75 in her savings account. She makes a withdrawal of $18. What is Tammy's total account balance after the withdrawal?

11. A submarine is positioned 310 feet below sea level. It descends 215 feet. How many feet below sea level is the submarine?

12. Bill lends his brother $95 from his savings account. His account now has $265. How much money did Bill's savings account have before he gave his brother the money?

13. Maggie says that the number of years between 510 BCE and 205 CE is 305 years. Tara says the number of years between 510 BCE and 205 CE is 715 years. Who is correct? Use the addition of integers to verify your answer.

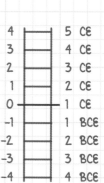

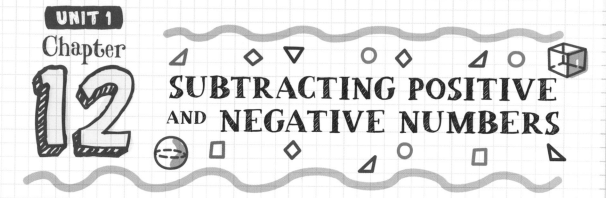

SUBTRACTING POSITIVE AND NEGATIVE NUMBERS

We already know that subtraction and addition are "opposites" of each other. So, we can use this strategy: Change a *subtraction sentence* to an *addition sentence* by using the **ADDITIVE INVERSE**, or **OPPOSITE**. Then follow the rules for adding positive and negative numbers.

EXAMPLE 1: 85 – 165 = ?

85 – 165 = ?   Subtraction sentence with integers + 85 and +165.

85 + (–165) = ?   **STEP 1:** The additive inverse or opposite of subtraction is addition. The opposite of +165 is –165.

85 + (–165) = ?   **STEP 2:** Follow the rules for addition: If the signs of the numbers you are adding are *different*, <u>subtract</u> the absolute value of each of the two numbers and use the sign of the number with the greatest absolute value for the sum.

$85 + (-165) = -80$

STEP 3: Subtract 85 from 165. Use the sign of the number with the *greater absolute value*: $|85| = 85$; $|-165| = 165$. So, the answer will be negative since 165 is greater than 85!

So, $85 - 165 = -80$. ◄

EXAMPLE 2: A meteorologist reported that the temperature in Miami, Florida, was 69°F while the temperature in Buffalo, New York, was -17°F. What was the difference between the temperatures?

To find the difference between the temperatures, subtract -17°F from 69°F.

$69 - (-17) = ?$	Subtraction sentence with integers + 69 and -17.
$69 + (+17) = ?$	The additive inverse or opposite of subtraction is addition. The opposite of -17 is 17.
$69 + 17 = ?$	Follow the rules for addition: When the signs are the *same*, <u>add</u> and keep the sign.
$69 + 17 = +86$	

So, the difference between the temperatures in Miami and Buffalo was 86 degrees. ◄

FIND THE DIFFERENCE.

1. 6 – (–2)

2. –15 – (–4)

3. –7 – 10

4. –9 – (–25)

5. –141 – 107

6. 15 – 132

7. –10 – (2) + (–16)

SOLVE THE PROBLEMS. USE WHAT YOU KNOW ABOUT SUBTRACTING POSITIVE AND NEGATIVE NUMBERS.

8. Brie is learning to play a new video game. In the first round, she earned 56 points. In the second round, she lost 78 points. What was Brie's total number of points after the second round?

9. A submarine descended 560 feet below sea level. If it then ascends 294 feet, what is its new position?

10. A coffee shop takes a loan for $1,750 to introduce a new line of drinks to its menu. Two shareholders also lend the coffee shop $335 each to help with the new drinks. How much total debt will the coffee shop acquire borrowing money for this project?

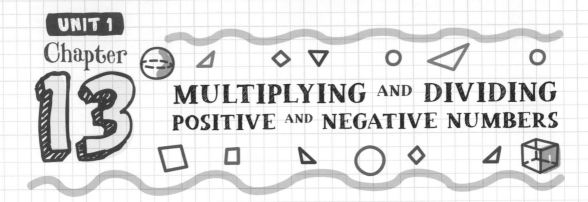

UNIT 1
Chapter 13
MULTIPLYING AND DIVIDING POSITIVE AND NEGATIVE NUMBERS

You can multiply or divide positive and negative numbers using patterns or rules!

If there are an **ODD NUMBER** of negative numbers, the product or quotient is **NEGATIVE**.

$(+5) \cdot (-6) = (-30)$ *or* $(-5) \cdot (+6) = (-30)$

$(+5) \cdot (+5) \cdot (-1) = (-25)$

$(-25) \div (-5) \div (-5) = -1$ ← There are 3 negative numbers, so the answer is negative.

If there are an **EVEN NUMBER** of negative numbers, the product or quotient is **POSITIVE**.

$(-5) \cdot (-6) = (+30)$

$(-25) \div (-5) = (+5)$ ← There are 2 negative numbers, so the answer is positive.

$(-25) \div (+5) \cdot (-5) = +25$

EXAMPLE: XYZ stock plummeted a total of 63 points in 7

decreased

days. If the stock decreased at the same rate, what is the rate of
decrease each day?

To find the rate of decrease, divide the total point decrease
by 7 days or -63 points ÷ 7 days = ?

-63 ÷ 7 = ?   Division sentence with -63 and +7.

-63 ÷ 7 = -9   Divide as you do with whole numbers. Since there is
               only 1 negative number (an odd number), the quotient
               is negative.

So, the rate of decrease each day
was -9 points.

THINK:

Division and multiplication are _inverse
operations_. This means you can check your
answer to this problem by multiplying!
-9 points x 7 days = -63 points

COMPUTE.

1. −7 (−7)

2. −40 • 22

3. 300 • −10

4. 96 ÷ −12

5. −110 ÷ −110

6. $\dfrac{-48}{6}$

7. $\dfrac{108}{-9}$

SOLVE THE PROBLEMS. USE WHAT YOU KNOW ABOUT MULTIPLYING AND DIVIDING POSITIVE AND NEGATIVE NUMBERS.

8. Aaron borrowed $7 a day to buy his lunch. He owes $56 total for his lunches. How many days did Aaron borrow money?

9. The temperature in Antarctica is –27°C. If the temperature drops by 4°C every hour between 6 p.m. and 9 p.m., how many degrees did the temperature drop? What is the temperature at 9 p.m.?

10. Tina says that the multiplication expression (–2) • (–2) • (–2) • (–2) • (–2) • (–2) has a product that is a positive number because there is an even number of factors. Matt says Tina is incorrect because all the factors are negative. Who is correct? How do you know?

Chapter 14. INEQUALITIES

An **INEQUALITY** is a mathematical sentence that compares quantities and uses the signs <, >, ≠, ≤, or ≥.

REMEMBER: Place the sign between numbers, with the open side toward the *greater quantity* and the vertex side toward the *lesser quantity*.

5 < 10
5 is *less than* 10.

n ≤ 10   n is *less than <u>or equal to</u>* 10.

THINK: n can be 10, 9, 8, 7, 6, 5, 4, 3, 2, 1, 0, -1...

10 > 5
10 is *greater than* 5.

n ≥ -5   n is *greater than <u>or equal to</u>* -5.

THINK: n can be -5, -4, -3, -2, -1, 0, 1, 2 ...

5 ≠ 10
5 *is not equal to* 10.

THE MATH MONSTER ALWAYS WANTS TO EAT THE GREATER AMOUNT!

Compare $^-3$ and 4.

Make a number line to compare: $^-3$ and 4.

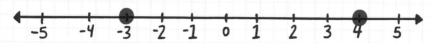

Write the inequality: $^-3 < 4$ *or* $4 > ^-3$

> **REMEMBER:**
> Negative numbers are less than zero. Positive numbers are greater than zero.

▶ Compare $-\dfrac{5}{9}$ and $-\dfrac{2}{3}$.

To compare fractions, first rewrite the fractions so they have the same denominators. Use the LCM.

The LCM of 9 and 3 is 9. So, you only need to rewrite $-\dfrac{2}{3}$.

$$-\dfrac{2 \times 3}{3 \times 3} = -\dfrac{6}{9}$$

Make a number line to compare:

$-\dfrac{5}{9}$ and $-\dfrac{6}{9}$

Write the inequality: $-\dfrac{5}{9} > -\dfrac{2}{3}$ *or* $-\dfrac{2}{3} < -\dfrac{5}{9}$

EXAMPLE: Express each situation as an inequality.

Vincent runs *at least* 10 miles a week.

Make a number line to show all the possible number of miles Vincent could have run.

THINK:
"At least" 10 miles means Vincent could have run 10 miles _or_ _greater_ than 10 miles. (10, 11, 12, 13, 14 ...)

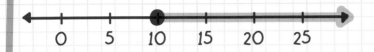

Let n = the number of miles Vincent runs.

Write the inequality: $n \geq 10$

EXAMPLE: Kim is thinking of a number *no greater than* $-2\frac{1}{2}$.

Make a number line to show all the possible numbers Kim could be thinking of.

THINK:
"No greater than" $-2\frac{1}{2}$ means the number Kim is thinking of could be $-2\frac{1}{2}$ _or_ _less_ than $-2\frac{1}{2}$.
$(-2\frac{1}{2}, -3, -3\frac{1}{2}, -4 ...)$

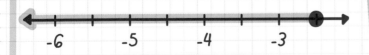

Let n = the number Kim is thinking about.

Write the inequality: $n \leq -2\frac{1}{2}$

ANSWER THE QUESTIONS. USE WHAT YOU KNOW ABOUT INEQUALITIES.

1. Write an inequality the number line illustrates.

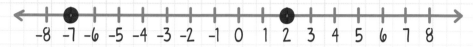

2. Compare 4 and –4.

3. Compare –1.8 and –1.75.

4. Compare $\frac{3}{5}$ and $\frac{2}{3}$.

5. Compare $-1\frac{1}{2}$ and $-1\frac{3}{7}$.

6. Which is a greater depth: 36 feet below sea level or 48 feet below sea level? Write a comparison to explain your answer.

7. Write the inequality for the statement: Nancy is at least 14 years old. (Hint: Let n = Nancy's age.)

8. Explain why $x \leq -1\frac{1}{8}$ is false when x is 0.

9. Explain the difference between $y \geq 10$ and $y > 10$.

10. Jan needs to sell 85 rolls of wrapping paper to win a new watch. Jan reports she has sold at least 70 rolls. Is it possible Jan won the watch? How do you know?

Unit 2

Ratios, Proportions, and Percents

Chapter 15 RATIOS

A **RATIO** is a comparison of two quantities. You can write this comparison in words, as a ratio, or as a fraction. Ratios help us understand data better. The ratio *a:b* is read as "the ratio of a to b."

> **GIVEN TWO QUANTITIES:**
> 3 roses and 8 flowers
> Words: 3 to 8   Ratio: 3:8
> Fraction: $\frac{3}{8}$

Look at the inventory chart below. There are three ways we can compare this data using ratios: a part *to* a part, a part *to* a whole, and a whole *to* a part.

The baseball and football jerseys represent "the part."

The total number of jerseys represent "the whole."

SCHOOL BOOKSTORE ATHLETIC JERSEY INVENTORY	QUANTITY
Total number of baseball jerseys	12
Total number of football jerseys	8
Total number of jerseys	20

part to part comparison:

football jerseys *to* baseball jerseys

$\frac{8}{12}$ or   8 to 12   or   8:12

Remember, you can simplify ratios: $\frac{8}{12} = \frac{2}{3}$

$\frac{2}{3}$ or   2 to 3   or   2:3

So, for every 2 football jerseys, there are 3 baseball jerseys.

part to whole comparison:

baseball jerseys *to* total number of jerseys

$\frac{12}{20}$ or   12 to 20   or   12:20

Simplify: $\frac{12}{20} = \frac{3}{5}$

$\frac{3}{5}$ or   3 to 5   or   3:5

So, for every 3 baseball jerseys, there are 5 jerseys in the bookstore.

whole to part comparison:

total number of jerseys *to* football jerseys

$\frac{20}{8}$ or   20 to 8   or   20:8

Simplify: $\frac{20}{8} = \frac{5}{2}$

$\frac{5}{2}$ or   5 to 2   or   5:2

So, for every 5 jerseys in the bookstore, there are 2 football jerseys.

FOR 1 THROUGH 6, WRITE EACH COMPARISON AS A FRACTION TO DESCRIBE EACH SITUATION. SIMPLIFY THE FRACTION IF POSSIBLE.

1. Nio's store sells 6 black ink pens for every 8 blue ink pens.

2. Ms. Ron's class had 15 out of 27 students participate in the school talent show.

3. A baker uses 21 ounces of milk for every 14 cups of cake mix.

4. Every 5 days, Nidia earns a total of $55 for tutoring math.

5. 27 mountain bicycles to 39 hybrid bicycles

6. 68 bottles of water for every 34 participants

FOR 7 THROUGH 12, WRITE EACH COMPARISON AS A RATIO IN THE FORMAT A:B TO DESCRIBE EACH SITUATION.

7. A survey of Belville residents shows 110 people want a new park and 175 do not.

8. Rick uses 52 cups of water for every 8 bags of cement mix.

9. For every 50 bags of apples sold at Pete's Produce, 20 bags are organic.

10. Fran can download 15 audiobooks for $150.

11. A city planner creates a map with a scale of 2 centimeters for every 30 miles.

12. A hospital places an order for medical supplies. It bought 105 boxes of bandages, 45 thermometers, 20 stethoscopes, and 95 boxes of disposable gloves. What was the ratio of thermometers to stethoscopes? What was the ratio of bandages to gloves?

Chapter 16 UNIT RATE AND UNIT PRICE

A **RATE** is a special kind of ratio where the *two amounts* being compared have *different units*.

EXAMPLE: 10 dollars for 5 avocados

Dollars and *avocados* are *different units*. So, this ratio is a rate!

A **UNIT RATE** is a rate that has a 1 in the denominator.

When the unit rate describes a *price*, it is called **UNIT PRICE**. When you are calculating unit price, be sure to put the price in the numerator!

> Rate: 10 dollars for 5 avocados
>
> UNIT RATE: $\frac{10 \text{ dollars}}{5 \text{ avocados}} = \frac{2 \text{ dollars}}{1 \text{ avocado}} = 2$ dollars
>
> To find a unit rate set up a ratio as a *fraction* and then *divide* the numerator (10) *by* the denominator (5).
>
> $\frac{10 \text{ dollars}}{5 \text{ avocados}} = 10 \div 5 = 2 = \frac{2}{1}$
>
> So, the unit rate and the unit price are 2 dollars for 1 avocado.

EXAMPLE: Michelle is looking to buy an efficient solar panel water pump and is calculating unit rates to find the best one. The pump she chooses can move $\frac{9}{10}$ of a gallon of water in $\frac{3}{4}$ of a minute. What is the unit rate of this water pump?

To find the unit rate, first write the rate: $\dfrac{\frac{9}{10} \text{ gallon}}{\frac{3}{4} \text{ minute}}$.

Then divide to determine the unit rate: $\frac{9}{10}$ gallon of water ÷ $\frac{3}{4}$ minute.

$$\frac{\frac{9}{10}}{\frac{3}{4}} = \frac{9}{10} \div \frac{3}{4} = \frac{9}{10} \cdot \frac{4}{3} = \frac{36}{30} = \frac{6}{5} = 1\frac{1}{5} = \frac{1\frac{1}{5} \text{ gallon of water}}{1 \text{ minute}}$$

Remember: The denominator will always be 1.

So, the water pump will move $1\frac{1}{5}$ gallons of water every minute.

This is the unit rate.

FOR 1 THROUGH 10, FIND THE UNIT RATE OR THE UNIT PRICE.

1. An airline's policy states that for every 30 passengers there needs to be 2 flight attendants on board.

2. The winner of the fundraiser baked and sold 450 muffins every 15 days.

3. A manufacturing plant can produce 72 bags of trail mix every 18 seconds.

4. A popular online clothing store sells 144 T-shirts every 12 minutes.

5. A commercial kitchen uses $\frac{3}{4}$ of a cup of milk every $\frac{4}{6}$ of a minute.

6. An athlete swims $4\frac{1}{2}$ miles every 3 days.

7. The typical household in New Town uses 792 therms of gas every 12 months.

a unit of measure
for natural gas

8. The Riley family spent $902.60 for 4 weeks of groceries.

9. Gerald's store purchased 36 bottles of organic oil for $288.

10. A museum had 1,988 visitors to its new exhibit in the first 7 days.

PROPORTIONS

A **PROPORTION** is a number sentence where two ratios are equal. You can check if two ratios are proportional by using **CROSS PRODUCTS**. If both products are equal, then the two ratios are **EQUIVALENT FRACTIONS** and form a proportion!

Are the ratios $\frac{1}{3}$ and $\frac{2}{6}$ proportional?

$$\frac{1}{3} \diagdown \frac{2}{6}$$ ← Cross multiply.

$2 \cdot 3 = 6$ ← These are the cross products.
$1 \cdot 6 = 6$ ←

$6 = 6$ ← Cross products are equal.

So, $\frac{1}{3} = \frac{2}{6}$. This is a proportion because the ratios are equal.

| $\frac{1}{3}$ | $\frac{1}{3}$ | $\frac{1}{3}$ |

| $\frac{1}{6}$ | $\frac{1}{6}$ | $\frac{1}{6}$ | $\frac{1}{6}$ | $\frac{1}{6}$ | $\frac{1}{6}$ |

| $\frac{2}{6}$ | $\frac{2}{6}$ | $\frac{2}{6}$ |

EXAMPLE: A recipe uses 2 tablespoons of salt and 8 cups of flour. The baker accidentally puts in 3 tablespoons of salt. How many cups of flour should the baker now use?

▶ To find how many cups of flour the baker should now use, write a proportion, and solve for the unknown quantity: x.

RATIO: $\dfrac{2 \text{ tbsp salt}}{8 \text{ cups flour}}$

PROPORTION: $\dfrac{2 \text{ tbsp salt}}{8 \text{ cups flour}} = \dfrac{3 \text{ tbsp salt}}{x \text{ cups flour}}$

Use x for the amount of flour the baker needs.

SOLVE: $\dfrac{2}{8} \diagdown \dfrac{3}{x}$ ← Cross multiply

$2x = 3 \cdot 8$ Multiply

$2x = 24$

$2x \div 2 = 24 \div 2$

Divide each side of the equation by 2 to find x.

$x = 12$ ← This is the amount of flour the baker needs. 12 cups!

$\dfrac{2 \text{ tbsp salt}}{8 \text{ cups flour}} = \dfrac{3 \text{ tbsp salt}}{12 \text{ cups flour}}$

So, the baker will need to use 12 cups of flour.

THINK:

Look at the table. The proportion of _salt_ to _flour_ stays the same even in different scenarios. Every tablespoon of salt is multiplied by 4, and that product tells us the number of cups of flour. This is known as the **CONSTANT OF PROPORTIONALITY.**

TBSP. SALT		CUPS FLOUR
1	× 4	4
2	× 4	8
3	× 4	12
4	× 4	16
5	× 4	20
6	× 4	24

SOLVE THE PROBLEMS.

1. Do the ratios $\frac{10}{6}$ and $\frac{5}{3}$ form a proportion? Show why or why not using cross products.

2. Do the ratios $\frac{8}{9}$ and $\frac{7}{8}$ form a proportion? Show why or why not using cross products.

3. Which two ratios form a proportion? Show why using cross products.

$$\frac{3}{5}, \frac{7}{12}, \frac{9}{15}$$

4. Which two ratios form a proportion? Show why using cross products.

$$\frac{20}{32}, \frac{5}{8}, \frac{4}{14}$$

5. Solve for the unknown: $\dfrac{4}{x} = \dfrac{16}{36}$

6. Solve for the unknown: $\dfrac{7}{11} = \dfrac{y}{22}$

7. Solve for the unknown: $\dfrac{n}{3.10} = \dfrac{2.5}{5}$

8. At Nell's Grocery Store, you can buy 3 oranges for $1.25. Kalvin has $8.75. How many oranges can he purchase?

9. For every 12 minutes of aerobic exercise, an instructor allocates 2 minutes of stretching. Her boot camp class is 60 minutes long. How many minutes do the class members spend stretching?

10. An art teacher can purchase 7 containers of paint for $35. Her class uses 8 containers of paint each week. If the class runs for 10 weeks, how much will the teacher spend on paint? Explain how you know.

Chapter 18 ✏️ CONVERTING MEASUREMENTS

There are two **SYSTEMS OF MEASUREMENT**: **STANDARD** and **METRIC**. We can convert, or change, measurements of length, weight, and capacity within one system. We can also convert between measurement systems.

To change from one unit of measurement to another unit, use ratios and proportions.

EXAMPLE: An engineer is inspecting a highway that is 8.05 kilometers long. She needs to write a report using measurements in yards. What is the length of the highway in yards?

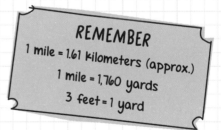

REMEMBER
1 mile = 1.61 kilometers (approx.)
1 mile = 1,760 yards
3 feet = 1 yard

▶ To find the length of the highway in yards, set up proportions and solve.

STEP 1: You know 1 mile = 1.61 kilometers, and 1 mile = 1,760 yards. So, 1,760 yards = 1.61 kilometers.

Convert kilometers to yards.

$$\frac{1.61 \text{ kilometers}}{1,760 \text{ yards}} = \frac{8.05 \text{ kilometers}}{x \text{ yards}}$$ ← Proportion: kilometers *to* yards.

$1.61x = 8.05 \cdot 1,760$ ← Cross multiply to solve for x.

$1.61x \div 1.61 = 14,168 \div 1.61$ ← Divide both sides by 1.61 to isolate x on one side of the equal sign.

$x = 8,800$ ← 8.05 kilometers = 8,800 yards

Now that you know 8.05 kilometers = 8,800 yards, find how many feet are equal to 8,800 yards.

That will tell you the number of feet that are equivalent to 8.05 kilometers.

STEP 2: You know 1 yard = 3 feet.

Convert yards to feet.

$$\frac{1 \text{ yard}}{3 \text{ feet}} = \frac{8,800 \text{ yards}}{x \text{ feet}}$$ ← Proportion: yards *to* feet.

$1x = 3 \cdot 8,800$ ← Cross multiply to solve for x.

$x = 26,400$ ← 8,800 yards = 26,400 feet

So, the length of the highway is 26,400 feet.

FOR 1 THROUGH 7, WRITE THE EQUIVALENT MEASUREMENTS. ROUND ALL MEASUREMENTS TO THE NEAREST WHOLE NUMBER.

Length

12 inches (in) = 1 foot (ft)

3 feet (ft) = 1 yard (yd)

1,760 yards (yd) = 1 mile (mi)

10 millimeters (mm) = 1 centimeter (cm)

100 centimeters (cm) = 1 meter (m)

1,000 meters (m) = 1 kilometer (km)

1 inch (in) = 2.54 centimeters (cm)

3.28 feet (ft) = 1 meter (m) (approximately)

1 yard (yd) = 0.9144 meter (m)

1 mile (mi) = 1.61 kilometers (km) (approximately)

Weight

1 pound (lb) = 16 ounces (oz)

1 ton (t) = 2,000 pounds (lb)

1,000 milligrams (mg) = 1 gram (g)

1,000 grams (g) = 1 kilogram (kg)

1 ounce (oz) = 28.349 grams (g) (approximately)

1 pound (lb) = 453.592 grams (g) (approximately)

1 pound (lb) = 0.454 kilograms (kg) (approximately)

Capacity

1 tablespoon (tbsp) = 3 teaspoons (tsp)

1 fluid ounce (oz) = 2 tablespoons (tbsp)

1 cup (c) = 8 fluid ounces (oz)

1 pint (pt) = 2 cups (c)

1 quart (qt) = 2 pints (pt)

1 gallon (gal) = 4 quarts (qt)

1 fluid ounce (fl oz) = 29.574 milliliters (ml) (approximately)

1 pint (pt) = 473.177 milliliters (ml) (approximately)

1 pint (pt) = 0.473 liters (l) (approximately)

1 gallon (gal) = 3.785 liters (l) (approximately)

1. 2.5 tons = _____ pounds

2. _____ gallons = 48 cups

3. 9,000 centimeters = _____ meters

4. _____ ounces = 4.75 pounds

5. 75.5 feet = _____ inches

6. 38 kilometers = _____ miles

7. _____ pounds = 5 kilograms

FOR 8 THROUGH 10, SOLVE THE PROBLEM USING WHAT YOU KNOW ABOUT CONVERTING MEASUREMENTS. ROUND ALL MEASUREMENTS TO THE NEAREST WHOLE NUMBER.

8. A commercial for an amusement park states that the tallest point of the roller coaster is 19.2 meters high. What is the tallest point of the roller coaster in feet?

9. Zack rents a camper for a road trip. At the gas station, he fills the tank with 40 liters of gas. The amount of gas Zack needs to reach his first destination is 53 gallons of gas. How many more liters of gas does Zack need to reach his first destination? Explain how you know.

10. Which is greater, 27 inches or 50.8 centimeters? Explain how you know.

19 PERCENT

PERCENT means *per hundred* or *out of 100*. Percentages are ratios that compare a quantity to 100. They use the symbol %.

You can write a percentage using a ratio, fraction, or decimal.

25% =
25 out of 100; $\frac{25}{100} = \frac{1}{4}$; 0.25

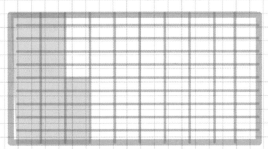

50% =
50 out of 100; $\frac{50}{100} = \frac{1}{2}$; 0.50

75% =
75 out of 100; $\frac{75}{100} = \frac{3}{4}$; 0.75

100% =
100 out of 100; $\frac{100}{100} = 1$

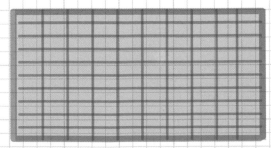

EXAMPLE: In a survey of 130 high school freshmen, 78 students sleep in on weekends. What percentage of freshmen **DO NOT** sleep in on weekends?

▶ To find what percentage of freshmen **DO NOT** sleep in on weekends, you can divide or set up a proportion.

THINK:

You are told 78 out of 130 freshmen sleep in on weekends. That means: 130 − 78 = 52 or 52 out of 130 freshmen DO NOT sleep in on weekends.

METHOD 1: Divide

Write the ratio: 52 out of 130 as a fraction. Then divide.

$$\frac{52}{130} = 52 \div 130 = 0.4$$

Move the decimal two spaces to the right and include a percent sign. Remember we do this because *percent* means "per 100" or $\frac{40}{100}$.

0.4 = 40%

So, 40% of freshmen DO NOT sleep in on weekends.

METHOD 2: Write a Proportion

Write the ratio: 52 out of 130 as a fraction. Then write the ratio: x out of 100.

$$\frac{52}{130} \diagdown \diagup \frac{x}{100}$$

130 · x = 52 · 100 ← Cross multiply

$130x = 5{,}200$ ← Divide both sides by 130 so you can isolate x.

$x = 40$

Notice: We get the same answer! So, 40% of freshmen DO NOT sleep in on weekends.

FOR 1 THROUGH 3, WRITE THE PERCENT AS A FRACTION. SIMPLIFY THE FRACTION IF POSSIBLE.

1. 32%

2. 9.2%

3. 48%

FOR 4 THROUGH 6, WRITE THE PERCENT AS A DECIMAL.

4. 84%

5. 110.5%

6. 0.016%

FOR 7 THROUGH 8, WRITE THE FRACTION AS A PERCENT.

7. $\frac{42}{60}$ is what percent?

8. $\frac{230}{100}$ is what percent?

SOLVE THE PROBLEMS.

9. A car salesman sold 5 cars for every 9 people coming into the car showroom. What was the car salesman's percentage of sales?

   (Hint: Round to the nearest percentage.)

10. At the state zoo, 110 out of 145 visitors buy ice cream at the zoo's concession stand. What percentage of visitors do not buy ice cream at the zoo? Explain how you know.

11. A local newspaper reported that 4 out of 10 people in town own a cat, and 3 out of 5 people own a dog. What percent of the town owns cats? What percent of the town owns dogs? Do more people own cats than dogs? Explain how you know.

12. A survey in a newspaper reported that 39 out of 50 people prefer coffee to tea. After reading the survey, a barista says 68% of people prefer coffee to tea. Is the percentage given by the barista correct? Explain how you know.

PERCENT WORD PROBLEMS

The key to solving percent word problems is translating the words in the problem accurately, writing a number sentence, performing calculations carefully, and *always* checking your work!

- *Is* means "equals."
- *What* or *What number* means "an unknown number."
- *Of* means "multiply"; *remaining* means "subtract."
- Represent an unknown number with a variable, like *x*.
- A percent can be written as a decimal. Simply move the decimal point two spaces to the left and get rid of the percent sign.

EXAMPLE: Every summer, Neilsville holds a carnival to raise money for community programs. On the first night, 348 of the 400 people in attendance each donated more than $30, and the remaining people gave less than $30. What percent of the people in attendance gave less than $30?

To find what percent of the people gave less than $30, write a number sentence and solve by using what you know about percent.

STEP 1: Write a number sentence. Look for the key words in the problem.

"Remaining" is a clue that a subtraction sentence will be needed.

THINK:
We know 348 of the 400 people gave *more* than $30.

That means: 400 - 348 = 52 or 52 people gave *less* than $30.

STEP 2: Solve.

What percent of the people in attendance gave less than $30?

$x \cdot 400$ people in attendance = 52 people gave less than $30

$x \cdot 400 = 52$ ← Number sentence that represents the problem.

$x \cdot \dfrac{400}{400} = \dfrac{52}{400}$ ← Divide both sides by 400 to isolate the unknown, x.

$x = 0.13$ ← This is the answer. Rewrite the answer as a percent by moving the decimal two spaces to the right and including a % sign.

$x = 13\%$

STEP 3: Check your work.

If 13% gave *less than* $30, that would mean: 100% – 13% = 87%, or 87% gave *more than* $30.

Write a proportion to check:

$\dfrac{348}{400} = \dfrac{x}{100}$

$400x = 34{,}800$

$400x \div 400 = 34{,}800 \div 400$

$x = 87$

$\dfrac{87}{100} = 0.87 = 87\%$ ← This answer is correct! 87% of the people in attendance gave *more than* $30.

> **COMMON ERROR:**
> Do not forget to check the REASONABLENESS OF YOUR ANSWER! Think: If only 52 people out of 400 gave *less than* $30, would a percentage larger than 13% make sense?

So, 13% of the people in attendance gave less than $30.

SOLVE EACH PROBLEM. CHECK YOUR ANSWERS.

1. What is 19% of 300?

2. What is 32% of 50?

3. What is 15% of 66?

4. 147 is what percent of 210?

5. 48 is what percent of 96?

6. 7 is what percent of 35?

7. 1.80 is what percent of $2.40?

CHAPTER 20

8. Chris received a 75% on his science test. He answered 24 questions correctly. How many questions were on the science test?

9. A food pantry received 12 boxes of rice. This is 30% of their weekly donation goal. How many boxes of rice does the pantry still need to meet its weekly donation goal?

10. There are 600 seats in the university's auditorium. The student life committee sells tickets for 520 seats to the next variety show. What percent of the seats are still available?

Chapter

21

TAXES AND ⊞
⊜ □ FEES ○ ◁

TAXES are fees charged by the government to improve our states and neighborhoods. There are many kinds of taxes. One type of tax is **SALES TAX**, a fee charged on items purchased. Some **FEES** work like taxes— a fee amount can be determined by a percentage of something else.

TAXES: Ms. Dobs purchases a used 3-D printer for the school's media room. The price is $765 plus a 7% state sales tax and an $18 shipping fee. How much does Ms. Dobs pay in total for the 3-D printer?

STEP 1: Change 7% to a decimal.

7% = 0.07

STEP 2: Multiply 0.07 and $765.

$765 • .07 = sales tax
$53.55 = sales tax ← tax on $765

STEP 3: To find how much Ms. Dobs pays in total for the 3-D printer, write an equation that adds the cost, tax, and shipping fee.

$765 + $53.55 + $18 = $836.55

So, Ms. Dobs pays a total of $836.55 for the 3-D printer.

FEES: Jessica recently joined a new health club. The club has a monthly charge that includes a 12% fee for group exercise classes. What is the monthly cost for membership without the fee for classes if Jessica pays $101.36?

STEP 1: Add the percent of the cost of the monthly membership (100%) and the percent of the fee (12%) to get the total cost percent.

100% + 12% fee = 112%

STEP 2: Convert the total cost percent to a decimal.

112% = 1.12

STEP 3: Write an equation to solve for the monthly cost *without* the fee for classes.

$101.36 = 1.12x$

$101.36 \div 1.12 = 1.12x \div 1.12$ ← Divide both sides of the equation by 1.12 to get x alone.

$90.50 = x$

So, the monthly cost for membership without the group class fee is $90.50.

SOLVE EACH PROBLEM. ROUND YOUR ANSWERS TO THE NEAREST CENT.

1. The cost of a skateboard is $125.36. The state sales tax is 8.5%. What is the total cost of the skateboard with tax?

$125.36 + TAX

2. The cost of a textbook is $55.10. The state sales tax is 5%. What is the total cost of the textbook with tax?

3. The cost of a pizza party was $230.41. There was a state sales tax of 9.2%. What was the amount of tax paid?

4. The Chen family has a monthly electric bill of $85 on a budget plan. The electricity usage tax is 2.25% in their state. What is the monthly amount of usage tax on the electric bill?

5. Aditi spent $35.74 on music downloads. There was a 6.8% state sales tax included. What was the cost of the music downloads without the state sales tax?

6. The total cost of a Jet Ski rental was $286.78. There was a 15% late fee included. What was the cost of the Jet Ski rental without the late fee?

7. A painter charges $580 and a 7% sales tax for painting a studio apartment. What is the total cost of painting the apartment?

8. ABC Mechanics will fix most cars for $60 an hour, plus the cost of new parts, and a 6.5% sales tax. If Sarah gets an estimate from the shop of 4 hours to fix her car, what is the estimated cost, including tax, and without any new parts?

9. Miguel purchased a mailbox for his new home from an online store. The cost of the mailbox was $55 with a 7.5% sales tax and a $15 shipping fee. What was the total cost of Miguel's purchase?

10. Jake wins $2,000,000 in the lottery! According to the lottery website, Jake will need to pay 36% in taxes when claiming his winnings. How much money will Jake pay in taxes? How much money will Jake receive after paying taxes?

Chapter 22 · DISCOUNTS AND MARKUPS

Calculating a **DISCOUNT** is like calculating taxes or fees, but because you are *saving money*, you *subtract* it from the original price.

On the other hand, it is important to remember that businesses exist to make money. So, more often than we realize, businesses *increase our costs*. These increases are known as **MARKUPS**. For example, a new pillow may cost $10 to make, but $50 to buy. That is a 400% markup!

DISCOUNT

Wayne purchases a smartphone for $422.50. This purchase price was a good deal because he received 45% off the manufacturer's retail price. What was the manufacturer's retail price of the smartphone?

STEP 1: This is a discount. So, *subtract* the percent of the discount from the percent of the original cost.

100% − 45% = 55% ← Think: He only paid 55% of the manufacturer's retail price.

STEP 2: Change the percent to a decimal.

55% = 0.55 ← Move the decimal point two spaces to the left.

STEP 3: Write a number sentence. Then solve for the manufacturer's retail price of the smartphone.

$422.50 is 55% of what number
$422.50 = 0.55 • x
$422.50 ÷ 0.55 = 0.55$x$ ÷ 0.55 ← Divide both sides of the equation
by 0.55 to get x alone.

x = $768.18 ← Round to the nearest cent.

So, the manufacturer's retail price of the smartphone was $768.18.

MARKUP

A hardware store purchases a package of solar panel lights for $8.85. To make a profit, the store will mark up the original price by 90%. What is the markup? What is the store's selling price of the solar panel lights?

STEP 1: Change the percent discount to a decimal.

90% = 0.90 ← Move the decimal point two spaces to the left.

STEP 2: Determine the markup. Multiply the decimal by the original cost.

$8.85 • 0.90 = $7.97 ← Multiply. Round to the nearest cent.

So, the markup is $7.97.

STEP 3: Add the markup to the original cost.

$8.85 + $7.97 = $16.82 ← Add. This is the selling price.

So, the selling price of the solar panel lights is $16.82.

SOLVE EACH PROBLEM. ROUND YOUR ANSWERS TO THE NEAREST CENT.

1. Manny's Music Store is having a 35% off sale on all guitars. The guitar Shondra chooses is priced at $199.99. Find the discount and the final price of the guitar.

2. Sabrina wants to learn a new language. She downloads an app and sees that it comes with an immediate discount of 55% off a yearly membership. If the yearly membership costs $139.99, how much money will Sabrina save? How much money will the yearly membership with the discount cost?

3. David buys new ice skates for the hockey season. He pays $78.63, receiving a 25% discount for showing his student ID. What was the original price of the ice skates?

4. Gia purchases supplies from a new vendor. Her total order comes to $410. Because Gia operates a family-owned business, the vendor gives her a 45% discount and an additional 10% off her first purchase. How much will the supplies cost after the discounts are applied?

5. Kenji wants to buy a video game at a warehouse store. The game is priced at $81.36 but comes with a discount of 20%. He searches online and finds the same game being sold for $71.25, and that offer comes with a 5% discount and free shipping. Which offer is a better deal? How do you know?

6. A home store purchases autumn wreaths for $11 a wreath. To make a profit, the manager will mark up the price by 82% percent. Find the markup amount and the new selling price.

7. Fit Health Club purchases reusable water bottles for $4 a case. The club will mark up the price by 95% percent. Find the markup amount and the new selling price of one case of water bottles.

8. A furniture store charges $554.60 for a recliner. They mark up the chair by 88% to make a profit. What was the original cost of the chair?

9. At an electronics store, a wireless mouse priced at $38.65 is marked 25% off. The marked price of the mouse included a markup of 75%. What is the original cost of the mouse? What is the sale price?

10. Sharron's Shirt Shack bought long-sleeve and short-sleeve shirts. The long-sleeve shirts cost Sharron $12.50 each, and the short-sleeve shirts cost her $9.85 each. Sharron made a markup of 55% to the long-sleeve shirts and a 60% markup to the short-sleeve shirts. Which shirt will cost more? Explain your answer.

Chapter 23 GRATUITY AND COMMISSION

A **GRATUITY** is a "tip" or a "gift" in the form of money. We usually talk about tips or gratuity regarding servers at restaurants.

> The more your bill costs, the more the gratuity or commission will be—they have a proportional relationship!

A **COMMISSION** is a fee paid for selling a product or service. We usually talk about commissions regarding salespeople at stores.

In both cases, how much is paid is typically dependent on the total cost of the services or the items sold. You can calculate gratuity and commission just like sales tax.

UH-OH...

EXAMPLES:

GRATUITY

The Kay family is celebrating the end of the school year at their favorite restaurant. The final bill for the dinner is $386.94. Ms. Kay gives an 18% gratuity. How much is the gratuity? What is the total cost of the family dinner?

STEP 1: Convert the percent to a decimal.

18% = 0.18 ← Move the decimal point two spaces to the left.

STEP 2: Determine the gratuity. Multiply the decimal by the final bill for the dinner.

$386.94 • 0.18 = $69.65 ← Multiply. Round to the nearest cent.

So, the gratuity is $69.65.

STEP 3: Add the gratuity to the final bill for the dinner.

$386.94 + $69.65 = $456.59 ← Add. This is the total cost of dinner.

So, the total cost of the family dinner is $456.59.

COMMISSION

Jackson sells many types of automobiles at Amari's Car Dealership. In the first quarter of the year, he made $256,000 in car sales. Jackson's commission is 11%. How much did he earn in commission?

METHOD 1:

STEP 1: Convert the percent discount to a decimal.

11% = 0.11 ← Move the decimal point two spaces to the left.

STEP 2: Determine the commission. Multiply the decimal by the total dollar amount of car sales.

$256,000 • 0.11 = $28,160 ← Multiply.

METHOD 2:

STEP 1: $\frac{11}{100} = \frac{x}{256,000}$ ← Set up a proportion. Cross multiply.

$100x = 256,000 • 11$

STEP 2: $100x ÷ 100 = 2,816,000 ÷ 100$ ← Divide both sides of the equation by 100 to get x alone.

$x = $28,160$ ← Both methods resulted in the same answer. This is a good way to check your work!

So, Jackson earned $28,160 in commission.

ANSWER THE QUESTIONS. USE WHAT YOU KNOW ABOUT GRATUITY AND COMMISSION. ROUND YOUR ANSWERS TO THE NEAREST CENT.

1. Emilia's Pizzeria has several deliveries ready to leave the restaurant. Unfortunately, the computer went offline leaving Emilia to calculate customers' receipts by hand. Complete Emilia's Pizzeria's delivery receipt chart.

CUSTOMER'S NAME	PIZZERIA BILL	GRATUITY PERCENTAGE	FINAL COST
Harold M.	$38.56	18%	
Maria's family	$66.89	20%	
Chailai S.		15%	$31.91
Campanella family	$84.22	18%	
Duante J.		19%	$50.37

2. Freddy's Furniture Store has five associates. The store manager keeps record of every associate's weekly furniture sales and their commission. Complete Freddy's Furniture Store's commission chart.

ASSOCIATE'S NAME	WEEKLY FURNITURE SALES	COMMISSION PERCENTAGE	TOTAL COMMISSION
Tiffany	$5,445	10%	
Johanan	$7,256	8%	
Diego	$6,523	12%	
Frida	$10,998	12%	
Sharon	$8,235	11%	

3. Celine's Bakery hires Bart's Appliance Company to install a new double wall oven. The cost of the installation is $575, and the bakery wants to give a 30% tip. How much is the tip, and how much does the bakery pay in total to Bart's Appliance Company?

4. Karen pays $487.56 for a company luncheon. This included a 16% gratuity. Karen needs to report the cost of the lunch without the gratuity to receive a reimbursement from her manager. How much was the cost of the luncheon without the gratuity?

PASTA PALACE

TOTAL PLUS 16%
GRATUITY : $487.56

5. Abel's Discount Suit Store offers its employees two compensation plans: 9% commission or a salary of $10 per hour. If Carl works 20 hours a week and sells $2,000 in suits every week, which is the better compensation plan? Explain your answer.

6. Martin and Athena are waiters at Francesco's Bistro. Martin receives a 22% gratuity from a table whose bill is $307.12. Athena receives a 18% gratuity from a table whose bill is $398.26. Who receives the greater amount of money? Explain your answer.

24 SIMPLE INTEREST

SIMPLE INTEREST is the amount of dollars paid by a *borrower* on a fixed amount of money given by a *lender*, for an established amount of time, in years.

You can use the **SIMPLE INTEREST FORMULA** to determine the total amount of interest to be paid on money borrowed or loaned.

> **INTEREST (I):** The amount of money that is collected in return for lending money.
>
> **PRINCIPAL (P):** The amount of money that is being borrowed.
>
> **INTEREST RATE (R):** The percentage that will be paid for every year the money is borrowed.
>
> **TIME (T):** The amount of time that the money will be borrowed.

Interest = Principal × Interest Rate × Time
$$I = P \cdot R \cdot T$$

EXAMPLES:

INTERESTING...

▶ Hanan deposits $7,200 in a savings account that offers an annual interest rate of 2.5%. How long does she need to leave this money in the account to earn $900?

STEP 1: Find the interest, principal, interest rate, and time.

I = $900

P = $7,200

R = 2.5% = 0.025 ← Move the decimal point two spaces to the left.

T = ? ← Note: The amount of time is to be determined. So, use T to represent the unknown variable.

STEP 2: Use the Simple Interest Formula and solve for T, the time in years.

Interest = Principal • Interest Rate • Time

$I = P \cdot R \cdot T$

$900 = 7,200 \cdot 0.025 \cdot T$ ← Substitute.

$900 = 180 \, T$ ← Multiply.

$900 \div 180 = 180 \, T \div 180$ ← Divide both sides of the equation by 180 to get T alone.

$5 = T$ ← The amount of time to earn $900.

So, Hanan needs to leave her money in the savings account for 5 years to earn $900.

Sally's Hair Salon borrows $25,000 to open a new location. The length of the loan will be for 6 years at an annual interest rate of 10.8%. What is the total amount of money the salon will pay back to the lender?

STEP 1: Find the principal, interest rate, and time.

$P = \$25,000$

$R = 10.8\% = 0.108 \leftarrow$ Move the decimal point two spaces to the left.

$T = 6$

STEP 2: Use the Simple Interest Formula.

Interest = Principal • Interest Rate • Time

$I = P \cdot R \cdot T$

$I = 25,000 \cdot 0.108 \cdot 6 \leftarrow$ Substitute.

$I = \$16,200 \leftarrow$ Multiply. This is the total interest to be paid on the 6-year loan.

STEP 3: To find the total amount of money the salon will pay back to the lender, add the principal and the interest.

$\$25,000 + \$16,200 = \$41,200$

So, the total amount of money the salon will pay back to the lender is $41,200.

ANSWER THE QUESTIONS. USE WHAT YOU KNOW ABOUT SIMPLE INTEREST. ROUND YOUR ANSWERS TO THE NEAREST CENT.

1. Complete the following chart.

INTEREST	PRINCIPAL	INTEREST RATE	TIME
	$2,158.60	6.5%	5 years
	$64,155	11%	8 years
$33,710.40	$37,456	9%	
$5,578.20	$5,165	18%	

2. Dylan is applying for a loan to purchase a new boat. The cost of the boat is $37,260. He wants to take out a loan for the full amount and is quoted an interest rate of 4.5%. The term of the loan is 8 years. How much interest will Dylan pay on this loan? How much money will he pay in total for the new boat?

3. Anika is saving for a new home. She deposits $54,895 in a 3-year high-yield CD account that has an annual interest rate of 3.25%. How much money will Anika have in her account after 3 years?

4. A family who owns a pet store borrows $45,000 to purchase a new van for grooming animals. The loan is for 6 years and has an interest rate of 5.5%. How much interest will the family pay on the loan? How much money will the family pay back in full for the loan?

5. The Young family is replacing their central air-conditioning with a high-efficiency unit that costs $11,798. The family is offered a 48-month loan without interest. If the family is not able to pay back the full amount in 48 months, they will be charged 8% interest on the purchase amount. How much money in total will the Young family pay if they take longer than 48 months? (Think: 48 months is 4 years.)

6. Jan needs to save $7,500 to remodel her sunroom. She has $6,000 and decides to deposit her money in a savings account that has an annual interest rate of 5%. How long will it take for Jan's savings account to earn $1,500 in interest?

7. Valentina deposits $1,350 in a savings account at a 5% interest rate. Neil deposits $1,150 at a 7% interest rate. If both high school students keep their money in the savings account for 5 years, who earns more money, Valentina or Neil? How much more money is earned? Explain your answer.

8. Salvatore borrows $4,800 at an 8% interest rate. Riley borrows $6,150 at a 6% interest rate. If both business owners take this loan for 8 years, who pays more interest at the end of their loan, Salvatore or Riley? How much more? Explain your answer.

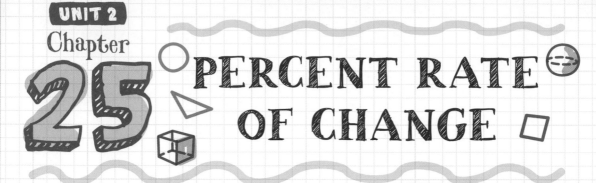

Chapter 25: PERCENT RATE OF CHANGE

We use **PERCENT RATE OF CHANGE** to show how much an amount has changed in relation to the original amount.

We can show percent rate of change by setting up a ratio.

> **AMOUNT INCREASE (ORIGINAL PRICE GOES UP)**
> March 1: skateboard $129
> June 1: skateboard $199
>
> **AMOUNT DECREASE (ORIGINAL PRICE GOES DOWN)**
> April 1: wireless printer $89
> July 1: wireless printer $59

$$\text{percent rate of change} = \frac{\text{amount of increase or decrease in quantity}}{\text{original quantity}}$$

Percent Increase

In March, a sporting goods store sells a skateboard for $129. In June, the same skateboard sells for $199. What is the skateboard's *percent increase* in price from March to June?

STEP 1: To calculate the **PERCENT INCREASE** in price, set up a ratio.

THINK:
The change or increase in price is the *difference* between the original price and the new price. So, subtract $129 from $199.

$$\text{percent increase} = \frac{\text{price } increase}{\text{original price}}$$

$$\text{percent increase} = \frac{199 - 129}{129} = \frac{70}{129}$$

STEP 2: Divide. Round to the nearest cent.

$\frac{70}{129} = 70 \div 129 = 0.54$

STEP 3: Move the decimal point two spaces to the right and insert the percent symbol.

$0.54 = 54\%$

So, the percent increase in price is 54%.

Percent Decrease

In April, an electronics store sells a wireless printer for $89. In July, the same wireless printer sells for $59. What is the printer's *percent decrease* in price from April to July?

STEP 1: To calculate the **PERCENT DECREASE** in price, set up a ratio.

percent decrease = $\frac{price\ decrease}{original\ price}$

Think: The "change or decrease in price" is the *difference* between the original price and the new price. So, subtract $59 from $89. Write that amount in the numerator.

percent decrease = $\frac{89 - 59}{89} = \frac{30}{89}$

STEP 2: Divide. Round to the nearest cent.

$\frac{30}{89} = 30 \div 89 = 0.34$

> For percentages, round decimals to the nearest hundredths place.
> .47587 = .48 = 48%

STEP 3: Move the decimal point two spaces to the right and insert the percent symbol.

$0.34 = 34\%$

So, the percent decrease in price is 34%.

ANSWER THE QUESTIONS. USE WHAT YOU KNOW ABOUT PERCENT RATE OF CHANGE. (REMEMBER: ROUND DECIMALS TO THE NEAREST HUNDREDTHS PLACE.)

1. A university's enrollment in January is 7,959 students. In September, the total enrollment changes to 8,834 students. What is the percent rate of change in the university's enrollment?

2. Scottie's Grocery Store receives 56 crates of apples in early fall. At the end of the fall season, the store receives 24 crates. What is the percent rate of change in the number of crates of apples the store receives?

3. An online merchant posts the latest smartphone on their website. In the first hour, they sell 1,168 smartphones. In the second hour, they sell 2,227 smartphones. What is the percent rate of change in the number of smartphones sold?

4. Chen rents his apartment for $1,050 a month. His landlord increases his rent to $1,275 a month. What is the percent rate of change for the rent?

5. This time last year, 4,026 cars were driving to Seashell Beach each day. This year, that number changed to 2,084 cars. What is the percent rate of change for the number of cars traveling to Seashell Beach?

6. Nathan purchases antique picture frames for his home goods store for $8.85 each. He sells them for $16.25 each. What is the percentage rate of change for the price of a picture frame?

7. Julia has 14.8 shares of RCS stock. She sells some of her shares and now has a total of 9.2 shares. What is the percentage rate of change for the shares of stock?

8. What is the difference between a rate of change that increases and a rate of change that decreases?

Chapter 26 TABLES AND RATIOS

We can use tables to compare **RATIOS** and **PROPORTIONS**. They are helpful in organizing equivalent ratios and solving problems that involve proportional relationships.

Top Fit Yoga Studios provides its members with free classes for every package of classes purchased. The table below is displayed next to the cashier. How many free classes will a member receive for purchasing 8 classes? What is the least number of classes a member must purchase to get 1 free class? Note: The ratio of purchased classes to free classes is proportional.

Number of Yoga Classes Purchased	Number of Free Classes
8	?
24	6
40	10

▶ We can find how many free classes a member receives for purchasing 8 classes by writing a proportion.

$$\frac{8}{x} = \frac{24}{6}$$

← A proportion is made up of two equivalent ratios. In this case, we are comparing the number of purchased classes to the number of free classes.

$8(6) = 24x$ ← Cross multiply.

$48 = 24x$

$48 \div 24 = 24x \div 24$ ← Divide both sides of the equation by 24 to get x alone.

$2 = x$

So, a member will receive 2 free classes for purchasing 8 classes.

▶ To determine the least number of classes a member must purchase to get 1 free class, find the unit rate.

$$\frac{8}{2} = \frac{x}{1}$$ ← Cross multiply.

$8 = 2x$ ← Divide both sides of the equation by 2 to get x alone.

$x = 4$

REMEMBER:
A unit rate is a rate that has a 1 in the denominator.

So, a member needs to purchase at least 4 classes to get 1 class free.

FILL IN THE MISSING NUMBERS. THEN ANSWER THE QUESTION.

An art supply manufacturer keeps track of its daily production in minutes using the tables below. The daily production is always constant.

1.

NUMBER OF CRAYONS	MINUTES
1,250	2
2,500	
7,500	6
	8

2.

NUMBER OF COLORED MARKERS	MINUTES
3,000	
6,000	20
	30
12,000	40

3.

NUMBER OF WATERCOLOR PAINT PALLETS	MINUTES
	3
2,250	
3,375	9
4,500	12

4.

NUMBER OF DRAWING PENCILS	MINUTES
2,130	6
4,260	
6,375	18
	24

5. Which art supply can the manufacturer produce the fastest in 1 minute? Explain your answer. (Hint: Find the unit rate for each art supply.)

FOR 6 THROUGH 8, USE THE TABLES AND WHAT YOU KNOW ABOUT RATIOS AND PROPORTIONS TO SOLVE THE PROBLEMS.

6. The Hollifield School Marching Band is holding a raffle to raise money for their next performance trip. They sell 4 tickets for $6.00, and record the raffle ticket sales in the given table. How many tickets will the team need to sell to make $375?

NUMBER OF RAFFLE TICKETS	COST
4	$6
50	$75
100	$150
150	$225
	$375

7. The student government is planning a trip to an amusement park. The number of buses needed depends on the number of students going on the trip. To keep track of the required number of buses, they create the given table. If one bus can hold 28 students, how many buses will the school need if all 840 students go on the trip?

NUMBER OF BUSES	NUMBER OF STUDENTS
1	28
12	336
	840

8. At a commercial kitchen, a robotic mixer can make 4 batches of muffin batter in 270 seconds. The manager of the kitchen records its progress hourly in the given table. How many muffin batter batches will the robotic mixer make in 3,510 seconds?

NUMBER OF MUFFIN BATTER BATCHES	NUMBER OF SECONDS
4	270
20	1,350
32	2,160
44	2,970
	3,510

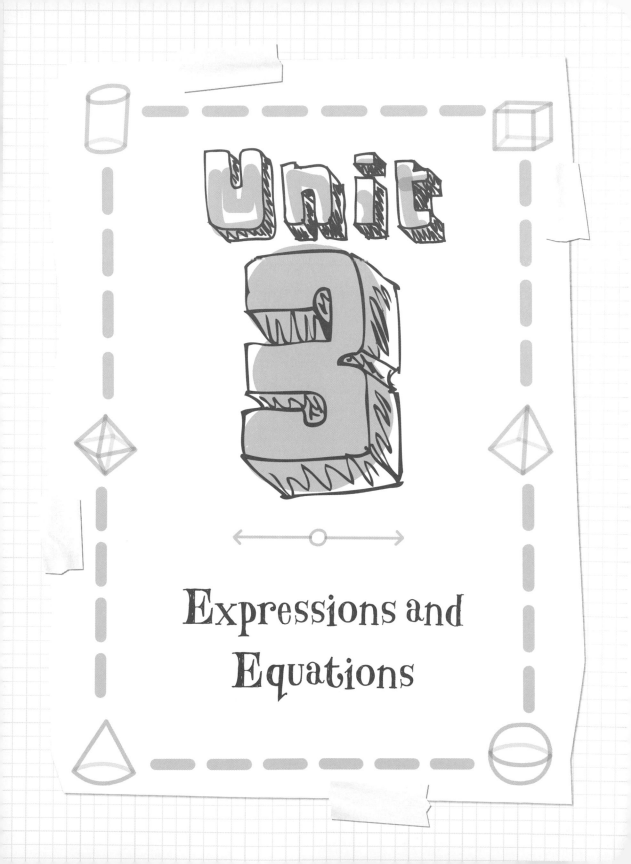

Unit

3

Expressions and
Equations

27. EXPRESSIONS

In math, an **EXPRESSION** is a mathematical phrase that contains numbers. An expression is made up of one or more **TERMS**.

An *algebraic expression* is a mathematical phrase that contains one or more **VARIABLES** (letters that represent an unknown quantity) and mathematical **OPERATORS** (+, −, •, ÷). Sometimes, it may contain numerals as well, called **CONSTANTS**.

A term is a number by itself or the product of a number and variable(s). In this diagram, the terms are $25n$ and 16. Terms can be negative or positive.

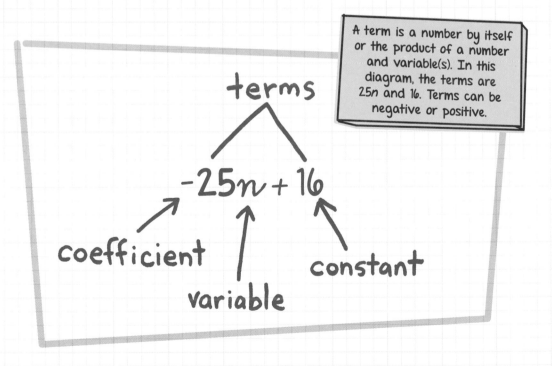

terms

$$-25n + 16$$

coefficient

variable

constant

You can say or write algebraic expressions in different ways.

Algebraic Expressions	Word Phrases
Addition Expression $-4b + 19$	negative four times b *plus* 19 the *product* of negative four and b *added to* 19 negative four multiplied by b *increased by* 19 the *sum* of negative four times b and 19
Subtraction Expression $y - \dfrac{1}{5}$	y *minus* one-fifth the *difference* between y and one-fifth y *decreased by* one-fifth y *minus* one divided by five one-fifth *subtracted* from y
Multiplication Expression $g(2); \ g \cdot 2; \ 2g$	the *product* of g and 2 g *times* 2 g *multiplied by* 2
Division Expression $36 \div -7r; \ \dfrac{36}{-7r}$	36 *divided by* negative 7 times r 36 *divided by* the product of negative 7 and r the *quotient* of 36 and negative 7 multiplied by r

FOR 1 THROUGH 3, LIST THE TERMS OF THE EXPRESSIONS.

1. $6w \div 55$

2. $-75 + 98d$

3. $8h + \dfrac{1}{16} - 18$

FOR 4 THROUGH 6, NAME THE VARIABLE(S), COEFFICIENT(S), AND CONSTANT(S).

4. $52 - 1.9x \div c$

5. $(8,022m) (d - 4) + 1.23$

no number in front of the variable means that the coefficient is 1

6. $3y \cdot \dfrac{4}{2r}$

FOR 7 THROUGH 9, WRITE THE EXPRESSIONS.

7. The product of two-thirds and h added to 26

8. The quotient of w and sixty-six hundredths

9. The product of 11 and c subtracted from the addition of r and 5

FOR 10 THROUGH 15, WRITE AN ALGEBRAIC EXPRESSION THAT ILLUSTRATES EACH SITUATION. USE x TO REPRESENT THE UNKNOWN QUANTITY.

10. Jonathan is 5 years older than his sister.

11. Double the number of students from last year will participate in this year's annual talent show.

12. Half of the people who live in our community like to shop at the new big-box store.

13. The store manager increased the stock of milk containers by 250 containers.

14. On field day, Danielle divided 30 juice boxes among all the children.

15. The online electronics store sells 73 of its personal computers in stock.

Chapter 28 PROPERTIES

PROPERTIES are like a set of math rules that always hold true.

Properties of Addition and Multiplication

ADDITION PROPERTIES	MULTIPLICATION PROPERTIES
Identity Property of Addition	**Identity Property of Multiplication**
$5 + 0 = 5 \leftarrow$ (add zero to any number and it stays the same)	$5 \cdot 1 = 5 \leftarrow$ (multiply any number by 1 and it stays the same)
Commutative Property of Addition	**Commutative Property of Multiplication**
$5 + 2 = 2 + 5 \leftarrow$ equivalent expressions both = 7	
$7 = 7$	$5 \cdot 2 = 2 \cdot 5 \leftarrow$ equivalent expressions both = 10
	$10 = 10$
Associative Property of Addition	**Associative Property of Multiplication**
$(5 + 4) + 2 = 5 + (4 + 2)$	
$9 + 2 = 5 + 6$ equivalent expressions	$(5 \cdot 2) \cdot 3 = 5 \cdot (2 \cdot 3) \leftarrow$ equivalent expressions
$11 = 11 \leftarrow$ It doesn't matter in what order you add the numbers. The answer is the same.	$10 \cdot 3 = 5 \cdot 6$
	$30 = 30 \leftarrow$ both = 30

The **DISTRIBUTIVE PROPERTY** allows us to simplify an expression by taking out the parentheses.

> **Distributive Property of Multiplication over Addition**
>
> $5(3x + 2) = (5 \cdot 3x) + (5 \cdot 2) = 15x + 10$
>
> $5(3x + 2) = 15x + 10$ ← equivalent expressions
>
> ---
>
> **Distributive Property of Multiplication over Subtraction**
>
> $5(3x - 2) = (5 \cdot 3x) - (5 \cdot 2) = 15x - 10$
>
> $5(3x - 2) = 15x - 10$ ← equivalent expressions

FACTORING is the reverse of the distributive property! It puts the parentheses back.

$2b + 2c = 2(b + c)$

$15x + 25y - 50 = ?$

Find the GCF of the terms: 15, 25, and 50. That is 5!

Divide each term by 5.

$15 \div 5 = 3$

$25 \div 5 = 5$

$50 \div 5 = 10$

$15x + 25y - 50 = 5(3x + 5y - 10)$

FOR 1 THROUGH 8, WRITE THE EQUIVALENT EXPRESSIONS. THEN IDENTIFY THE NAME OF THE PROPERTY ILLUSTRATED.

Expression	Equivalent Expression	Name of Property
1. $m + 5$		
2. $h(6 - d)$		
3. $18 \cdot c$		
4. $(n \cdot 2) \cdot 3$		
5. $9(x + 6)$		
6. $-y + (8 + 11)$		
7. $g + 0$		
8. ab		

FOR 9 THROUGH 11, WRITE EQUIVALENT EXPRESSIONS BY USING THE DISTRIBUTIVE PROPERTY.

9. $8(2x + 3.5)$

10. $4(x - 7y + 16)$

11. $\frac{2}{3}(3m + 24n + r)$

FOR 12 THROUGH 14, FACTOR THE EXPRESSIONS.

12. $8m + 32$

13. $7y - 28x + 14$

14. $6a + 12b + 30c$

SOLVE THE PROBLEM.

15. Sue's store sells 6 packages of 4 trail mix containers for $5.50. Darleen's store sells 4 packages of 6 trail mix containers for $5.50. Which store has the better buy or more trail mix for your money? Explain how you know.

Chapter 29

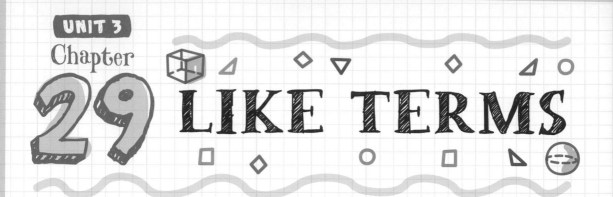

LIKE TERMS

A **TERM** is a number by itself or the product of a number and a variable (or more than one variable).

Coefficients

$$6n^2 + 12mn + 24mn - 48$$

Variables

Constant

> We can *collect* or *combine* like terms to simplify an expression—meaning we rewrite the expression so that it contains fewer numbers, variables, and operations.
>
> $6n^2 + 12mn + 24mn - 48 = 6n^2 + 36mn - 48$
>
> like terms

Terms: $6n^2$; $12mn$; $24mn$; -48

Simplify the expressions.

STEP 1: Identify like terms.

$-x + 4x - 7x + 11x + 28$

STEP 2: Combine like terms.

$-x + 4x + (-7x) + 11x + 28$

STEP 3: Review equivalent expression. Arrange in descending order.

$7x + 28$

STEP 1: Identify like terms.

$8a + 7xy + ba - 3xy + 5ab$ Think: We are adding a negative number.

STEP 2: Combine like terms.   Think: Because of the Commutative Property $ba = ab$.
So, we can combine ba and $5ab$.

$8a + 7xy + ba + (-3xy) + 5ab$

STEP 3: Review equivalent expression. Arrange in descending order.

$8a + 6ab + 4xy$

STEP 1: Identify like terms.

$2(cd + 6) - 12cd + 3$

STEP 2: Combine like terms.

$2cd + 12 + (-12cd) + 3$

STEP 3: Review equivalent expression. Arrange in descending order.

$-10cd + 15$

STEP 1: Identify like terms.

$5mn - 3mn + 3 + m - 11m^2$

STEP 2: Combine like terms.

$5mn + (-3mn) + 3 + m - 11m^2$ Think: We cannot combine m and m^2.
They are not alike. m^2 is $m \bullet m$.

STEP 3: Review equivalent expression.

Arrange in descending order.

$-11m^2 + m + 2mn + 3$ ⟵ REMEMBER: Since m^2 has the greatest exponent, we usually put it first in the equivalent expression. The constant always comes last.

FOR 1 THROUGH 3, LIST THE TERMS IN EACH EXPRESSION.

1. $y^2 - 9y + 6$

2. $5cd - 3d + 11$

3. $14mn + m^2 - 7m + 8$

FOR 4 THROUGH 6, LIST THE COEFFICIENTS AND THE CONSTANT IN EACH EXPRESSION.

4. $9x^2 + 25xy - 3$

5. $2ab^3 - 13a^2c - 8$

6. $1.52h^2 + \frac{2}{3}h + 36$

FOR 7 THROUGH 12, SIMPLIFY EACH EXPRESSION.

7. $h - 41h$

8. $15 - 7w + w - 52$

9. $-6x - 2x + x^2 + 22$

10. $4(x + 6) - 2x + 3.2$

11. $9y + 5t^2 + hg - 32 + 5gh$

12. $-ab + 3(ab - 1) + 18$

An **EXPONENT** is the number of times the **BASE NUMBER** is multiplied by itself.

> **COMMON ERROR:**
> The expression 3^5 does NOT mean 3×5.

exponent

$$3^5 = 3 \times 3 \times 3 \times 3 \times 3 = 243$$

base   5 threes

3^5 is read "three to the fifth power."

> **REMEMBER:**
> Any base that does not have an exponent has an unwritten exponent of 1: $5 = 5^1$

THAT'S **390,625** MORE POWER THAN THE AVERAGE 5!

Exponent Rules	Simplified Expressions
$x^5 = x \cdot x \cdot x \cdot x \cdot x$	$-7^5 = -(7 \cdot 7 \cdot 7 \cdot 7 \cdot 7) = -16{,}807$
$x^0 = 1$	$16^0 = 1$
$x^a \cdot x^b = x^{a+b}$	$10^2 \cdot 10^4 = 10^{2+4} = 10^6 = 1{,}000{,}000$
$x^a \div x^b = \dfrac{x^a}{x^b} = x^{a-b}$	$8^6 \div 8^5 = \dfrac{8^6}{8^5} = 8^{6-5} = 8^1 = 8$
$(x^a)^b = x^{a \cdot b}$	$-(4^2)^3 = -(4^{2 \cdot 3}) = -(4^6) = -4{,}096$
$(xy)^a = x^a \cdot y^a$	$(15xy)^2 = 15^2 \cdot x^2 \cdot y^2 = 225x^2y^2$
$x^{-a} = \dfrac{1}{x^a}$, where $x \neq 0$	$9^{-4} = \dfrac{1}{9^4} = \dfrac{1}{6{,}561}$
$\dfrac{1}{x^{-a}} = x^a$, where $x \neq 0$	$\dfrac{24x}{6x^{-3}} = \dfrac{24}{6} \cdot \dfrac{x}{x^{-3}} = 4 \cdot (x \div x^3) =$
	$4 \cdot (x^{1-3}) = 4 \cdot x^{-2} = \dfrac{4}{x^2}$

SIMPLIFY EACH OF THE FOLLOWING EXPRESSIONS.

1. 9^3

2. $(\frac{1}{3})^3 \cdot -(10^2)$

3. $(7p)^2$

4. $-(5^4)$

5. $m^{11} \div m^8$

6. $-6y^3 \cdot 3y \cdot -y^4$

7. $(\frac{-3}{4})^3$

8. $\dfrac{48h^{12}}{-8h^{-2}}$

9. $\dfrac{16a^9b^7}{3a^4b^2}$

10. $-(2^4)^3$

11. $(6m^2n^5)^4$

12. $\dfrac{r^{-4}s^6}{r^4s^7}$

Chapter 31

ORDER OF OPERATIONS

The **ORDER OF OPERATIONS** is an agreed-upon order to evaluate mathematical expressions.

1st

Any calculations inside parentheses or brackets should be performed first.

Parentheses **( )**
Brackets **[ ]**
Braces **{ }**

2nd

Exponents roots and absolute value are calculated left to right.

Exponents x^a
Square Roots $\sqrt{}$
Absolute Value $|\ |$

Multiplication and division—whichever comes first when you calculate left to right

Addition and subtraction—whichever comes first when you calculate left to right

EXAMPLE

Simplify: $6^2 + 5 \cdot (10 - 7)^2 \div 9$

To simplify, use the Order of Operations.

$6^2 + 5 \cdot (10 - 7)^2 \div 9$ ← Evaluate the innermost parentheses.

$6^2 + 5 \cdot 3^2 \div 9$ ← Evaluate the exponents.

$36 + \overrightarrow{5 \cdot 9 \div 9}$ ← Multiply then divide from left to right.

$36 + 45 \div 9 = 36 + 5$

$36 + 5 = 41$ ← Add.

So, $6^2 + 5 \cdot (10 - 7)^2 \div 9$ simplifies to 41.

FOR 1 THROUGH 8, SIMPLIFY EACH OF THE FOLLOWING EXPRESSIONS.

1. $5 + 3^3 \cdot 6$

2. $300 \div (11 \cdot 1)^2$

3. $-2^5 + 3 - 4(8)$

4. $6 + 2(9 - 5) \div -2$

5. $10 + (-1)^3 \cdot 3 - 4(12 + 7)$

6. $(56 \div 7) \cdot 5 - 18 \div 2$

7. $\dfrac{4^2 + (59 - 3^3)}{-16}$

8. $|24 - 40| - [(8 + 6) \cdot 4]^2$

FOR 9 THROUGH 10, INSERT PARENTHESES TO MAKE EACH NUMBER SENTENCE A TRUE STATEMENT.

9. $6 + 26 - 2 \div 8 = 9$

10. $36 \div 2^2 \cdot 3 + 10 \cdot 0.5 = 32$

FOR 11 THROUGH 13, SOLVE THE PROBLEMS.

11. The cafeteria at the stadium has 11 bottles of mustard in the supply room. It receives 10 boxes of 12 bottles and 8 boxes of 6 bottles. Before the manager could do inventory, 18 bottles of mustard were removed from the supply room. What is the total number of mustard bottles the cafeteria has remaining in the supply room? Explain how you got your answer.

12. Stephan has $165 in his savings account. He saves $50 a week for 36 weeks, and in week 37 he makes a withdrawal of $475 to purchase a mountain bike. What is the total amount of money in Stephan's account after this withdrawal?

13. Jillian and Brian simplify the same expression. However, Jillian gets a very different answer from Brian. Who is correct? Explain how you know.

JILLIAN	BRIAN
$-12 \cdot 8 + 4^2 \cdot (63 \div 7) - 3$	$-12 \cdot 8 + 4^2 \cdot (63 \div 7) - 3$
$-96 + 16 \cdot 9 - 3$	$-12 \cdot 8 + 16 \cdot 9 - 3$
$-80 \cdot 9 - 3$	$-96 + 144 - 3$
$-720 - 3$	$48 - 3$
-723	45

Chapter 32 · SCIENTIFIC NOTATION

SCIENTIFIC NOTATION is a shortened way of writing very small or very large numbers using powers of 10. This notation is commonly used by scientists, mathematicians, and engineers.

CONVERT: Standard Notation to Scientific Notation.

Standard Notation: 8,340,000	**Standard Notation:** 0.00000834
8.340000 ← Move the decimal point 6 spaces *to the left* to get a number between 1 and 10.	0.000008.34 ← Move the decimal point 6 spaces *to the right* to get a number between 1 and 10.
Scientific Notation: $8.34 \cdot 10^6$ The standard number is *greater than 1*, so the exponent of 10 is positive 6.	**Scientific Notation:** $8.34 \cdot 10^{-6}$ The standard number is *less than 1*, so the exponent of 10 is negative 6.

CONVERT: Scientific Notation to Standard Notation.

Scientific Notation:	Scientific Notation:
$2.98 \cdot 10^5$	$2.98 \cdot 10^{-5}$
298,000 ← The exponent 5 is positive, so move the decimal five spaces *to the right* (and fill with zeros).	0.0000298 ← The exponent 5 is negative, so move the decimal five spaces *to the left* (and fill with zeros).
Standard Notation: 298,000	Standard Notation: 0.0000298

Calculating Numbers in Scientific Notation.

$(8 \cdot 10^{-3})(5 \cdot 10^{-6})$

$8 \cdot 10^{-3} \cdot 5 \cdot 10^{-6}$ ← Keep the base 10 and add the exponents
$10^{-3+(-6)} = 10^{-9}$.

$8 \cdot 5 \cdot 10^{-9}$ ← Multiply: 8 and 5.

$40 \cdot 10^{-9} = 0.000000040$

$\dfrac{12 \cdot 10^6}{6 \cdot 10^{-2}}$

$\dfrac{12}{6} \cdot \dfrac{10^6}{10^{-2}}$ ← Keep the base 10 and subtract the exponents
$10^{6-(-2)} = 10^8$.

$\dfrac{12}{6} \cdot 10^8$ ← Divide 12 by 6.

$2 \cdot 10^8 = 200,000,000$

To change a negative number to scientific notation, count how many places you have to move the decimal point so that there is only a number between 0 and –10 remaining.

FOR 1 THROUGH 3, WRITE IN SCIENTIFIC NOTATION.

I APPROVE!

1. 320,000,000

2. 80,610,000

3. 0.000000129

FOR 4 THROUGH 6, WRITE IN STANDARD NOTATION.

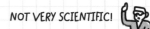

NOT VERY SCIENTIFIC!

4. $9.48 \cdot 10^6$

5. $3.07 \cdot 10^{-8}$

6. $5.56 \cdot 10^{11}$

FOR 7 THROUGH 9, FIRST CONVERT TO STANDARD NOTATION. THEN CIRCLE THE GREATER QUANTITY.

7. $1.25 \cdot 10^4$ | $8.16 \cdot 10^3$

8. $-3.08 \cdot 10^6$ | $-7.9 \cdot 10^7$

9. $6.31 \cdot 10^{-8}$ | $9.4 \cdot 10^{-5}$

FOR 10 THROUGH 15, EVALUATE. WRITE YOUR ANSWERS IN SCIENTIFIC NOTATION.

10. $(6.4 \cdot 10^2)(8.59 \cdot 10^7)$

11. $(4.04 \cdot 10^{-9})(-1.075 \cdot 10^5)$

12. $(-5.15 \cdot 10^{-4})(2.06 \cdot 10^{-9})$

13. $\dfrac{1.2 \cdot 10^5}{0.6 \cdot 10^{-8}}$

14. $\dfrac{36 \cdot 10^2}{9 \cdot 10^8}$

15. $\dfrac{2.25 \cdot 10^{12}}{0.15 \cdot 10^3}$

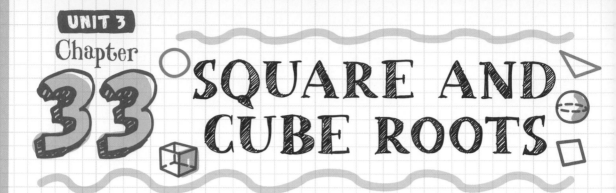

SQUARE AND CUBE ROOTS

To **SQUARE** a number, raise it to the **POWER OF 2**.

The *opposite* of squaring a number is to take a number's **SQUARE ROOT** ($\sqrt{}$). Study the chart. Look for patterns.

Notice the square root of a number can have two answers.
For example: $5^2 = 5 \cdot 5 = 25$ and $(-5^2) = -5 \cdot -5 = 25$.

So, $\sqrt{25} = +5$ *or* -5, or ± 5.

Square a Number	Perfect Squares	Square Root
$1^2 = 1 \cdot 1 = 1$	1	$\sqrt{1} = \pm 1$
$2^2 = 2 \cdot 2 = 4$	4	$\sqrt{4} = \pm 2$
$3^2 = 3 \cdot 3 = 9$	9	$\sqrt{9} = \pm 3$
$4^2 = 4 \cdot 4 = 16$	16	$\sqrt{16} = \pm 4$
$5^2 = 5 \cdot 5 = 25$	25	$\sqrt{25} = \pm 5$
$6^2 = 6 \cdot 6 = 36$	36	$\sqrt{36} = \pm 6$
$7^2 = 7 \cdot 7 = 49$	49	$\sqrt{49} = \pm 7$
$8^2 = 8 \cdot 8 = 64$	64	$\sqrt{64} = \pm 8$
$9^2 = 9 \cdot 9 = 81$	81	$\sqrt{81} = \pm 9$
$10^2 = 10 \cdot 10 = 100$	100	$\sqrt{100} = \pm 10$

To **CUBE** a number, raise it to the **POWER OF 3**.

The *opposite* of cubing a number is to take a number's
CUBE ROOT ($\sqrt[3]{}$). ← Unlike with cube root, we do not include the number 2, in the upper left corner when writing the square root symbol.

Study the chart. Look for patterns.

Cube a Number	Perfect Cubes	Cube Root
$1^3 = 1 \cdot 1 \cdot 1 = 1$	1	$\sqrt[3]{1} = 1$
$2^3 = 2 \cdot 2 \cdot 2 = 8$	8	$\sqrt[3]{8} = 2$
$3^3 = 3 \cdot 3 \cdot 3 = 27$	27	$\sqrt[3]{27} = 3$
$4^3 = 4 \cdot 4 \cdot 4 = 64$	64	$\sqrt[3]{64} = 4$
$5^3 = 5 \cdot 5 \cdot 5 = 125$	125	$\sqrt[3]{125} = 5$
$6^3 = 6 \cdot 6 \cdot 6 = 216$	216	$\sqrt[3]{216} = 6$
$7^3 = 7 \cdot 7 \cdot 7 = 343$	343	$\sqrt[3]{343} = 7$
$8^3 = 8 \cdot 8 \cdot 8 = 512$	512	$\sqrt[3]{512} = 8$
$9^3 = 9 \cdot 9 \cdot 9 = 729$	729	$\sqrt[3]{729} = 9$
$10^3 = 10 \cdot 10 \cdot 10 = 1,000$	1,000	$\sqrt[3]{1,000} = 10$

Perfect cubes can also be negative numbers.
Example: $\sqrt[3]{-64} = -4$
(Read aloud as "cube root of negative 64,"
which equals $-4 \cdot -4 \cdot -4$.)

FOR 1 THROUGH 5, LIST THE SQUARE ROOT OF EACH NUMBER.

1. 49

2. 121

3. 225

4. $\frac{1}{36}$

5. 20.25

FOR 6 THROUGH 8, EVALUATE THE EXPRESSIONS. USE ONLY THE POSITIVE SQUARE ROOT OF EACH NUMBER.

6. $-(\sqrt{9}) + 2.5$

7. $\sqrt{169} \cdot \sqrt{81}$

8. $\sqrt{\dfrac{64}{16}}$

FOR 9 THROUGH 11, LIST THE CUBE ROOT OF EACH NUMBER.

9. −512

10. 1,728

11. $\dfrac{-1}{729}$

FOR 12 THROUGH 14, EVALUATE EACH EXPRESSION. USE ONLY POSITIVE CUBE ROOTS.

12. $-\sqrt[3]{64} + 1.85$

13. $\sqrt[3]{343} \cdot \sqrt[3]{216}$

14. $\sqrt[3]{\dfrac{-125}{1,000}}$

SOLVE THE PROBLEM.

15. Nelson says that to find the square root of a number all you must do is divide by 2. For example: $\sqrt{4} = 2$ because $4 \div 2 = 2$. Is he correct? Explain how you know.

The simplest way to compare **IRRATIONAL NUMBERS** is to round or use **APPROXIMATIONS**.

> **IRRATIONAL NUMBERS:** numbers that *cannot be written* as a simple fraction (because the decimal goes on forever without repeating)

For example, **PI** or π is commonly rounded to 3.14. Square roots of perfect squares are easy to find. However, we can also find the *approximate values* of irrational numbers.

Look at the chart of square roots. Notice the pattern. Highlighted numbers are *perfect squares*. Irrational numbers are rounded to the nearest hundredth.

$\sqrt{1}$ = 1	$\sqrt{11}$ = 3.31	$\sqrt{21}$ = 4.58	$\sqrt{31}$ = 5.57
$\sqrt{2}$ = 1.41	$\sqrt{12}$ = 3.46	$\sqrt{22}$ = 4.69	$\sqrt{32}$ = 5.66
$\sqrt{3}$ = 1.73	$\sqrt{13}$ = 3.61	$\sqrt{23}$ = 4.80	$\sqrt{33}$ = 5.74
$\sqrt{4}$ = 2	$\sqrt{14}$ = 3.74	$\sqrt{24}$ = 4.90	$\sqrt{34}$ = 5.83
$\sqrt{5}$ = 2.24	$\sqrt{15}$ = 3.87	$\sqrt{25}$ = 5	$\sqrt{35}$ = 5.92
$\sqrt{6}$ = 2.45	$\sqrt{16}$ = 4	$\sqrt{26}$ = 5.10	$\sqrt{36}$ = 6
$\sqrt{7}$ = 2.65	$\sqrt{17}$ = 4.12	$\sqrt{27}$ = 5.20	$\sqrt{37}$ = 6.08
$\sqrt{8}$ = 2.83	$\sqrt{18}$ = 4.24	$\sqrt{28}$ = 5.29	$\sqrt{38}$ = 6.16
$\sqrt{9}$ = 3	$\sqrt{19}$ = 4.36	$\sqrt{29}$ = 5.39	$\sqrt{39}$ = 6.24
$\sqrt{10}$ = 3.16	$\sqrt{20}$ = 4.47	$\sqrt{30}$ = 5.48	$\sqrt{40}$ = 6.32

FOR 1 THROUGH 6, COMPUTE. USE WHAT YOU KNOW ABOUT IRRATIONAL NUMBERS AND APPROXIMATIONS.

1. $-\frac{2}{3}\pi$

2. $\sqrt{16} + \sqrt{50}$

3. $-(\sqrt{82}) - \sqrt{38}$

4. $\sqrt{50} \cdot \pi$

5. $\dfrac{\pi}{3}$

6. $\sqrt{47} + 3^2 + \sqrt{88}$

FOR 7 THROUGH 10, ANSWER THE QUESTIONS.

7. Order the numbers from *least* to *greatest.* $\sqrt{95}$, 2π, $\sqrt{29}$

WHO ARE
YOU CALLING
IRRATIONAL?

8. Order the numbers from *greatest* to *least*. $-\sqrt{74}$, -4^3, $-\sqrt{68}$

9. What is the approximate value of $\sqrt{110}$ to the hundredths place?

10. Draw a number line and place the following numbers in the correct location.

2.25, $-\sqrt{8}$, -0.5, $3\frac{3}{4}$, 0

Chapter

35 EQUATIONS

An **EQUATION** is a mathematical sentence with an equal sign.

To solve an equation, find the missing number, or VARIABLE, that makes the sentence true. That number is called the SOLUTION.

DEPENDENT VARIABLE
(the one you solve for)

$$y = 2x + 9$$

INDEPENDENT VARIABLE
(the one you substitute for)

The value of y depends on the value of x.

EXAMPLE: Evaluate $\dfrac{4mn + 2}{r^2 - 7}$ when $m = -11$, $n = 5$, and $r = 3$.

STEP 1: Substitute.

$$\frac{4mn + 2}{r^2 - 7} = \frac{(4 \cdot -11 \cdot 5) + 2}{3^2 - 7}$$

STEP 2: Solve using the Order of Operations.

$$\frac{(4 \cdot -11 \cdot 5) + 2}{3^2 - 7}$$

$$= \frac{-220 + 2}{9 - 7}$$

$$= \frac{-218}{2} = -109$$

EXAMPLE: Solve for w in the equation $w = -4z - 19$ when $z = -12$.

STEP 1: Substitute.

$w = -4z - 19$

$w = (-4 \cdot -12) - 19$

STEP 2: Solve using the Order of Operations.

$w = (-4 \cdot -12) - 19$

$w = 48 - 19$

$w = 29$

STEP 3: Check your work.

$w = -4z - 19$

$29 = (-4 \cdot -12) - 19$

$29 = 48 - 19$

$29 = 29 \leftarrow$ The answer is correct!

199

FOR 1 THROUGH 6, EVALUATE EACH EQUATION.

1. $h - 15$, when $h = 31$

2. $78 + 3m$, when $m = -6$

3. $\frac{5}{8} k + 11$, when $k = 48$

4. $|7mn|$, when $m = -1$ and $n = 32$

5. $-6s + 4v^2$, when $s = -3$ and $v = 4$

6. $\dfrac{2xy - 8}{xy + 15}$, when $x = -2$ and $y = 7$

FOR 7 THROUGH 12, SOLVE FOR d IN EACH EQUATION. CHECK YOUR WORK.

7. $d = -c + 11$, when $c = 18$

8. $d = 22 - |3p|$, when $p = -5$

9. $d = 16m^3$, when $m = -3$

10. $125 - z \div 12 = d$, when $z = 60$

11. $d = \dfrac{5c - a}{b + 21}$, when $a = -4$, $b = -8$, and $c = -13$

12. $7v(4w^2 - 92) = d$, when $w = 5$ and $v = -10$

Chapter 36 SOLVING FOR VARIABLES

Solving an **EQUATION** is like asking, "What value of the variable makes this equation true?" To answer that question, *isolate the variable* on one side of the equal sign using the INVERSE OPERATION.

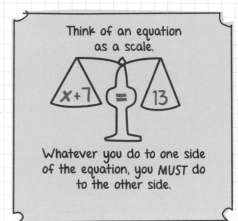

Think of an equation as a scale.

$x + 7 = 13$

Whatever you do to one side of the equation, you MUST do to the other side.

The chart below shows different types of equations and how to solve them.

ADDITION EQUATION:	SUBTRACTION EQUATION:
To solve, use the inverse operation, SUBTRACTION.	To solve, use the inverse operation, ADDITION.
$x + 25 = 19$ Isolate x on one side of the equation.	$n - 11 = 36$ Isolate n on one side of the equation.
$-25 = -25$ Subtract 25 from both sides of the equation.	$+ 11 = + 11$ Add 11 to both sides of the equation.
$x - 0 = -6$	$n - 0 = 47$
$x = -6$	$n = 47$

MULTIPLICATION EQUATION:

To solve, use the inverse operation, **DIVISION**.

$4m = 52$ Isolate m on one side of the equation.

$\frac{4m}{4} = \frac{52}{4}$ Divide each side of the equation by 4.

$1m = 13$

$m = 13$

DIVISION EQUATION:

To solve, use the inverse operation, **MULTIPLICATION**.

$\frac{h}{6} = -210$ Isolate h on one side of the equation.

$\frac{h}{\cancel{6}_1} \cdot \frac{\cancel{6}^1}{1} = -210 \cdot \frac{6}{1}$ Multiply each side of the equation by 6.

$h = -1{,}260$

EQUATION WITH SQUARING (EXPONENT OF 2):

To solve, undo the squaring by finding the square root.

$k^2 = 225$ Isolate k on one side of the equation.

$\sqrt{k^2} = \sqrt{225}$ Find the square root of each side of the equation.

$k = \pm 15$

EQUATION WITH CUBING (EXPONENT OF 3):

To solve, undo the cubing by finding the cube root.

$y^3 = 512$ Isolate y on one side of the equation.

$\sqrt[3]{y^3} = \sqrt[3]{512}$ Find the cube root of each side of the equation.

$y = 8$

SOLVE FOR EACH VARIABLE.

1. $r + 21 = -148$

2. $x - 9 = 33$

3. $14n = -70$

4. $-62 + s = -218$

5. $9g = 117$

6. $-81 = -3p$

7. $\dfrac{y}{4} = 196$

8. $w \div 22 = 60$

9. $\dfrac{1}{2}d = -52$

10. $c^2 = 400$

11. $216 = b^3$

12. $m^2 = 343$

Chapter

37. SOLVING MULTISTEP EQUATIONS

MULTISTEP EQUATIONS are equations that require several steps to isolate a variable. Here are some ways to isolate a variable on one side of the equal sign:

> DISTRIBUTIVE PROPERTY: $4(x + 5) = (4 \cdot x) + (4 \cdot 5) = 4x + 20$
> COMBINE LIKE TERMS: $(x^2 + x^2) + (2x - x) + (5 - 3) = 2x^2 + x + 2$
>
> | Operation | Inverse Operation |
> |---|---|
> | Addition: $x + 5 = 10$ | Subtraction: $x + 5 - 5 = 10 - 5$ |
> | Subtraction: $x - 5 = 10$ | Addition: $x - 5 + 5 = 10 + 5$ |
> | Multiplication: $5x = 10$ | Division: $(5x) \div 5 = 10 \div 5$ |
> | Division: $x \div 5 = 10$ | Multiplication: $(x \div 5) \bullet 5 = 10 \bullet 5$ |

▶ Use the distributive property
▶ Combine like terms
▶ Use inverse operations as many times as necessary

EXAMPLE: Solve $8(w + 6) + 2w - 7 = 3w + 13$.

$(8 \bullet w + 8 \bullet 6) + 2w - 7 = 3w + 13$ ← Use the distributive property.

$8w + 48 + 2w - 7 = 3w + 13$

$(8w + 2w) + (48 - 7) = 3w + 13$ ← Combine like terms on the left side of the equation.

$10w + 41 = 3w + 13$

$10w + 41 = 3w + 13$ ← Use inverse operations to get the variable alone on one side of the equation. Subtract $3w$.

$-3w \qquad -3w$

$7w + 41 = 0 + 13$

$7w + 41 = 0 + 13$ ← Use inverse operations again to get the numbers on one side of the equation. Subtract 41.

$\qquad -41 \qquad -41$

$7w + 0 = -28$

$7w = -28$ ← Use inverse operations again.

$\dfrac{7w}{7} = \dfrac{-28}{7}$ ← Undo multiplication. Divide by 7.

$w = -4$ ◄

CHECK YOUR WORK! Insert your answer into the original equation.

Check: $8(w + 6) + 2w - 7 = 3w + 13$

Plug in your answer: $w = -4$.

$8(-4 + 6) + 2(-4) - 7 = 3(-4) + 13$

$8(2) \quad - 8 \quad - 7 = -12 + 13$

$16 \quad - 15 = -12 + 13$

$1 = 1$

Since both sides of the equation are equivalent, $1 = 1$, your answer is correct!

SOLVE FOR EACH VARIABLE. CHECK YOUR WORK.

1. $8r + 16 = 96$

2. $-3x - 25 = -100$

3. $11y + 3 - 6y + 28 = 96$

4. $17n + 8 = 104 + 5n$

5. $\dfrac{d}{4} + 17 = -3$

6. $74 - 2m = -5(m - 4)$

7. $2r - 7 + r = 1 + 4r$

8. $(b + 7)(-12) = 48$

9. $12 = -(a + 14) + 8$

10. $\frac{2}{3}(4x - 16) = -8$

Chapter

38

SOLVING AND GRAPHING INEQUALITIES

To solve an inequality, just follow the same steps as solving an equation. The only difference is when you *multiply* or *divide* by a negative number, REVERSE the direction of the inequality sign.

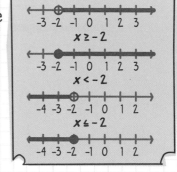

Solve and Graph: $-7(x + 2) + 6 \le 27$

$-7(x + 2) + 6 \le 27$

$(-7 \cdot x) + (-7 \cdot 2) + 6 \le 27$ ← Use the distributive property.

$-7x + (-14) + 6 \le 27$

$-7x + (-14) + 6 \le 27$ ← Combine like terms.

$-7x - 8 \le 27$ ← Use inverse operations to get the variable alone on one side of the equation. Add 8 to both sides.

$ + 8 + 8$

$-7x + 0 \le 35$

$-7x \leq 35$ ← Use inverse operations again.

$\dfrac{-7x}{-7} \geq \dfrac{35}{-7}$ ← Isolate x. Divide by -7. Reverse the direction of the inequality symbol since we are dividing by a negative number.

$x \geq -5$ ← Graph the solution.

Graph: $x \geq -5$

CHECK YOUR ANSWER:

Because our answer says that x is greater than or equal to -5, test points greater than -5.

Let $x = -2$.

$-7(-2 + 2) + 6 \leq 27$

$6 \leq 27$ This is true.

Let $x = 0$.

$-7(0 + 2) + 6 \leq 27$

$-8 \leq 27$ This is true. Therefore, your answer is correct.

FOR 1 THROUGH 3, GRAPH THE INEQUALITY ON A NUMBER LINE.

1. $r > 4$

2. $h < -1$

3. $p \geq -3$

FOR 4 THROUGH 6, WRITE THE INEQUALITY THAT THE NUMBER LINE REPRESENTS. USE *n* AS YOUR VARIABLE.

4.

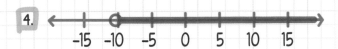

5.

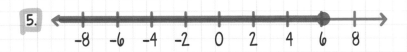

6.

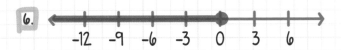

FOR 7 THROUGH 9, SOLVE AND GRAPH EACH INEQUALITY. THEN CHECK YOUR WORK.

7. $3a - 2 \geq a + 4$

8. $-\dfrac{1}{6}(m + 12) \leq 8$

9. $-17 + 6b \geq -4b + 11$

SOLVE THE PROBLEM.

10. Sasha solved the inequality below. Her teacher said she made an error at step 2. What was Sasha's error? Explain.

Step 1: $-3(x - 1) < -39$

Step 2: $\dfrac{-3(x - 1)}{-3} < \dfrac{-39}{-3}$

Step 3: $x - 1 < 13$

$\ + 1 \quad + 1$

$\ x < 14$

Chapter 39

WORD PROBLEMS WITH EQUATIONS AND INEQUALITIES

The key to solving real-world problems is accurately translating the words in the situation into a mathematical equation or inequality.

KEY WORDS

is means =
is greater than means >
is less than means <
at least means ≥
at most means ≤

EXAMPLE: Peter downloaded three audiobooks, each for the same price. On the same website, he also purchased a new set of wireless headphones for $110. The total cost was $176. What was the cost of one audiobook?

STEP 1: What info is known?
- Three audiobooks were downloaded for the same price.
- Wireless headphones cost: $110.
- Total cost was $176. (*was* means =)

STEP 2: What info is unknown?
- The cost of one audiobook.
- Let a = the cost of one audiobook.

STEP 3: Write an equation.
$$3a + \$110 = \$176$$

STEP 4: Solve the equation.
$$3a + 110 = 176$$

Use inverse operations to get the variable alone on one side of the equation. Subtract.

$$3a + 110 = 176$$
$$-110 - 110$$
$$3a = 66$$

Use inverse operations again. Divide.

$$\frac{3a}{3} = \frac{66}{3}$$

The cost of one audiobook.

$$a = 22$$

So, the cost of one audiobook was $22.

EXAMPLE: Airport Cars charges a flat fee of $15 in addition to $2.00 per mile. The Wilson family wants to pay at most $75 to get to the airport. How many miles can the family travel without spending more than $75?

STEP 1: What info is known?
▸ Flat fee: $15
▸ Cost per mile: $2.00.
▸ Spend at most $75.
   (at most means ≤)

STEP 2: What info is unknown?
▸ The number of miles the family can travel.
▸ Let x = the number of miles the family can travel.

STEP 3: Write an inequality.
$$\$15 + \$2x \le \$75$$

STEP 4: Solve the inequality.
$$\$15 + \$2x \le 75$$

Use inverse operations to get the variable alone on one side of the equation. Subtract.

$$15 + 2x \le 75$$
$$-15 \qquad\quad -15$$
$$2x \le 60$$

Use inverse operations again. Divide.

$$\frac{2x}{2} \le \frac{60}{2}$$

The number of miles the family can travel.

$$x \le 30$$

So, the family can travel at the most 30 miles.

SOLVE EACH PROBLEM USING AN EQUATION OR INEQUALITY. CHECK YOUR WORK.

1. Great Ocean Middle School has an incoming class of 652 students. 319 of those students will be enrolled in marine studies, 168 in computer science, and the remaining in a traditional academic program. How many students will be enrolled in the traditional academic program?

2. Carolyn has $956 in her savings account. She made 4 withdrawals that were each the same amount. Carolyn's balance after the withdrawals is $656. What was the amount of each withdrawal?

3. Simon purchases a subscription to a monthly puzzle club. To join he must pay a sign-up fee of $20 and a fee for every month he participates in the subscription. Simon has a coupon for $5.00 off and wants to make a purchase for 12 months. How much will he pay monthly if the total cost for the subscription is $399?

4. The school athletic department is advertising a concert that will raise money for new gym equipment. They print 4,500 flyers publicizing the event. The coach separates the flyers into 18 stacks to be distributed by each department member. How many flyers are in each stack?

5. Tamera is saving money for a new computer that costs $1,008. She babysits 14 hours a week and earns $12 an hour. What is the least amount of weeks Tamera must babysit to purchase this computer?

6. Adrian wants to purchase graphic T-shirts from an online retailer. Each T-shirt costs $16. The retailer offers a $10 off coupon for all purchases over $50, and Adrian plans to spend at least $86. How many T-shirts can Adrian purchase?

7. Marla is planning a graduation luncheon. Her budget is $1,620. What is the greatest number of people Marla can invite if the restaurant charges $16 per person, and there are no additional fees?

8. Tickets to the annual school musical for 1 adult and 1 child cost $23. An adult ticket is $5 more than a child's ticket. What is the cost of a child's ticket?

9. Jamel's Bikes charges a flat fee of $15 to rent a bike and $5 for every hour the bike is used. If Maron pays $45, how many hours did she use the bike?

10. Christy's weekly income was less than or equal to $890. Her base pay was $350 with an hourly rate of $12. How many hours did Christy possibly work?

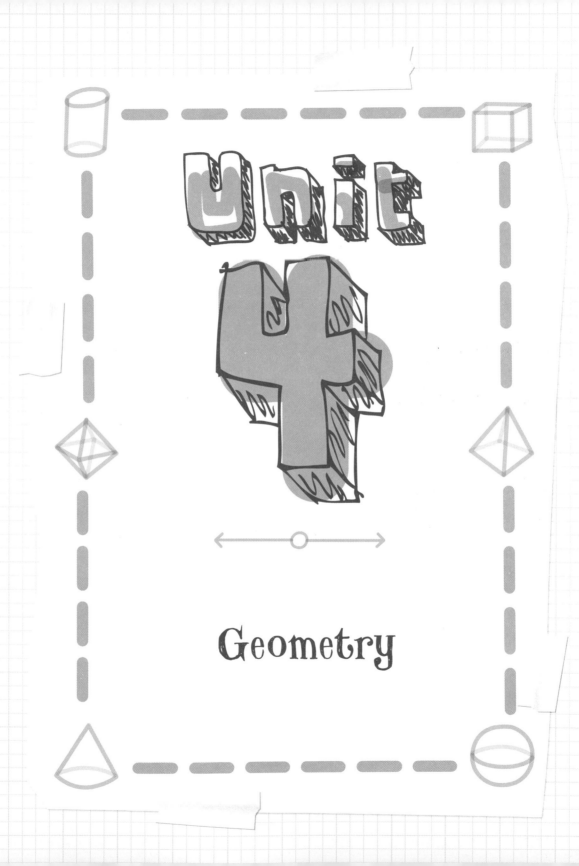

Unit 4

Geometry

INTRODUCTION TO GEOMETRY

GEOMETRY is the branch of mathematics that deals with lines, shapes, and space.

Here are some key geometry terms:

TERM	DEFINITION
Line Segment	a part of a line that has two endpoints
Line	a line that continues forever in both directions
Ray	a line with only one endpoint
Point	a location
Parallel Lines	Lines that are always the same distance apart. They NEVER intersect.
Perpendicular Lines	two lines that form a right angle
Congruent Lengths	line segments with the same measure
Angle	formed by two rays with the same endpoint
Vertex	the point of intersection of rays or lines that form an angle
Right Angle	a 90-degree angle

TERM	DEFINITION
Acute Angle	an angle smaller than a right angle, or smaller than 90°
Obtuse Angle	an angle greater than 90° and less than 180°
Two-Dimensional Shape (Polygon)	a closed figure with at least three segments
Three-Dimensional Shape (polyhedron)	the intersection of three or more polygons

We can use a protractor to measure angles. What is the measure of each angle?

Are these two angles congruent? Why or why not?

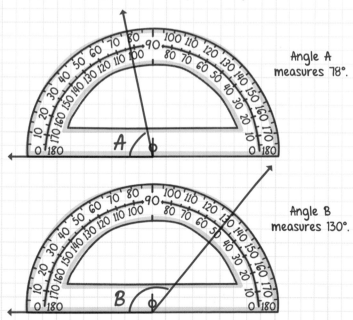

Angle A measures 78°.

Angle B measures 130°.

Angles that are congruent have the same angle measure. Since angles A and B have different measures, they are NOT congruent.

FOR 1 THROUGH 3, IDENTIFY THE GEOMETRIC CONCEPT.

1. Look at the angle below. Name the vertex and the two rays that form ∠ABC.

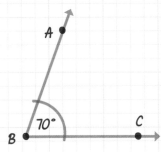

vertex: _____

ray: _____

ray: _____

2. Look at the lines below. Identify the **line**, **ray**, and **line segment**.

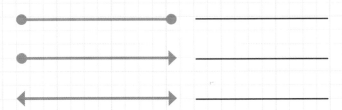

_____

_____

_____

3. Look at the angles below. Name the acute angle and the obtuse angle.

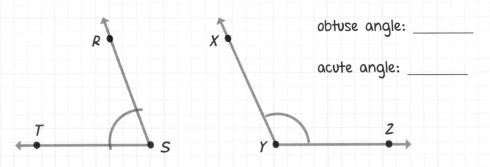

obtuse angle: _____

acute angle: _____

4. Look at the figures below. Identify the polygon (two-dimensional figure) and the polyhedron (three-dimensional figure).

pyramid: _____   heptagon: _____

5. Use a ruler to draw a line segment that is 8 centimeters long. Then draw a line segment that is 5 inches long.

6. Use a protractor to draw an angle that is 125°.

7. Use a protractor to draw an angle that is 70°.

8. Use a set square to draw a line perpendicular to the one below.

9. Use two set squares and a ruler to draw two parallel lines.

10. Use a protractor to draw two congruent acute angles.

ANGLES

An **ANGLE** (∠) is formed by two rays with a common endpoint. We use **DEGREES** (°) to measure the size of an angle. Some of the most common angles are shown below.

Acute Angle:
Measures less than 90°

Right Angle:
Measures 90°

Straight Angle:
Measures 180°

Obtuse Angle:
Measures more than 90° but less than 180°

360° Angle:
Complete rotation

Adjacent Angles:
Two angles that share a vertex and a common side

Vertical Angles:
Opposite angles that are = in measure

Complementary Angles:
Two angles whose sum = 90°

Supplementary Angles:
Two angles whose sum = 180°

Congruent Angles:
Angles that are = in measure

ACUTE ANGLE

RIGHT ANGLE

OBTUSE ANGLE

STRAIGHT ANGLE

We can use various properties of angles to find the measure of unknown angles.

Find the measures of the following angles:

∠ACB and ∠DCE.

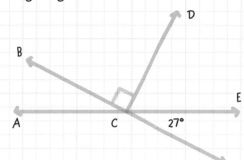

STEP 1: Find ∠ACB.

∠ACB and ∠FCE are
VERTICAL ANGLES. They are opposite angles equal in measure.

∠FCE = 27°, so ∠ACB = 27°.

STEP 2: Find ∠DCE.

$\overleftrightarrow{AE}$ is a straight line, so it measures 180°.

∠BCD is a right angle, or 90°.

We found ∠ACB = 27°.

Therefore, ∠ACB + ∠BCD + ∠DCE = 180°.

$27 + 90 + x = 180$ — the missing angle

$$117 + x = 180$$

$$\begin{array}{r} -117 \qquad -117 \\ \hline x = 63 \end{array}$$

So, ∠DCE = 63°

COMPLETE THE SENTENCES BELOW. USE WHAT YOU KNOW ABOUT ANGLES.

1. _____ angles are greater than 90° but less than 180°.

2. _____ angles are two angles that add up to 90°.

3. _____ angles are two angles that share a vertex and a common side.

FOR 4 THROUGH 7, FIND THE MEASURE OF EACH ANGLE.

4. In the diagram below, $\angle A = 136°$ and $\angle B = 44°$. What are $\angle C$ and $\angle D$?

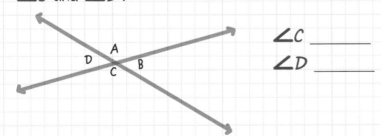

$\angle C$ _____

$\angle D$ _____

5. In the diagram below, $\angle x$ and $\angle y$ are complementary. If $\angle y$ is 65°, what is $\angle x$?

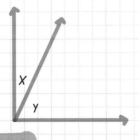

$\angle x$ is _____

6. In the diagram below, ∠FHG is a right angle. ∠GHI is 35°. What is ∠JHI?

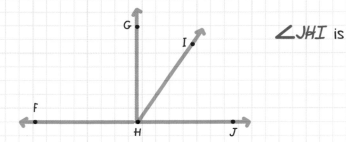

∠JHI is _____

7. If ∠R is 140° and ∠R is congruent to ∠H, what is the measure of ∠H?

FOR 8 THROUGH 10, USE THE DIAGRAM BELOW.

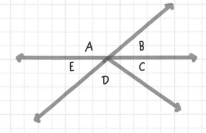

8. Name two angles that are adjacent angles.

_____   _____

9. Name three angles that form a straight angle.

_____   _____   _____

10. If ∠A is 145°, what is ∠B?

_____

Chapter 42
QUADRILATERALS AND AREA

A **QUADRILATERAL** is a polygon, or 2-D figure, with four sides. Look at the quadrilateral tree diagram. Notice the rhombus, rectangle, and square are three types of parallelograms.

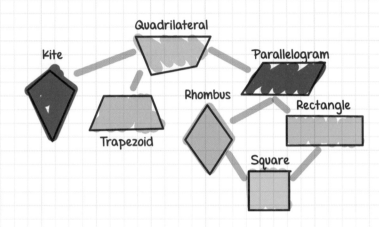

Kite

Quadrilateral

Trapezoid

Rhombus

Parallelogram

Rectangle

Square

Find the **perimeter**, the distance around a quadrilateral, by adding up the lengths of all four sides.

Find the **area**, the amount of space inside a quadrilateral, by using these formulas:

Area of a parallelogram: A = base • height

Area of a trapezoid: A = $\frac{base_1 + base_2}{2}$ • height

Area is written in "units squared," or units^2.

Calculate the perimeter and the area of the trapezoid.

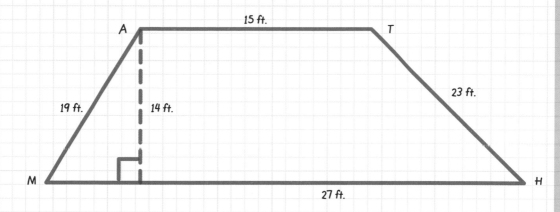

Perimeter = $\overline{MA}$ + $\overline{AT}$ + $\overline{TH}$ + $\overline{HM}$

P = 19 + 15 + 23 + 27

P = 84 ft.

So, the perimeter of the trapezoid MATH is 84 ft.

Area = $\dfrac{\text{base}_1 + \text{base}_2}{2}$ • height

A = $\dfrac{15 + 27}{2}$ • 14

A = $\dfrac{42}{2}$ • 14

A = 21 • 14

A = 294 ft.^{2}

So, the area of the trapezoid MATH is 294 ft.^{2}

FOR 1 THROUGH 5, CALCULATE THE AREA FOR EACH OF THE FOLLOWING QUADRILATERALS.

QUADRILATERAL	AREA
1. 8 cm / 3 cm	
2. 12 in. / 7 in.	
3. 9 ft. / 16 ft.	
4. 10.5 m / 10.5 m / 10.5 m / 10.5 m	
5. 8 cm / 6.5 cm / 5 cm / 6.5 cm / 16 cm	

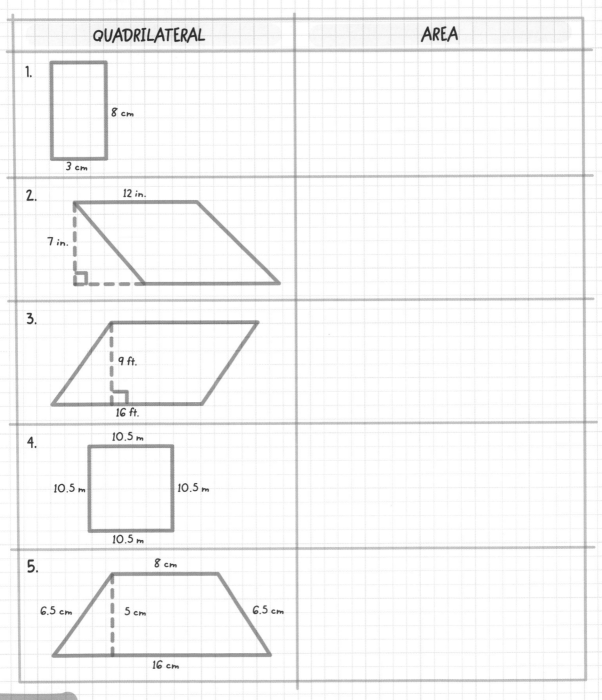

FOR 6 THROUGH 10, SOLVE THE PROBLEMS.
SHOW YOUR WORK.

6. Pedro made this drawing of his first-floor living space. He needs to find the area of the entire space to determine how many square feet of flooring to order. What is the area of Pedro's living space?

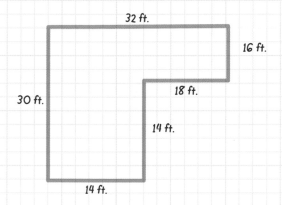

7. Malcom needs to determine the perimeter of his backyard to install new fencing around his property. The backyard is the shape of a quadrilateral with opposite sides parallel and equal in length. The measure of one side of the yard is 18.288 meters. The measure of another side is 15.24 meters. What is the perimeter of the property?

8. Mason Middle School is replacing the grass on their football field. To calculate the cost of the new turf, the athletic director needs to know the square footage of the field. The field is rectangular and has the following dimensions: 360 feet in length and 160 feet in width. What is the square footage of the football field?

9. A new sandbox is being designed for the school playground. It will be in the shape of a trapezoid. Shown below is a model of the sandbox. How many square feet is the sandbox?

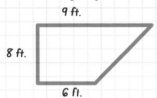

10. In math class, Cheryl is given the two trapezoids shown below. She says the perimeter of the trapezoids will be identical in measure. However, the area of the trapezoids will not be the same. Is Cheryl correct? How do you know?

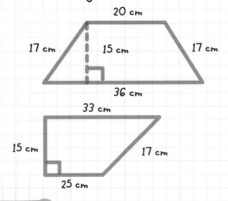

43 ⊜ TRIANGLES AND AREA

A **TRIANGLE** is a polygon, or 2-D figure, with three sides and three angles. We classify triangles by their sides and angles.

Find the **AREA**, the amount of space inside a triangle, by using this formula:

Area of a triangle:

$$\left\{ A = \frac{1}{2} \cdot base \cdot height \right\}$$

or

$$\left\{ A = \frac{1}{2}bh \right\}$$

The base and height must always form a right triangle.

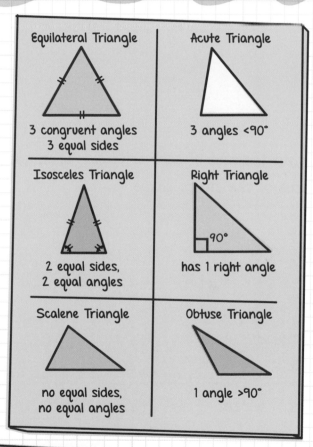

Equilateral Triangle	Acute Triangle
3 congruent angles 3 equal sides	3 angles <90°
Isosceles Triangle	Right Triangle
2 equal sides, 2 equal angles	has 1 right angle · 90°
Scalene Triangle	Obtuse Triangle
no equal sides, no equal angles	1 angle >90°

Area is always expressed in square units or units².

Find the area of this shape.

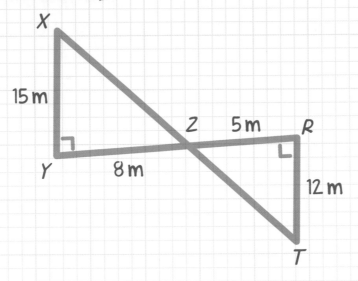

Find the area of each triangle. Then add those areas together to get the area of the entire shape.

Area of $\triangle XYZ = \frac{1}{2}bh$	Area of $\triangle TRZ = \frac{1}{2}bh$	Area of the entire shape:
$A = \frac{1}{2} \cdot 15 \cdot 8$	$A = \frac{1}{2} \cdot 12 \cdot 5$	$60\,m^2 + 30\,m^2 = 90\,m^2$
$A = \frac{1}{2} \cdot 120$	$A = \frac{1}{2} \cdot 60$	
$A = 60\,m^2$	$A = 30\,m^2$	

FOR 1 THROUGH 5, CALCULATE THE AREA FOR EACH OF THE FOLLOWING TRIANGLES. SHOW YOUR WORK.

TRIANGLE	AREA
1. 9 yd. 14 yd.	
2. 8 mm 5 mm	
3. 2 yd. 14 yd.	
4. 2 yd. 14 yd.	
5. 10 ft. 18 ft.	

CHAPTER 43

FOR 6 THROUGH 10, SOLVE THE PROBLEMS. SHOW YOUR WORK.

6. An architect is designing a new garage. Shown below is the top of the garage. It is the shape of an equilateral triangle. What is its area?

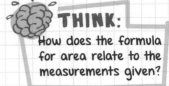

THINK:
How does the formula for area relate to the measurements given?

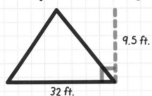

9.5 ft.

32 ft.

7. Emily is repaving her backyard patio space in the shape shown below. To order the correct number of concrete pavers, she needs to calculate the area of the patio. What is the area of Emily's patio?

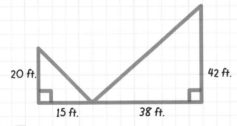

20 ft.

42 ft.

15 ft.   38 ft.

8. Mark is making a new sail for his family's boat and needs to calculate its area to purchase the material. The sail is in the shape of an isosceles triangle. The height of the sail will be 16.25 feet and the width 8 feet. What is the area of the sail?

9. In Hapeville, a triangular open space between three roads is being beautified with trees, flowers, and a waterfall. To determine costs, the mayor requested the area of the space from the city planner. What is the area of the space?

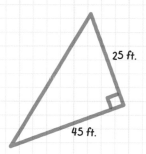

10. Robert says that you can find the area of the triangle below by first finding the areas of △ABD and △CBD and then adding them together. Bella says all you need to do is find the area of △ABC. Who is correct? How do you know?

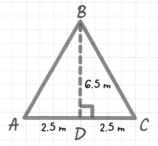

Chapter 44 THE PYTHAGOREAN THEOREM

A right triangle has two "legs" and a hypotenuse. The hypotenuse is always the longest side. The **PYTHAGOREAN THEOREM** is used to find the length of a side of a right triangle. This is the theorem:

$$a^2 + b^2 = c^2$$

a and b are the lengths of the legs, and c is the length of the hypotenuse.

Square the lengths of a and b. Then add. This will give you the square of length c.

The Larsons drew a map of their family road trip. They drove **15 miles** from their home to the science museum and then **12 miles** from the science museum to the mountain preserve. Finally, they drove home from the mountain preserve using Bleeker Boulevard. What is the distance from the mountain preserve to the Larson home?

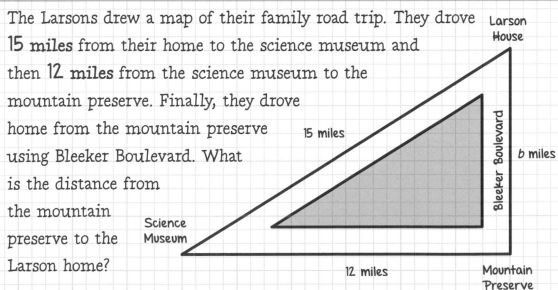

To find the distance from the mountain preserve to their home, use the Pythagorean Theorem and solve it just like an equation.

$a^2 + b^2 = c^2$

$12^2 + b^2 = 15^2$ Substitute.

$144 + b^2 = 225$

-144 -144 Inverse operation. Subtract to isolate the variable.

$b^2 = 81$

$\sqrt{b^2} = \sqrt{81}$ Take the square root of both sides of the equation.

$b = 9$

So, the distance from the mountain preserve to the Larson home is **9 miles.**

FOR 1 THROUGH 5, FIND THE UNKNOWN LENGTH.

1.

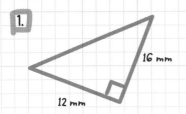

16 mm

12 mm

2.

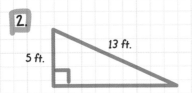

13 ft.

5 ft.

3.

6 cm

7 cm

4.

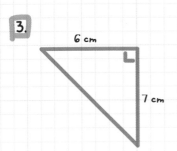

24 in.

25 in.

5.

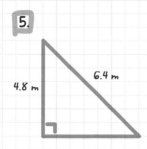

6.4 m

4.8 m

FOR 6 THROUGH 10, SOLVE THE PROBLEMS. SHOW YOUR WORK.

6. Mr. Jones leans a 13-foot ladder against a home. The ladder is 5 feet away from the wall. If the height of the home from the ground to the roof is 20 feet, will the ladder reach the roof? Explain your answer.

251

7. A technician is standing 9 feet away from a 40-foot telephone pole. He fastens a wire attached to the top of the telephone pole to the ground where he stands. How long is the wire?

8. An oak tree in front of Esme's house casts a shadow of 4 feet. The length from the top of the tree to the end of the shadow is 10 feet. How tall is the oak tree?

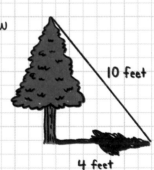

10 feet

4 feet

9. Mayville High School is installing a new ramp to the entrance of the gymnasium. The length of the ramp is 35 feet. When it is placed against the building, it reaches 3 feet in height. What is the distance between the base of the ramp and the building?

10. Paul says that the three measures 14 meters, 15 meters, and 16 meters represent the lengths of a right triangle. Is he correct? How do you know?

Chapter 45

CIRCLES, CIRCUMFERENCE, AND AREA

A **CIRCLE** is the set of all points that are equal distance from a point that is called the **CENTER**.

To find the **CIRCUMFERENCE OF A CIRCLE**, use:

$$\{ C = \pi \cdot \text{diameter} \}$$

or

$$\{ C = 2 \cdot \pi \cdot \text{radius} \}$$

To find the **AREA OF A CIRCLE**, use:

$$\{ A = \pi \cdot \text{radius}^2 \}$$

AREA

REMEMBER:

Pi (π): The ratio of a circle's circumference to its diameter:

$$\pi = \frac{\text{circumference}}{\text{diameter}} \quad \text{or} \quad \pi = \frac{c}{d}$$

EXAMPLE: Cole is designing a reusable water bottle for his soccer team. The diameter of the bottle is 2.5 inches. In order to design the bottlecap, he needs to calculate the distance around the top of the bottle and its area. How can Cole find these measures? Use 3.14 as the approximation of π.

▶ Find the distance around the water bottle:

$C = π \cdot d$	formula
$C = 3.14 \cdot d$	Substitute 3.14 for π.
$C = 3.14 \cdot 2.5$	Substitute 2.5 for diameter.
$C = 7.85$ in.	Multiply.

So, the distance around the top of the bottle is about 7.85 inches.

▶ Find the area for the top of the water bottle:

$A = π \cdot radius^2$	formula
$A = 3.14 \cdot radius^2$	Substitute 3.14 for π.
$2.5 ÷ 2 = 1.25$	The radius is half the diameter.
$A = 3.14 \cdot (1.25)^2$	Substitute 1.25 for the radius.
$A = 3.14 \cdot 1.5625$	Multiply 1.25 × 1.25.
$A ≈ 4.90625$ in.^{2}	Multiply by 3.14.

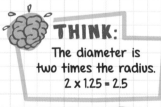

THINK:
The diameter is two times the radius.
2 × 1.25 = 2.5

So, the area of the top of the bottle is about 4.9 in.^{2}

1. Draw a circle. Label the parts of the circle with the terms **chord**, **center**, diameter, **radius**, and **circumference**.

FIND THE CIRCUMFERENCE OF EACH CIRCLE.

2. Use 3.14 as the approximation for π.

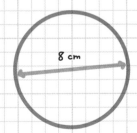

8 cm

3. Use $\frac{22}{7}$ as the approximation for π.

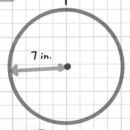

7 in.

4. Find the circumference of a circle with a diameter of 4.25 centimeters. (Use 3.14 as the approximation of π. Round your answer to the hundredths place.)

FIND THE AREA OF EACH CIRCLE.

5. Find the area of a circle with a radius of 6.5 centimeters. (Use 3.14 for the approximation of π. Round your answer to the hundredths place.)

6. Find the area of a circle with a radius of 3 inches. (Use $\frac{22}{7}$ for the approximation of π.)

7. Find the area of a circle with a diameter of 16 centimeters. (Use 3.14 for the approximation of π.)

USE WHAT YOU KNOW ABOUT CIRCUMFERENCE AND AREA TO SOLVE THE PROBLEMS.

8. An architect would like to build a circular patio. She wants the patio to have a diameter of 12 yards. What would the patio's area be? (Use 3.14 as the approximation of π.)

9. An artist must cut a circle out of a piece of canvas to create a portrait. The diameter of the circular portrait is 6 feet. What is the circumference of the circle to be cut? (Use 3.14 as the approximation of π.)

10. A girl wants to find the circumference of the top of her cupcake. She knows the cupcake's diameter is 7 centimeters. What is the circumference? (Use $\frac{22}{7}$ for the approximation of π.)

11. A gardener wants to find the area of a circular geranium plant so that he can purchase the correct size pot. The radius of the plant is 9 inches. What is the area of the plant? What is the circumference? (Use 3.14 for the approximation of π.)

12. An electrician is installing a circular light fixture that lays flat against the ceiling. To complete the work, the electrician must first mark the area with a circle. If the fixture has a radius of 10 inches, what is the area that must be marked? (Use 3.14 for the approximation of π.)

THREE-DIMENSIONAL FIGURES

Solid shapes are **THREE-DIMENSIONAL** (3-D) figures that have length, width, and height.

> **POLYHEDRON:**
> A 3-D figure with plane faces that are polygons
>
> **REGULAR POLYHEDRON:**
> A 3-D figure where all the faces are identical polygons

Prisms

Rectangular Prism   Square Prism (cube)   Triangular Prism   Hexagonal Prism

Pyramids

Triangular Pyramid   Rectanglar Pyramid   Hexagonal Pyramid   Pentagonal Pyramid

3-D figures with CURVED SURFACES

Cone

Cylinder   Sphere

vertical cross section: rectangle

horizontal cross section: circle

You can slice any 3-D figure open and get a different 2-D shape depending how you slice it. These new faces are called **CROSS SECTIONS**.

FOR 1 THROUGH 8, MATCH EACH SHAPE WITH ITS NAME OR DESCRIPTION.

1. Sphere: _____

2. Triangular prism: _____

3. A regular polyhedron where all the faces are identical squares: _____

4. A 3-D figure where all its lateral faces are triangles and so is its base: _____

5. A polyhedron that has all right angles, the bases are parallel, and the lateral faces are rectangles: _____

6. A 3-D figure with one circular base and one vertex (or point): _____

7. Rectangular pyramid: _____

8. A 3-D figure that has two parallel bases that are congruent circles: _____

A

B

C

D

E

F

G

H

9. Sketch a rectangular prism. Then draw and describe what a vertical and diagonal cross section look like.

10. Draw lines to show how you can cut the cone to get a triangle. Then draw lines to show how you can cut the rectangular pyramid to get a rectangle.

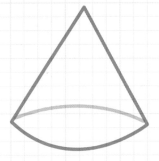

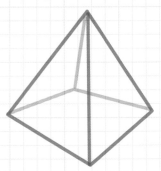

FOR 11 AND 12, ANSWER THE QUESTIONS. USE WHAT YOU KNOW ABOUT 3-D FIGURES.

11. How are pyramids and prisms the same? How are they different?

12. Name or draw one 3-D figure that is a regular polyhedron and one figure that is *not* a regular polyhedron. Tell how you know.

Chapter 47. VOLUME

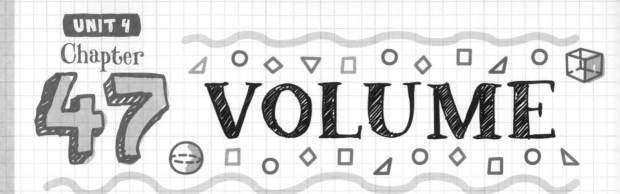

The **VOLUME** of a 3-D figure refers to the number of cubic units (units³) needed to fill the figure.

You can use formulas to find volume. Although the formulas are similar, each one is unique. So, be sure you use the correct formula!

> **THINK:**
> Think of volume as "How many cubes can fit inside each 3-D figure?"

Volume of Prisms

Cube or Rectangular Prism:

$V = (lw) \cdot$ *height of prism*

Triangular Prism:

$V = (\frac{1}{2}bh) \cdot$ *height of prism*

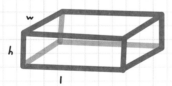

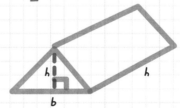

Volume of Pyramids

Rectangular Pyramid:

$V = (\frac{1}{3}B) \cdot$ *height of pyramid*

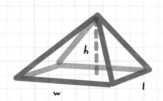

where B represents the area of the base

Volume of 3-D Figures with Curved Surfaces

Cylinder:

$V = (\pi r^2) \cdot$ *height of cylinder*

Cone:

$V = \frac{1}{3}(\pi r^2) \cdot$ *height of cone*

Sphere: $V = \frac{4}{3}(\pi r^3)$

EXAMPLE: Marla purchases a triangular prism planter for her balcony. To determine how many cubic feet of soil is needed to fill the planter, she must calculate the volume of the plant container. What is the volume of the planter?

Volume of a triangular prism formula:

$V = (\frac{1}{2}bh) \cdot$ *height of prism*

$V = (\frac{1}{2} \cdot 8 \cdot 12) \cdot 14$ ← substitute the measures into the formula: base of triangle = 8 ft., height of triangle = 12 ft., height of prism = 14 ft.

$V = \frac{96}{2} \cdot 14$ ← multiply

$V = \frac{1,344}{2}$ ← divide

$V = 672$ ← volume of planter

So, the volume of the planter is 672 cubic feet (672 ft.³).

FOR 1 THROUGH 7, FIND THE VOLUME OF EACH
FIGURE. ROUND TO THE NEAREST HUNDREDTH.
SHOW YOUR WORK.

1.

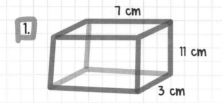

2.

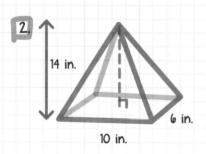

3.

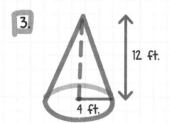

4.

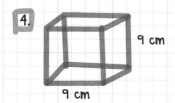

9 cm

9 cm

5.

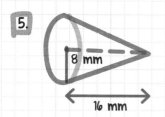

8 mm

16 mm

6.

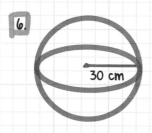

30 cm

7.

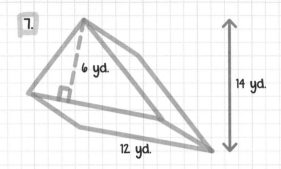

6 yd.

14 yd.

12 yd.

FOR 8 AND 9, SOLVE THE PROBLEMS.

8. Veronica is purchasing dog treats. Yum Treats and Tasty Treats sell for $5 each. Which treats are the better buy or give her more treats?

9. The Smith family installs a rectangular prism-shaped pool in their backyard. The pool has a length of 20 feet, a width of 10 feet, and a depth of 5 feet. How many cubic feet of water will the pool hold?

SURFACE AREA

SURFACE AREA is the area of a shape's surfaces. We can find the surface area of a 3-D figure by using a net (an unfolding of a figure). A net helps us calculate the sum of all the areas of a figure's surfaces.

What is the surface area of the triangular prism?

STEP 1: Use a net of the prism.

STEP 2: Find the area of each triangular base. Recall bases of a prism are parallel and congruent.

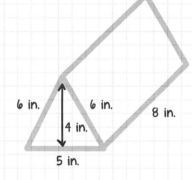

Base 1 and Base 2

$A = \frac{1}{2}bh$ height = $6^2 = 2.5^2 + h^2$

$A = \frac{1}{2}(5)(5.45)$ $h^2 = 29.75$

$A = 13.625$ in.^{2} $h = 5.45$

Net of triangular prism

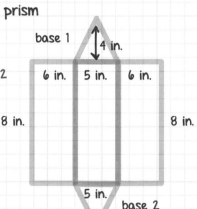

STEP 3: Find the area of each rectangular side.

SIDE 1	SIDE 2	SIDE 3
$A = lw$	$A = lw$	$A = lw$
$A = (8)(6)$	$A = (5)(8)$	$A = (8)(6)$
$A = 48$ in.^{2}	$A = 40$ in.^{2}	$A = 48$ in.^{2}

STEP 4: Add the surface areas of the bases and all the sides.

Surface Area = Base 1 + Base 2 + Side 1 + Side 2 + Side 3

Surface Area = 13.625 in.^{2} + 13.625 in.^{2} + 48 in.^{2} + 40 in.^{2} + 48 in.^{2}
$$= 163.25 \text{ in.}^2$$

So, the surface area of the triangular prism is 163.25 in.^{2}

What is the surface area of the cylinder?

STEP 1: Use a net of the cylinder.

First, find the width of the rectangular lateral area.
The width *is equal to* the circumference of the base.

Let $\pi = 3.14$. Round to the nearest whole number.

$C = \pi d$

$C = 3.14 (10)$

$C = 31.4$

$C \approx 31$ cm^2

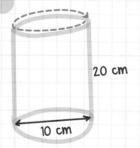

So, the width of the rectangular lateral area is approximately 31 cm^2.

STEP 2: Find the area of the rectangular lateral area.

Area of Rectangular Lateral Area

$A = lw$

$A = (20)(31)$

$A = 620 \text{ cm}^2$

STEP 3: Find the area of each circular base. Recall the bases are parallel and congruent. Round to the nearest whole number.

Area of the Bases

$A = \pi r^2$

$A = 3.14\ (5^2)$ ← The radius is half the diameter. Half of 10 is 5.

$A = 78.5$

$A \approx 79 \text{ cm}^2$

STEP 4: Add up the surface areas of the circular bases and the rectangular lateral area.

Surface Area = $620 \text{ cm}^2 + 79 \text{ cm}^2 + 79 \text{ cm}^2 = 778 \text{ cm}^2$

So, the surface area of the cylinder is 778 cm^2.

FOR 1 THROUGH 5, FIND THE SURFACE AREA OF EACH FIGURE.

1.

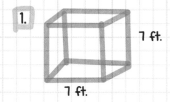

7 ft.

7 ft.

2.

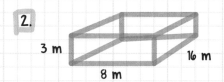

3 m

8 m

16 m

3.

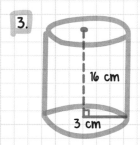

16 cm

3 cm

4.
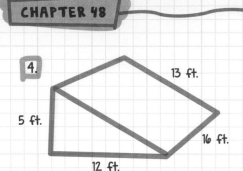
13 ft.

5 ft.

16 ft.

12 ft.

5.
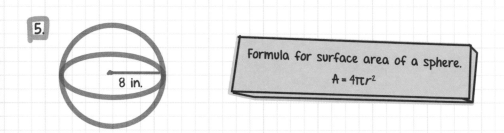

8 in.

Formula for surface area of a sphere.

$A = 4\pi r^2$

FOR 6 THROUGH 10, SOLVE THE PROBLEMS.

6. Nate is making a customized rectangular toy chest for his nephew. To determine how much paint to purchase, he needs to calculate its surface area. The toy box has a length of 6 feet, a width of 4 feet, and a height of 3 feet. What is the surface area of the toy chest?

7. Kathleen is making a cylindrical container using papier-mâché and wants to calculate how much papier-mâché she needs. The diameter of the cylinder is 6 inches and the height is 16 inches. What is the surface area of this container?

Papier-mâché = pieces of paper or pulp, mixed with a glue. It is used to cover the surface of other structures.

8. An artist is placing fabric around a sculpture shaped like the triangular prism shown below. He wants to wrap the figure with no overlap of fabric. How many square feet of fabric does the artist need?

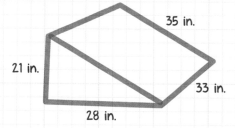

35 in.

21 in.

33 in.

28 in.

9. Darleen is purchasing wrapping paper to wrap 10 gift boxes that are 5.5 inches in length, width, and height. How many square inches of wrapping paper does Darleen need to purchase in order to wrap all 10 boxes completely with no overlap of wrapping paper?

10. A lighting company is making a glass spherical lighting fixture. How much glass will they need for the sphere if its radius is 7 inches? Use $A = 4\pi r^2$.

ANGLES, TRIANGLES, AND TRANSVERSAL LINES

The sum of a triangle's three **INTERIOR ANGLES** is always 180°.

> interior = inside
> exterior = outside

$A + B + C = 180°$

$50° + 60° + 70° = 180°$

EXTERIOR ANGLES are angles on the outside of the triangle. Angle D is an exterior angle. Angles B and D are supplementary to each other. $B + D = 180°$.

Angle D has the same value as the sum of the interior angles A and C.

$\angle D = 120°$ $\angle A + \angle C = 120°$

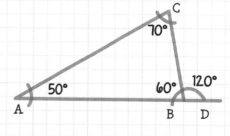

Parallel lines cut by a transversal:

A **TRANSVERSAL** is a line that cuts through two parallel lines.

A transversal line creates 8 angles. Some of the angles are congruent.

When parallel lines are cut by a transversal, the following types of angles are congruent:

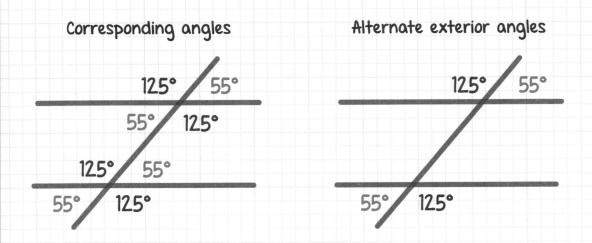

Corresponding angles

Alternate exterior angles

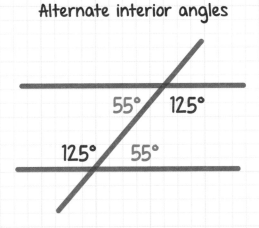

Alternate interior angles

ANSWER EACH QUESTION. USE WHAT YOU KNOW ABOUT ANGLES, TRIANGLES, AND TRANSVERSALS.

1. In △MAT, ∠M is 35° and ∠H is 76°. What is the measure of ∠A and ∠T?

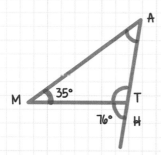

2. In △WXY, ∠W is 32° and ∠X is 43°. What is the measure of ∠Y and ∠Z?

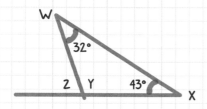

3. In △RLS, ∠R is 53°. What is the measure of ∠S?

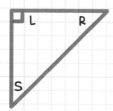

4. In the diagram below, line *m* is parallel to line *n*. Line *t* is the transversal. If ∠1 is 62°, determine the measure of each of the following angles.

∠2 = _____

∠3 = _____

∠4 = _____

∠5 = _____

∠6 = _____

∠7 = _____

∠8 = _____

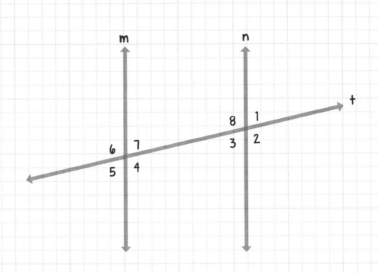

5. In the diagram below, line *P* is parallel to line *Q*. Line *R* is the transversal. If ∠O is 127°, determine the measure of each of the following angles.

∠H = _____

∠I = _____

∠J = _____

∠K = _____

∠L = _____

∠M = _____

∠N = _____

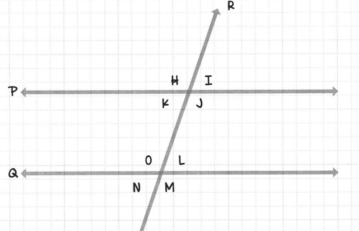

50. SIMILAR FIGURES AND SCALE DRAWINGS

SIMILAR FIGURES are figures that have the same shape but not necessarily the same size. The symbol for similar figures is ~.

If two figures are similar, their corresponding sides are proportional in size.

$\triangle MAT \sim \triangle QRS$. Find the missing lengths x and y.

$\dfrac{MT}{TA} = \dfrac{QS}{SR}$ Use their proportionality to find the missing measurements in both figures.

$\dfrac{x}{6} = \dfrac{16}{12}$ Use cross products to find the missing number.

$12x = 96$

$x = 8$

$\dfrac{MA}{TA} = \dfrac{QR}{SR}$ Use their proportionality to find the missing measurements in both figures.

$\dfrac{10}{6} = \dfrac{y}{12}$ Use cross products to find the missing number.

$6y = 120$

$y = 20$

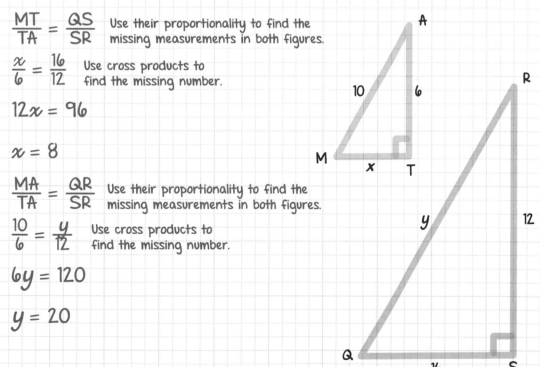

If two figures are similar, they have CONGRUENT ANGLES.

$\triangle EDF \sim \triangle HGI$. Find the missing $\angle F$.

$\angle E \cong \angle H = 66°$ and $\angle G \cong \angle D = 58°$.

Since all the angles of a triangle add up to $180°$,

$\angle E + \angle D + \angle F = 180°$

$66° + 58° + \angle F = 180°$

$124° + \angle F = 180°$

$\angle F = 56°$

You can use a proportion to find actual distances. This is used in scale drawings. A scale drawing is a drawing

that is similar to an actual object or place, just bigger or smaller. The SCALE is the ratio of the length in the drawing to the actual length.

EXAMPLE: An architect presents the school board with a blueprint of the new high school. The legend of the blueprint says that 5 inches represents 100 feet. If the distance on the blueprint between the auditorium and the gymnasium is 60 inches, what will be the actual distance?

key

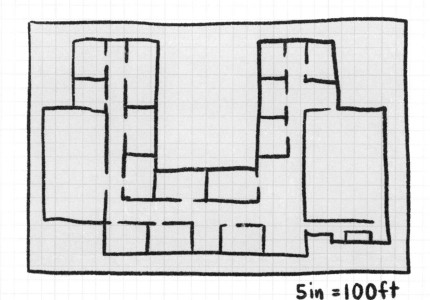

5in =100ft

Set up a proportion:

$$\frac{5 \text{ inches}}{100 \text{ feet}} = \frac{60 \text{ inches}}{x \text{ feet}}$$ Use cross products to find the missing number.

$5x = 6,000$

$x = 1,200$ feet

Therefore, the actual distance between the auditorium and the gymnasium is 1,200 feet.

ANSWER THE QUESTIONS. USE WHAT YOU KNOW ABOUT SIMILAR FIGURES AND SCALE DRAWINGS.

Note: largest side opposite largest angle

1. △QWP ~ △JLK. Find the value of x.

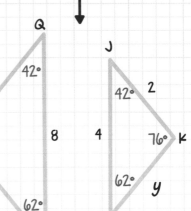

2. Using the triangles in question 1, find the value of y.

FOR 3 THROUGH 5, USE THE DIAGRAMS BELOW.

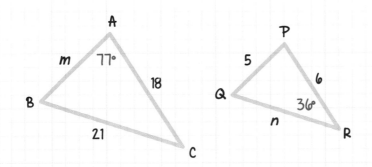

3. $\triangle ABC \sim \triangle PQR$. Find $\angle Q$.

4. $\triangle ABC \sim \triangle PQR$. Find the value of m.

5. Find the value of n.

SOLVE.

6. Jacob and his family are traveling to a ski lodge. The legend on the map says that 2 inches equals 12 miles. If the distance between Jacob's home and the ski lodge is 16 inches on the map, how many miles will Jacob and his family travel to get to the ski lodge?

7. Veronica is going to ride a new bike trail. The map of the trail states that 4 inches equals 2 miles. If the entire bike trail is represented by 36 inches, how many miles can Veronica ride?

8. Hill Farms is installing a new fence around their property. The project manager makes the following scale drawing of the property to assess its dimensions and cost. If 3 inches equals 36 feet, what is the actual perimeter of the property?

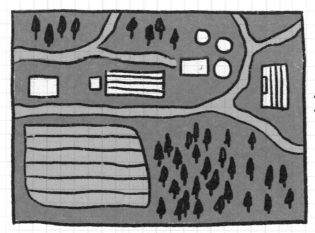

39 in.

48 in.

9. The Reillys are planning a renovation. They make a scale drawing of their den. The room is 32 feet long. The drawing indicates that 2 inches represent 4 feet. How many inches long is the room in the drawing?

10. The distance from Bart's house to his grandparents' house is 376 kilometers. Bart's mom shows him the route on a map. The map says that 2 centimeters represent 4 kilometers. How many centimeters is the distance between Bart's house and his grandparents' house in the drawing?

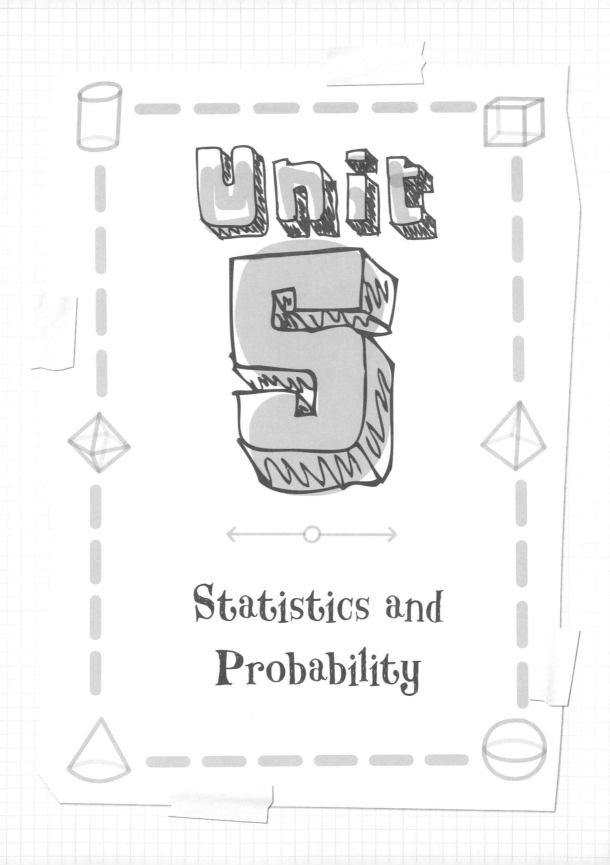

Unit 5

Statistics and Probability

INTRODUCTION TO STATISTICS

STATISTICS is the study of data. There are two types of data:

> quantitative—information you can count or measure, like "How many students attend your school?"
>
> qualitative—information you can observe, like "What is your favorite breakfast food?"

You can COLLECT DATA by asking a STATISTICAL QUESTION. This is a question that anticipates many different responses.

> Statistical question: "How tall is a professional athlete?" There can be different answers.
>
> Not a statistical question: "How tall is your principal?" There is only one answer.

Answers that vary have **VARIABILITY**.

Statistics can have *high* variability (data that is spread out) or *low* variability (data that is closely clustered).

SAMPLING is when we take a small part of a larger group to estimate characteristics about the whole group.

EXAMPLE: There are 2,785 students in the Builder Middle School District. The district surveys 500 students and asks if they are going to attend a sleepaway camp over the summer recess. The results show that 210 students are going to attend a sleepaway camp. Approximately how many students in the Builder Middle School District are going to attend a sleepaway camp?

Because 210 out of 500 students are going to attend a sleepaway camp, that means $\frac{210}{500} = \frac{21}{50}$ of the sample are going to attend sleepaway camp.

To apply this number to the entire middle school district population of 2,785 students, multiply:
$2,785 \cdot \frac{21}{50} = 1,169.7$.

So, we can estimate approximately 1,170 students are going to attend sleepaway camp over the summer recess.

ANSWER EACH QUESTION. USE WHAT YOU KNOW ABOUT STATISTICS.

1. Which of the following questions are statistical questions?

   A. What device do five friends use most often to access the internet?

   B. What mode of transportation do kids in your neighborhood take to get to school each day?

   C. Did your best friend do their homework last night?

   D. How many students in your school participate in after-school activities?

   E. What time did your family leave the museum last night?

2. State whether each of the following questions asks about qualitative or quantitative data.

   A. What is the most popular type of book borrowed from the school library?

   B. How many people attended the first basketball game of the season?

   C. How many times a week do you exercise?

   D. What is your favorite academic subject?

   E. How many hours do you spend playing video games each evening?

3. State whether each of the following situations has high or low variability.

   A. How much money do you spend on snacks every week?

   B. How many televisions does your family have?

   C. How many years has your family owned a car?

   D. What is the top score you achieved in a video game?

   E. How many classes do you attend in school each day?

4. Mr. Bart has 34 actors in his musical theater workshop. There are 14 actively performing in theatrical shows. If a total of 895 actors attended Mr. Bart's workshops this year, approximately how many of those actors are actively performing in theatrical shows?

5. Carol checks the quality of 45 jump ropes and needs to send back 6 to manufacturing. If Carol has a total of 315 jump ropes, about how many jump ropes can she expect to send back to manufacturing?

6. Jackson's car wash cleans 27 cars the first hour of its opening. If the car wash is open 9 hours, about how many cars will the car wash clean in one day?

7. The student council is planning a bake sale to raise money for the athletic teams. A local bakery donates a box containing 8 layers of assorted mini-muffins. If the top layer has 9 blueberry mini-muffins, about how many blueberry mini-muffins are in the box?

8. A new cartoon character exhibit at a museum attracts 1,881 people on its opening day. Carlton notices that 19 out of 100 people are dressed up as their favorite cartoon character. About how many of the 1,881 visitors at the exhibit are dressed as their favorite cartoon character?

Chapter 52 · MEASURES OF CENTRAL TENDENCY AND VARIATION

MEASURES OF CENTRAL TENDENCY: A single number that is a summary of all of a data set's values.

Mean: The arithmetic *average*, or central value of a data set.

Median: The *middle number* of a data set when all of the items are written in order, from least to greatest.

Minimum and Maximum: The *lowest* and *greatest* numbers in a data set.

Mode: The item that occurs the *most* in a data set.

MEASURES OF VARIATION describe how the values of a data set vary.

Range: The difference between the *minimum* and *maximum* values in a data set.

Outlier: A data value that is significantly *lower* or *higher* than all other values.

EXAMPLE: A data analyst for an online retailer created the chart below to showcase the sales of laptop computers for the first week of back-to-school sales.

Monday	Tuesday	Wednesday	Thursday	Friday	Saturday	Sunday
1,074	511	648	534	648	771	798

To analyze the data, calculate the measures of central tendency and the measures of variation.

▶ Find the **mean**, or average number, of computers sold daily.

$$\frac{1,074 + 511 + 648 + 534 + 648 + 771 + 798}{7} = \frac{4984}{7} = 712$$

▶ Find the **median**, or middle quantity, of computer sales.

511, 534, 648, (648,) 771, 798, 1,074

▶ Find the **minimum** and **maximum** number of daily sales. 511 computers sold on Tuesday. 1,074 computers sold on Monday.

THINK:
If the number of data values had been even, just divide the two middle numbers by 2 to find the median.

▶ Find the **mode**, or the amount of sales that occurred most. 648 laptop computer sales occurred on both Wednesday and Friday.

▶ Find the **range**, or the variation in sales.

1,074 − 511 = 563

▶ Find the **outlier**, or a variation that is lower or higher than the sales made on all days. Higher than typical sales occurred on Monday: 1,074.

This number is an exception and skews the average number of daily computers sold.

ANSWER EACH QUESTION. USE WHAT YOU KNOW ABOUT THE MEASURES OF CENTRAL TENDENCY AND VARIATION. ROUND ANSWERS TO THE NEAREST HUNDREDTH.

1. A university asked 10 recent graduates of the physical therapist program how much they earned per year at their first job. Below is the data collected.

$40,000	$74,250	$78,000	$74,250	$95,000
$64,500	$68,000	$72,000	$62,050	$58,950

A. Find the mean.

B. Find the median.

C. Find the mode.

D. Find the minimum and maximum.

E. Find the range.

F. Does there seem to be any outlier(s)? If so, what number(s)? Do you think the outlier(s) skew the mean?

2. Healthy Family Gym kept track of its daily usage by its members and guests from 5 a.m. to 11 p.m. over ten days. On the tenth day, the gym held an open house and 815 people stopped by.

558, 351, 316, 486, 510, 398, 600, 545, 510, 815

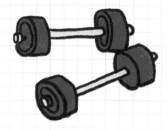

A. Find the mean.

B. Find the median.

C. Find the mode.

D. Find the minimum and maximum.

E. Find the range.

F. Does there seem to be any outlier(s)? If so, what number(s)? Do you think the outlier(s) skew the mean?

DISPLAYING DATA

Data that has been collected and organized can be displayed with tables, charts, graphs, or diagrams.

It is important to choose a visual display that best illustrates the data with no bias.

Box Plot

A box plot displays data along a number line and splits the data into quartiles (quarters), shown as boxes.

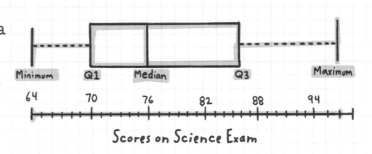

Scores on Science Exam

Data arranged in order:

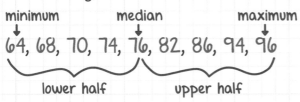

minimum   median   maximum

64, 68, 70, 74, 76, 82, 86, 94, 96

lower half   upper half

Line Plot

A line plot displays data by placing an "x" above numbers on a number line.

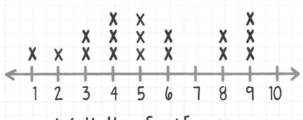

Weekly Hours Spent Exercising

Histogram

A histogram displays the frequency of data.

The horizontal scale uses a range of 5.

Two-Way Table

A two-way table displays data that has a relation between two categories.

	Owns a car	Does not own a car	Total
Lives in the city	5	12	17
Lives in the suburbs	18	2	20
Total	23	14	37

Scatter Plot

A scatter plot displays the relationship between two sets of data.

Scatter plots can show a positive correlation, a negative correlation, or no correlation.

A line of best fit can be drawn to roughly describe the given relationship.

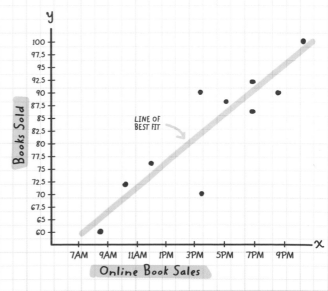

LINE OF BEST FIT

Online Book Sales

ANSWER EACH QUESTION. USE WHAT YOU KNOW ABOUT THE VARIOUS WAYS YOU CAN DISPLAY DATA.

1. Answer the questions based on the two-way table below. This data was collected from a random sample of middle school students.

	Reads every day	Does not read every day	Total
Plays video games every day	25	9	34
Does not play video games every day	11	6	17
Total	36	15	51

A. How many middle school students only play video games daily?

B. How many middle school students only read daily?

C. How many middle school students play video games and read daily?

D. How many middle school students do not play video games or read daily?

2. The physical education teacher asked her first-period class how many fruits and vegetables they typically eat every day. Create a line plot of the data the teacher collected.

5, 2, 3, 10, 8, 3, 3, 1, 6, 8, 7, 1, 3, 4, 5, 4, 5, 5, 6, 2, 3, 3, 4, 3, 4, 5, 9

3. Mac's science class keeps track of daily rainfall from March to May. Here are the recorded measures of rainfall in millimeters: 23, 22, 4, 2, 9, 38, 39, 9, 17, 18, 23, 44, 48, 49, 14, 17, 19, 18, 26, 31, 42, 31, 16, 12, 18, 27, 38, 39, 22, 2, 4, 8, 34, 34, 7, 11, 23, 27, 41.

▶ Create a histogram of this data. Use a range of 5 for the horizontal scale.

4. Sergio's Sneaker Store records the number of purchases made from its online website every minute from 7 p.m. to 7:20 p.m. Here are the number of purchases made every minute: 18, 75, 58, 60, 23, 35, 15, 26, 45, 35, 48, 78, 85, 12, 35, 21, 50, 70, 41, 76, 15.

▶ Find the median, the 1st quartile, and the 3rd quartile. Then create a box plot with the data.

5. Unionville College surveys 20 of its computer science majors, asking them approximately how many hours they spend online each school day. Here are the number of hours from the survey: 4, 12, 6, 7, 5, 4, 2, 5, 8, 6, 4, 3, 9, 10, 8, 11, 7, 10, 8, 7.

▶ Find the median, the 1st quartile, and the 3rd quartile. Then create a box plot with the data.

6. A car insurance company asked its customers approximately how many hours a week they drive. The table to the right shows the results.

Customer's age	Approximate number of hours spent driving each week
20	30
25	45
30	45
35	40
40	45
45	35
50	40
55	30
60	25
65	20
70	15
75	10
80	5

A. Create a scatter plot showing customer age (horizontal axis) and number of hours spent driving (vertical axis).

B. State whether the scatter plot illustrates a positive correlation, a negative correlation, or no correlation. Explain how you know.

Chapter 54 PROBABILITY

PROBABILITY is the likelihood something will happen. It is a number between 0 and 1 and can be written as a percent.

Impossible	Less Likely	Equally Likey	More Likely	Certain
0%	25%	50%	75%	100%

Use the ratio below to find out *how likely* it is that an event will occur.

> Sometimes to find all possible outcomes you may need to make a table or draw a tree diagram.

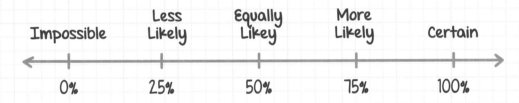

$$\text{Probability (Event)} = \frac{\text{number of favorable outomes}}{\text{number of possible outcomes}}$$

COMPLEMENTARY EVENTS are events that *cannot* happen at the same time, such as raining and not raining.

The sum of their likelihood of happening is always 1 or 100%.

Probability (event) + Probability (complement) = 1 or 100%

Chance of rain + Chance of no rain

30% + 70% = 100%

EXAMPLE: Darrell goes to his favorite deli to purchase the daily sandwich special. Today's special is a turkey sandwich with 1 choice of soup (chicken or vegetable), 1 choice of dessert (berry muffin or fruit cup), and 1 choice of drink (water or juice). What is the probability Darrell will choose a vegetable soup, fruit cup, and water with his turkey sandwich? What is the probability Darrell will *not* choose a vegetable soup, fruit cup, and water with his turkey sandwich?

STEP 1: Make a tree diagram to list all of the different possibilities.

Sandwich	Soup	Dessert	Drink
		Berry Muffin	Water
			Juice
	Chicken		
		Fruit Cup	Water
			Juice
Turkey Sandwich			
		Berry Muffin	Water
			Juice
	Vegetable		
		Fruit Cup	Water
			Juice

There are 8 possible choices or outcomes that Darrell can make.

STEP 2: Use the probability formula.

$$\text{Probability (Event)} = \frac{\text{number of favorable outcomes}}{\text{number of possible outcomes}} = \frac{1}{8} = 0.125 = 12.5\%$$

So, the probability that Darrell will choose a vegetable soup, fruit cup, and water with his turkey sandwich is 12.5%.

STEP 3: Use the complement of an event formula.

Probability (event) + Probability (complement) = 100%

12.5% + Probability (complement) = 100%

Probability (complement) = 100% − 12.5%

Probability (complement) = 87.5%

So, the probability that Darrell will *not* choose a vegetable soup, fruit cup, and water with his turkey sandwich is 87.5%.

DELI MENU
TURKEY SANDWICH...$5
VEGETABLE SOUP....$2
FRUIT CUP........$1
WATER..........$1

ANSWER EACH QUESTION. USE WHAT YOU KNOW ABOUT PROBABILITY.

1. Four siblings, Beth, Aaron, Mel, and Susanna, arrive at the front passenger door of their car at the same time. What is the probability Aaron gets into the car first? Hint: Make a tree diagram to find all the possible outcomes.

2. Willow flips a coin twice. The coin is colored red on one side and blue on the other side. What is the probability that Willow will flip blue twice? Hint: Make a table to list all the possible outcomes.

3. Kelly randomly gives each student a card with a math expression. Answer the following using these cards.

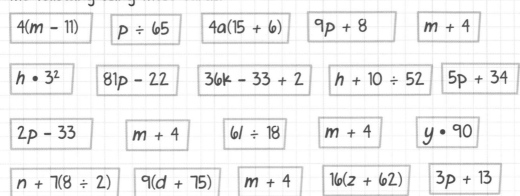

$4(m - 11)$ $P \div 65$ $4a(15 + 6)$ $9p + 8$ $m + 4$

$h \cdot 3^2$ $81p - 22$ $36k - 33 + 2$ $h + 10 \div 52$ $5p + 34$

$2p - 33$ $m + 4$ $61 \div 18$ $m + 4$ $y \cdot 90$

$n + 7(8 \div 2)$ $9(d + 75)$ $m + 4$ $16(z + 62)$ $3p + 13$

A. What is the probability that a student will receive a card with the expression $m + 4$?

B. What is the probability that a student will receive a card with an expression that contains parentheses?

C. What is the probability that a student will receive a card with an expression that contains the variable p?

D. What is the probability that a student will receive a card with an expression that contains an addition or division sign?

E. What is the probability that a student will receive a card with an expression that does *not* contain a subtraction sign?

4. Paola tosses a number cube with the numbers 1–6.

   A. What is the probability of tossing an even number?

   B. What is the probability of tossing a number greater than 2?

   C. What is the probability of *not* tossing an odd number?

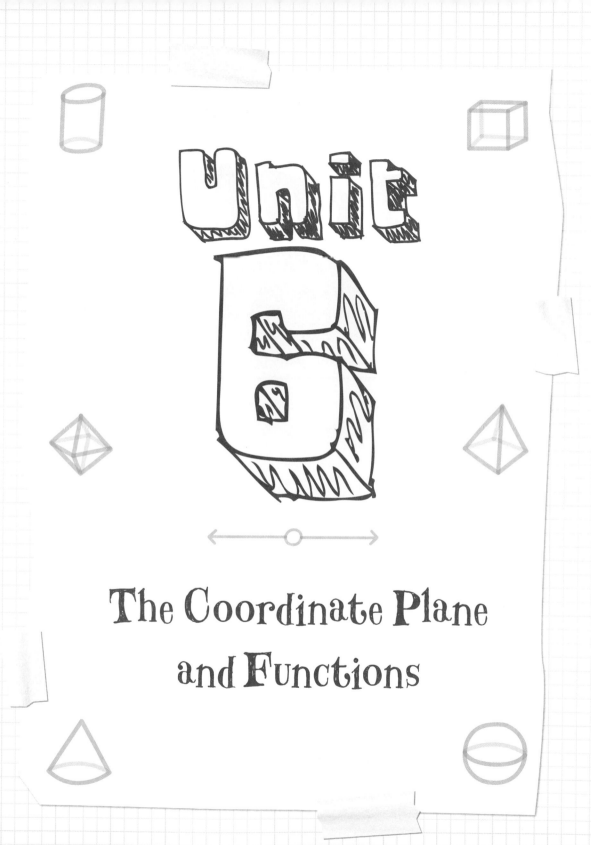

Unit

6

The Coordinate Plane and Functions

55 THE COORDINATE PLANE

The **COORDINATE PLANE** is a flat surface formed by the intersection of axes.

The horizontal number line is the x-axis. The vertical number line is the y-axis.

The x- and y-axes intersect at the origin. The coordinate plane is divided into four quadrants.

> An ORDERED PAIR gives the coordinates of a point. To plot a point such as (3, 5), follow the directions below:
>
> - For the x-coordinate: Start at the origin, (0, 0), then move 3 spaces to the right on the x-axis.
>
> - For the y-coordinate: Start at the origin, then move 5 spaces up on the y-axis.

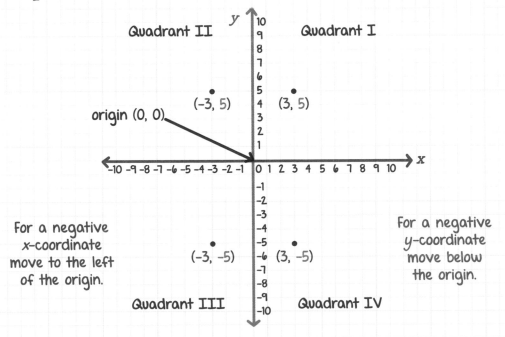

Quadrant II

Quadrant I

(–3, 5)

(3, 5)

origin (0, 0)

For a negative x-coordinate move to the left of the origin.

For a negative y-coordinate move below the origin.

(–3, –5)

(3, –5)

Quadrant III

Quadrant IV

You can find the distance between two points on the coordinate plane. There are two approaches.

When two points *share* an x- or y-coordinate, find the difference of the two different coordinates. Then calculate the absolute value of that number.

Find the distance between (–2, –8) and (5, –8). **shared y-coordinate**

–2 – (5) = –7   Subtract

|–7| = 7   Absolute value

So, these points are 7 units apart.

Find the distance between (4, 7) and (4, –3). **shared x-coordinate**

7 – (–3) = 10   Subtract

| 10 | = 10   Absolute value

So, these points are 10 units apart.

When two points *do not share* an x- or y-coordinate, use the Distance Formula.

$$d = \sqrt{(x_2 - x_1)^2 + (y_2 - y_1)^2}$$

Find the distance between (–4, 1) and (4, –5).

Assign values:

$x_1 = -4, \; y_1 = 1 \quad x_2 = 4, \; y_2 = -5$

Substitute these values into the formula. Use the Order of Operations to evaluate.

$$d = \sqrt{(x_2 - x_1)^2 + (y_2 - y_1)^2}$$

$$d = \sqrt{(4 - (-4))^2 + (-5 - 1)^2}$$

$$d = \sqrt{(8)^2 + (-6)^2}$$

$$d = \sqrt{64 + 36}$$

$$d = \sqrt{100}$$

$$d = 10$$

So, these points are 10 units apart.

1. Use the given coordinate plane to complete the table. In the first column, write the ordered pair for each given point. In the second column, write the location of that ordered pair on the coordinate plane: quadrants I, II, III, IV, *x*-axis, or *y*-axis.

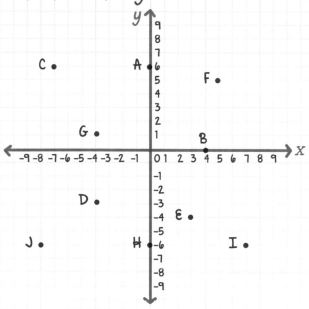

Coordinate Point	Ordered Pair	Quadrant
A		
B		
C		
D		
E		
F		
G		
H		
I		
J		

2. Plot the following ordered pairs on the given coordinate plane.

Q: (3, 0), R: (-8, -5), S: (4, 5), T: (-2, 3), V: (6, 1), Z: (-8, 0)

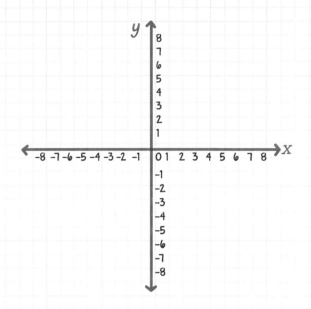

3. The coordinates of Point M are (-2, -5). The coordinates of Point N are (7, -5). What is the distance between Point M and Point N?

4. The coordinates of Point O are (-3, 2). The coordinates of Point P are (12, 10). What is the distance between Point O and Point P?

Chapter 56

RELATIONS, LINES, AND FUNCTIONS

A **RELATION** is a set of ordered pairs *(x, y)* that shows a relationship. Sometimes, when we are given several ordered pairs, we can connect them by drawing a straight line through all the points.

> You can determine if a relation is a function by graphing it and doing a VERTICAL LINE TEST.

A **FUNCTION** is a *special relation* where there is *only one y*-value (also known as the **RANGE**) for each *x*-value (also known as the domain).

The relation below is a function. The relationship between the *y*-value and the *x*-value is 12.

domain inches		range feet	(domain, range) (inches, feet)
12 in.	→	1 ft.	(12, 1)
24 in.	→	2 ft.	(24, 2)
36 in.	→	3 ft.	(36, 3)
48 in.	→	4 ft.	(48, 4)

This is what a function looks like algebraically: $y = 5x + 2$.
There is only one output *(y)* for each input *(x)*.

The relation below is *not* a function. There is more than one *y*-value for each *x*-value.

domain number of students per class		range average math score	(domain, range) (# of students, average score)
21	→	90	(21, 90)
26	→	87	(26, 87)
22	→	94	(22, 94)
26	→	82	(26, 82)

more than one value for 26

THINK:
The value of *y* depends on the value of *x*. (independent variable, dependent variable) (input, output)

EXAMPLE: Graph: $y = 5x + 2$.

STEP 1: Make an input/output chart.

Input (x)	Function: $y = 5x + 2$	Output (y)	Ordered Pair (x, y)
-2	$y = 5(-2) + 2$	-8	(-2, -8)
-1	$y = 5(-1) + 2$	-3	(-1, -3)
0	$y = 5(0) + 2$	2	(0, 2)
1	$y = 5(1) + 2$	7	(1, 7)

STEP 2: Use the chart to graph the equation of the line $y = 5x + 2$. Use the ordered pairs from the last column in the table.

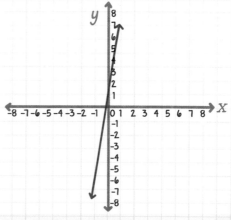

ANSWER THE QUESTIONS. USE WHAT YOU KNOW ABOUT RELATIONS, LINES, AND FUNCTIONS.

1. What numbers make up the domain of the relation? (0, 5), (3, 4), (5, 0), (−4, −3), (0, −5)

2. What numbers make up the range of the relation in question 1?

3. Is the relation in question 1 a function? Why or why not?

4. Graph the relation shown in the table. Is this relation a function? Why or why not?

Domain (x)	Range (y)
–4	–7
–2	–5
1	1
3	5

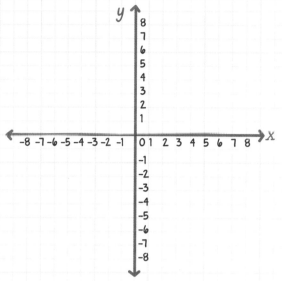

5. Complete the input/output and graph the function $y = x - 6$.

Input (x)	Function: $y = x - 6$	Output (y)	Ordered Pair (x, y)
–1			
0			
8			
10			

6. Complete the input/output and graph the function $y = \frac{1}{2}x - 1$.

Input (x)	Function: $y = \frac{1}{2}x - 1$	Output (y)	Ordered Pair (x, y)
–2			
0			
2			
4			

7. Complete the input/output and graph the function $y = -4x$.

Input (x)	Function: $y = -4x$	Output (y)	Ordered Pair (x, y)
-2			
-1			
1			
2			

8. Complete the input/output and graph the function $3x + y = -3$. Remember, isolate the y before you put in your x-values. Then, write your new function in the chart below.

Input (x)	Function:	Output (y)	Ordered Pair (x, y)
-3			
-2			
0			
2			

Chapter 57 ⬛ SLOPE ⊜

SLOPE is the ratio $\frac{\text{Rise}}{\text{Run}}$ that tells the steepness and direction of a line.

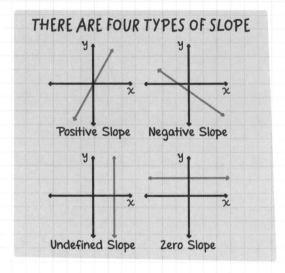

THERE ARE FOUR TYPES OF SLOPE

Positive Slope   Negative Slope

Undefined Slope   Zero Slope

There are two ways we can find the slope of a line.

Use a Slope Triangle

Find the slope of the given line.

STEP 1: Pick two points on the graph.

A: $(-6, 4)$ and B: $(-1, 0)$

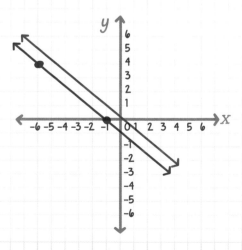

STEP 2: Draw a right triangle to get from A to B. Find the **RISE** and the **RUN**.

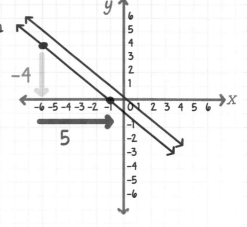

Rise = −4
(Because we moved down 4 spaces)

Run = 5
(Because we moved right 5 spaces)

STEP 3: Insert values into the ratio for slope.

$$\text{Slope} = \frac{\text{Rise}}{\text{Run}} = \frac{-4}{5} = -\frac{4}{5}$$

So, the slope of the given line is $-\frac{4}{5}$.

Use the Slope Formula

When you know two points on a line, you can find the slope of the line that goes through those points. For example: $(3, -2)$ and $(-2, 6)$.

$$\text{Slope } (m) = \frac{y_2 - y_1}{x_2 - x_1}$$

STEP 1: Label each given value as (x_1, y_1) and (x_2, y_2).

$x_1 = 3$ $y_1 = -2$

$x_2 = -2$ $y_2 = 6$

STEP 2: Use the slope formula and substitute the values.

$$\text{Slope } (m) = \frac{y_2 - y_1}{x_2 - x_1} = \frac{6 - (-2)}{-2 - 3} = \frac{8}{-5}$$

So, the slope of the line that goes through $(3, -2)$ and $(-2, 6)$ is $-\frac{8}{5}$.

ANSWER THE QUESTIONS. USE WHAT YOU KNOW ABOUT SLOPE. FOR QUESTIONS 1 THROUGH 4, USE THE GRAPHS A THROUGH D.

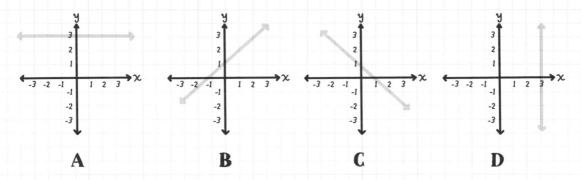

| A | B | C | D |

1. Which graph shows a line with a positive slope? _____

2. Which graph shows a line with a zero slope? _____

3. Which graph shows a line with a negative slope? _____

4. Which graph shows a line with an undefined slope? _____

5. Use a slope triangle to find the slope of this line.

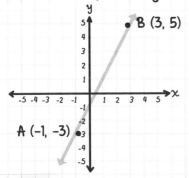

6. Use a slope triangle to find the slope of this line.

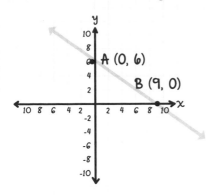

A (0, 6)

B (9, 0)

7. Use the slope formula to find the slope of the line that passes through the points (4, –1) and (–2, –3).

8. Use the slope formula to find the slope of the line that passes through the points (12, –9) and (–6, 11).

9. Draw the line that goes through $(2, -8)$ and has a slope of $-\dfrac{1}{4}$.

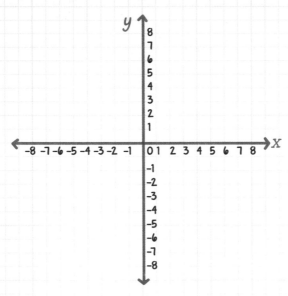

10. Draw the line that goes through $(5, 6)$ and has a slope of 3.

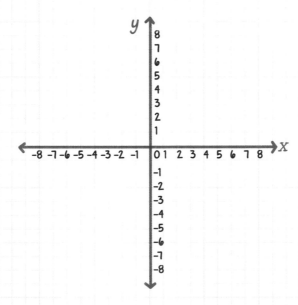

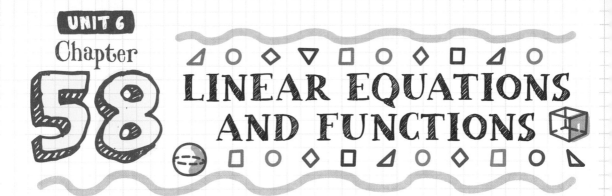

58 LINEAR EQUATIONS AND FUNCTIONS

A **LINEAR EQUATION** is an equation whose graph is a line. A linear equation always has the following form:

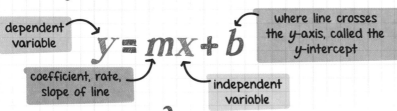

dependent variable

$$y = mx + b$$

where line crosses the y-axis, called the y-intercept

coefficient, rate, slope of line

independent variable

THINK: The graph of a linear equation is a straight line; this means that ALL linear equations are functions except for vertical lines!

Graph: $y - 6 = -\dfrac{2}{3}(x + 3)$.

STEP 1: Manipulate the equation so it is in $y = mx + b$ form.

$y - 6 = -\dfrac{2}{3}(x + 3)$

$y - 6 = -\dfrac{2}{3}x - 2$ Use the Distributive Property.

$\underline{+\, 6 \quad\; +\, 6}$ Add 6 to both sides of the equation to isolate y.

$y = -\dfrac{2}{3}x + 4$ Equation is in $y = mx + b$ form.

STEP 2: Identify the y-intercept and the slope.

$y = mx + b$ Linear equation

$y = -\dfrac{2}{3}x + 4$ m = slope and b = y-intercept

slope $(m) = -\dfrac{2}{3}$ y-intercept $(b) = 4$

STEP 3: Graph the line.

▶ First plot the y-intercept. $x = 0$ and $y = 4$ or $(0, 4)$

▶ From there, we know the slope is $-\frac{2}{3}$. Since the slope is negative, the rise is -2 and the run is 3.

▶ Continue to plot points until you form a line.

▶ Last, connect the points, and draw arrows on the ends of the line to show that it keeps going forever.

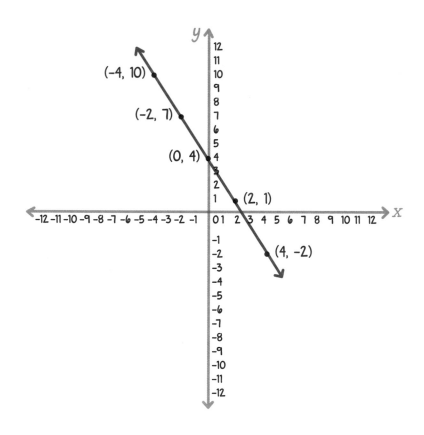

ANSWER THE QUESTIONS. USE WHAT YOU KNOW ABOUT LINEAR EQUATIONS. FOR QUESTIONS 1 THROUGH 5, IDENTIFY THE SLOPE AND THE Y-INTERCEPT OF EACH LINEAR EQUATION.

1. $y = -\dfrac{3}{5}x - 8$

2. $y = 5x + 7$

3. $\dfrac{1}{4}x = y$

4. $5x = 3y + 6$

5. $-x + 3 = \dfrac{y}{2}$

6. Graph $y = -\dfrac{1}{3}x + 2$

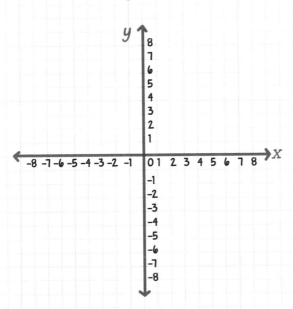

7. Graph $y = \dfrac{3}{5}x - 1$

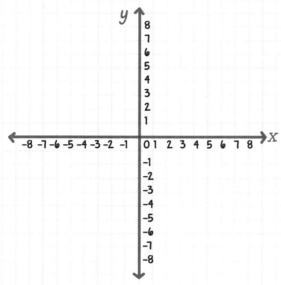

8. Graph $2x + 2y = 6$

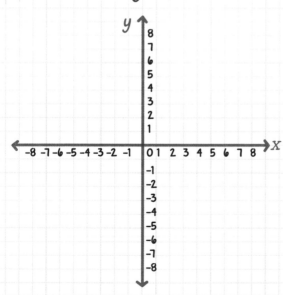

9. Graph $y + 3 = -1$

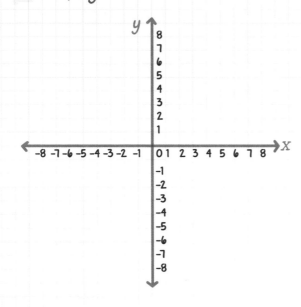

10. Graph $-6 + x = -4$

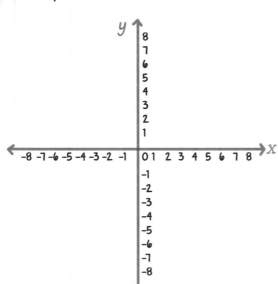

Chapter

59

SIMULTANEOUS LINEAR EQUATIONS AND FUNCTIONS

SIMULTANEOUS LINEAR EQUATIONS AND FUNCTIONS are a set of two or more equations that have variables in common.

You can find values that simultaneously satisfy both or all the equations by using one of three methods.

> Simultaneous equations can have one solution, no solution, or an infinite number of solutions.

EXAMPLE: Solve $\begin{cases} x - y = 5 \\ 3x - y = 7 \end{cases}$

Graphing Method

Graph the simultaneous equations to find the solution.

$x - y = 5$
$3x - y = 7$

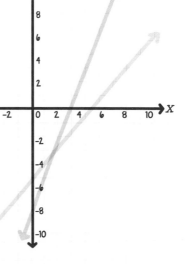

STEP 1: First rewrite each of the equations into $y = mx + b$ form:

$y = -x + 5$
$y = 3x - 7$

STEP 2: Then graph the equation using the y-intercept and slope from each.

The graph shows that the two lines intersect at $(1, -4)$, so the solution to the equation is $(1, -4)$.

Addition Method

STEP 1: Number the equations.

$x - y = 5$ ①
$3x - y = 7$ ②

STEP 2: Multiply Equation ② by -1 so that $-y$ in Equation ① will cancel out $+y$ in Equation ②.

$3x - y = 7$ Multiply each term by -1.
$-3x + y = -7$

STEP 3: Add Equations ① and ② together.

$x - y = 5$
$-3x + y = -7$ Addition Method

$-2x + 0 = -2$
$-2x = -2$
$\dfrac{-2x}{-2} = \dfrac{-2}{-2}$
$x = 1$

STEP 4: Substitute 1 for x into Equation ①. Solve for y.

$x - y = 5$
$1 - y = 5$
$\underline{-1 -1}$
$-y = 4$
$(-1)-y = (-1)\,4$ Multiply by -1.
$y = -4$

So, the solution is $(x, y) = (1, -4)$.

STEP 5: Check your solution.

336

Substitution Method

STEP 1: Number the equations.

$x - y = 5$ ①
$3x - y = 7$ ②

STEP 2: Rewrite Equation ① to isolate x.

$x - y = 5$
$ + y + y$

$x + 0 = 5 + y$
$ x = 5 + y$

STEP 3: Substitute $5 + y$ for x in Equation ②.

$3x - y = 7$
$3(5 + y) - y = 7$ Substitution Method
$15 + 3y - y = 7$
$ 15 + 2y = 7$
$ -15 -15$

$$2y = -8$$
$$\frac{2y}{2} = \frac{-8}{2}$$
$$y = -4$$

STEP 4: Substitute -4 for y into Equation ①. Solve for x.

$x - y = 5$
$x - (-4) = 5$
$x + 4 = 5$
$ -4 -4$
$ x = 1$

So, the solution is $(x, y) = (1, -4)$.

STEP 5: Check your solution.

ANSWER THE QUESTIONS. FOR QUESTIONS 1 THROUGH 4, SOLVE THE SIMULTANEOUS EQUATIONS BY USING THE GRAPHING METHOD.

1. $x - y = -4$

    $x + y = 2$

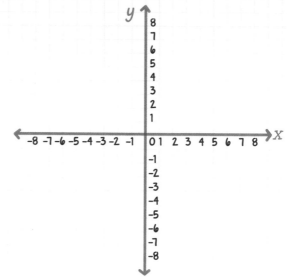

2. $-3x + y = -1$

    $-2x + y = 1$

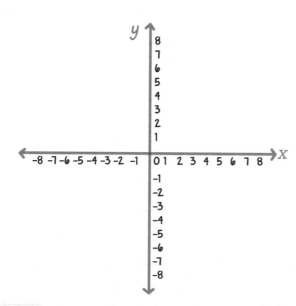

3. $-\frac{1}{4}x - y = -2$

   $-\frac{1}{4}x - y = -1$

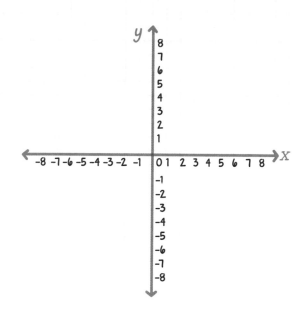

4. $\frac{1}{2}x + y = 0$

   $-3x - 2y = 4$

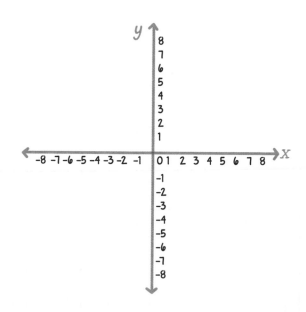

FOR QUESTIONS 5 AND 6, SOLVE THE SIMULTANEOUS EQUATIONS BY USING THE ADDITION METHOD.

5. $2x - y = 2$
   $-3x - 2y = -10$

6. $-3x + 3y = 6$
   $-4x + y = -4$

FOR QUESTIONS 7 AND 8, SOLVE THE SIMULTANEOUS EQUATIONS BY USING THE SUBSTITUTION METHOD.

7. $4x + 2y = 26$
   $x - y = -4$

8. $-2x - y = -7$
   $-4x + 4y = -8$

NONLINEAR FUNCTIONS

NONLINEAR FUNCTIONS are functions that do *not* form a straight line when graphed and are not in the form $y = mx + b$.

Two examples of nonlinear functions:

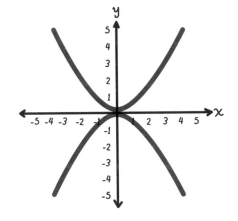

Quadratic Functions

When graphed, the result is a parabola, a U-shaped curve. A parabola can open upward or downward.

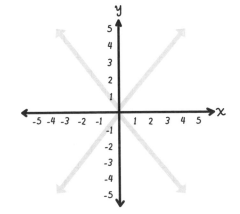

Absolute Value Functions

When graphed, the result is shaped like a "V." Absolute value functions can open upward or downward.

Complete the input/output chart and graph the quadratic function:
$y = 3x^2 + 1$.

Input (x)	Function	Output (y)	Coordinate Points (x, y)
-2	$3(-2)^2 + 1$ $3(4) + 1$ $12 + 1$	13	(-2, 13)
-1	$3(-1)^2 + 1$ $3(1) + 1$ $3 + 1$	4	(-1, 4)
0	$3(0)^2 + 1$ $3(0) + 1$ $0 + 1$	1	(0, 1)
1	$3(1)^2 + 1$ $3(1) + 1$ $3 + 1$	4	(1, 4)
2	$3(2)^2 + 1$ $3(4) + 1$ $12 + 1$	13	(2, 13)

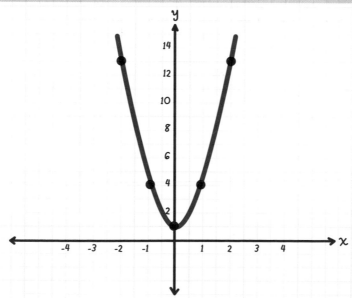

Complete the input/output chart and graph the absolute value function: $y = -|x| - 2$.

Input (x)	Function	Output (y)	Coordinate Points (x, y)
–5	$-\|-5\| - 2$ $-5 - 2$	–7	(–5, –7)
–3	$-\|-3\| - 2$ $-3 - 2$	–5	(–3, –5)
0	$-\|0\| - 2$ $0 - 2$	–2	(0, –2)
3	$-\|3\| - 2$ $-3 - 2$	–5	(3, –5)
5	$-\|5\| - 2$ $-5 - 2$	–7	(5, –7)

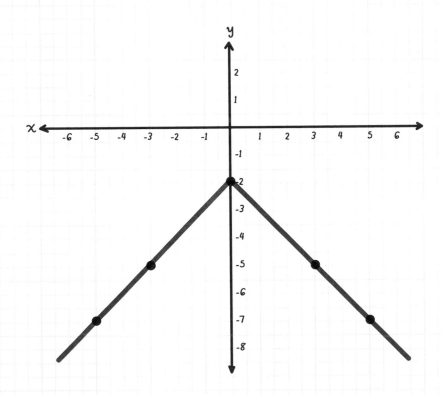

ANSWER THE QUESTIONS. USE WHAT YOU KNOW ABOUT GRAPHING QUADRATIC FUNCTIONS AND ABSOLUTE VALUE FUNCTIONS.

1. Create the input/output chart and graph: $y = 4x^2$.

Input (x)	Function $y = 4x^2$	Output (y)	Coordinate Points (x, y)
-2			
-1			
0			
1			
2			

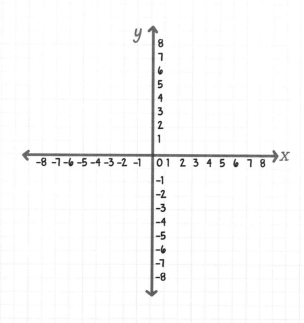

2. Create the input/output chart and graph: $y = -3x^2 - 1$.

Input (x)	Function $y = -3x^2 - 1$	Output (y)	Coordinate Points (x, y)
-2			
-1			
0			
1			
2			

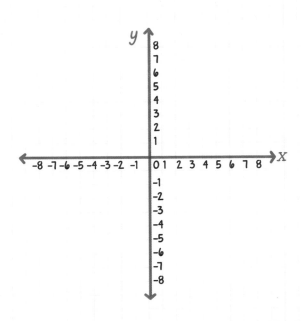

3. Create the input/output chart and graph: $y = -|2x|$.

Input (x)	Function $y = -|2x|$	Output (y)	Coordinate Points (x, y)
-4			
-2			
0			
2			
4			

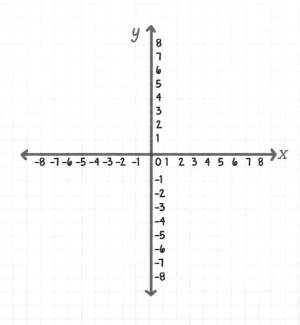

4. Create the input/output chart and graph: $y = -|3x| - 4$.

Input (x)	Function $y = -|3x| - 4$	Output (y)	Coordinate Points (x, y)
-4			
-2			
0			
2			
4			

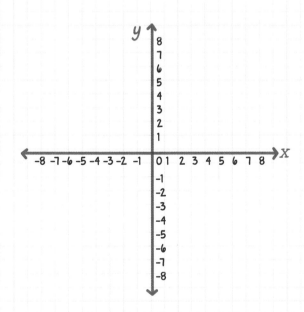

Chapter 61. POLYGONS AND THE COORDINATE PLANE

The coordinate grid can be used to draw polygons.

EXAMPLES

Plot the points (1, 4), (3, 2), (3, –1), (1, –3), (–2, –3), (–4, –1), (–4, 2), and (–2, 4). Connect the points and then identify the shape that is formed.

STEP 1: Plot the points on the coordinate plane.

STEP 2: Create the shape by connecting the points.

STEP 3: Identify the shape.

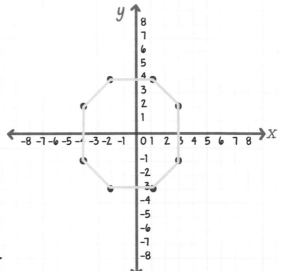

The shape has eight sides.

An eight-sided figure is an octagon.

A rectangle is plotted on a coordinate plane. Three of the vertices are M (–3, 4), A (–3, –2), and T (3, –2). What are the coordinates of point H, the 4th vertex?

STEP 1: Plot the points M (–3, 4), A (–3,–2), and T (3, –2) on the coordinate plane.

THINK:
Point M and Point A share the same x-coordinate. So, we can calculate the distance between the two points by finding the difference of the y-coordinates, which is 4 - (-2) = 6.

STEP 2: Locate the 4th vertex H.

Since a rectangle has opposite sides equal in length, we only have to find the length of the opposite side containing the points M (–3, 4) and A (–3, –2).

Because the distance between Point M and Point A is 6 units, the distance between point T and Point H must also be 6 units.

So, the coordinates for Point H are (3, 4).

STEP 3: Plot the 4th vertex H on the coordinate plane.

ANSWER THE QUESTIONS. USE WHAT YOU KNOW ABOUT GRAPHING POLYGONS ON THE COORDINATE PLANE.

1. Plot the points (–2, 2), (2, 2), (–5, –3), and (5, –3). Then identify the shape that is formed by the points.

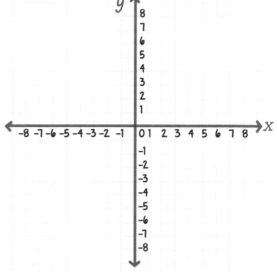

2. Plot the points (0, 6), (–5, 1), (0, –4), and (5, 1). Then identify the shape that is formed by the points.

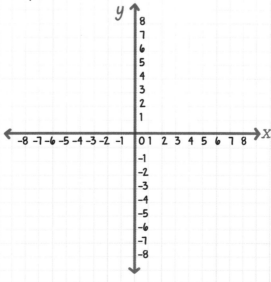

3. Plot the points (−4, 1), (4, 1), (7, 5), and (−7, 5). Then identify the shape that is formed by the points.

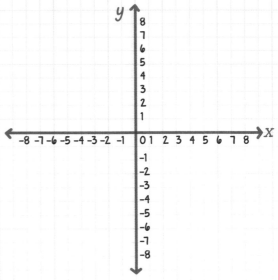

4. Plot the points (−5, −2), (1, −2), (3, 2), (−2, 5), and (−7, 2). Then identify the shape that is formed by the points.

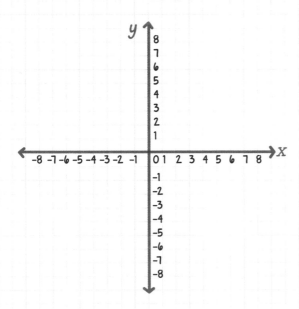

5. A square is plotted on a coordinate plane. Three of its vertices are at C (–3, 0), D (0, 0), and E (0, –3). What are the coordinates of Point F, the 4th vertex?

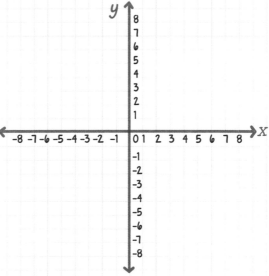

6. A rectangle is plotted on a coordinate plane. Three of its vertices are at K (–3, 2), J (6, 2), and R (–3, –3). What are the coordinates of Point T, the 4th vertex?

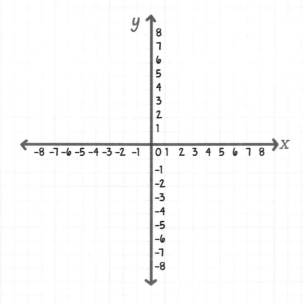

7. A rectangle is plotted on a coordinate plane. Three of its vertices are at M (2, 4), N (2, -4), and O (-2, -4). What are the coordinates of Point P, the 4th vertex?

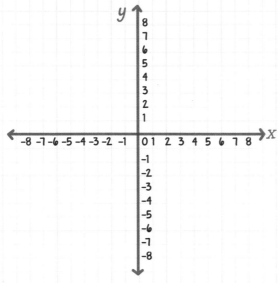

8. A square is plotted on a coordinate plane. Three of its vertices are at A (3, 5), B (8, 5), and C (8, 0). What are the coordinates of Point D, the 4th vertex?

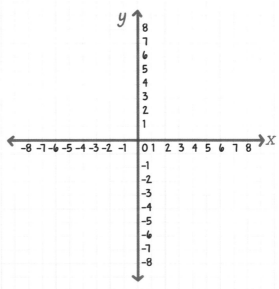

TRANSFORMATIONS

A **TRANSFORMATION** is a change of position or size of a figure. When a figure is transformed, it creates a new figure (the image) that is related to the original.

There are four types of transformations.

Translation: A transformation that moves all the figure's points the same distance and direction.

Given $\triangle ABC$, translate it as follows: $(x + 4, y - 9)$.

STEP 1: Write the original coordinates. $(-6, 1)$, $(-2, 7)$, and $(3, 5)$.

STEP 2: Calculate each translated point.

Original	Translation $(x + 4, y - 9)$	Image
$A\ (-6, 1)$	$(-6 + 4, 1 - 9)$	$A'\ (-2, -8)$
$B\ (-2, 7)$	$(-2 + 4, 7 - 9)$	$B'\ (2, -2)$
$C\ (3, 5)$	$(3 + 4, 5 - 9)$	$C'\ (7, -4)$

STEP 3: Plot and label the new image as A', B', C'.

> **Reflection:** A transformation that flips a figure over a Line of Symmetry.

Given the polygon *MATH*, reflect the shape over the *y*-axis.

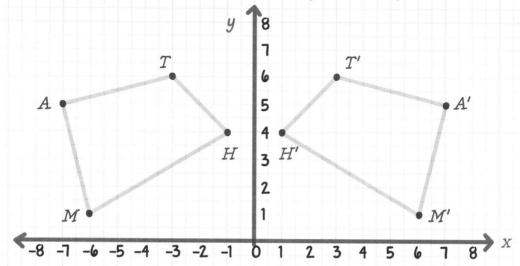

STEP 1: Count how many units each point is away from the line of symmetry (in this case the *y*-axis).

Original	Reflection over the *y*-axis	Image
M (–6, 1)	6 units from *y*-axis	*M'* (6, 1)
A (–7, 5)	7 units from *y*-axis	*A'* (7, 5)
T (–3, 6)	3 units from *y*-axis	*T'* (3, 6)
H (–1, 4)	1 unit from *y*-axis	*H'* (1, 4)

STEP 2: Draw the reflected points the same distance on the other side of the y-axis.

STEP 3: Plot and label the new image as *M'*, *A'*, *T'*, *H'*.

356

> Dilation: A transformation that enlarges or reduces a figure by a scale factor.

Given △ABC, draw the dilation image with the center of dilation at the origin (0, 0) and a scale factor of 2.

STEP 1: Write the coordinates of the original shape.

STEP 2: Since the center of dilation is the origin (0,0), simply multiply each coordinate of the original shape by the scale factor.

Original	Dilation (2)	Image
A (−2, −2)	(−2 • 2, −2 • 2)	A' (−4, −4)
B (1, −1)	(1 • 2, −1 • 2)	B' (2, −2)
C (0, 2)	(0 • 2, 2 • 2)	C' (0, 4)

STEP 3: Plot and label the new image as A', B', C'.

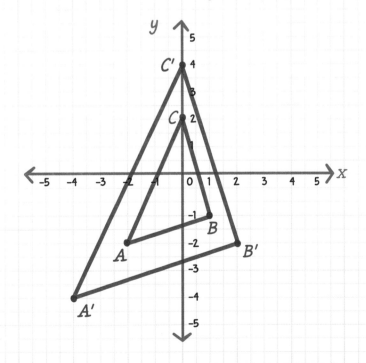

Rotation: A transformation that turns a figure around a fixed point called the center of rotation.

Rotate the polygon *RSTV* 180° clockwise around the origin (the center of rotation).

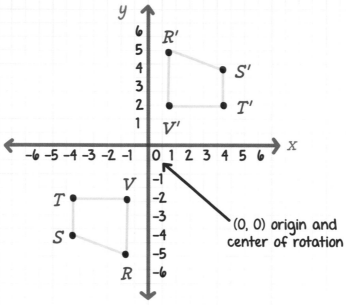

(0, 0) origin and center of rotation

STEP 1: Write the coordinates of the original shape.

STEP 2: Rotate each point 180° or two quadrants clockwise.

Original	Image
R (−1, −5)	R' (1, 5)
S (−4, −4)	S' (4, 4)
T (−4, −2)	T' (4, 2)
V (−1, −2)	V' (1, 2)

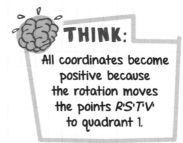

THINK:
All coordinates become positive because the rotation moves the points R'S'T'V' to quadrant 1.

STEP 3: Plot and label the new image as *R'S'T'V'*.

ANSWER THE QUESTIONS. USE WHAT YOU KNOW ABOUT TRANSFORMATIONS.

1. Graph a polygon with the following points: X (6, 0), Y (1, 1), and Z (3, 3). Then translate it as follows: $(x + 4, y + 7)$.

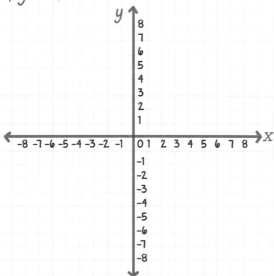

2. Graph a polygon with the following points: A (2, 1), B (1, 4), C (5, 4), and D (5, 2). Then translate it as follows: $(x - 3, y - 7)$.

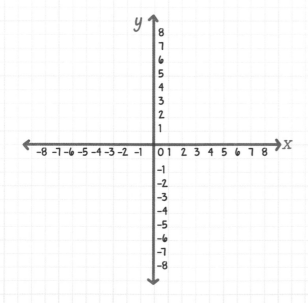

3. Graph a polygon with the following points: P (1, –3), Q (5, –3), R (5, –6), and S (1, –6). Then reflect that shape over the *x*-axis.

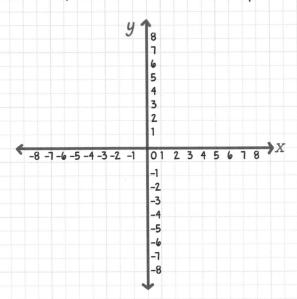

4. Graph a polygon with the following points: M (1, 2), A (3, –2), T (6, 0), and H (4, 4). Then reflect that shape over the *y*-axis.

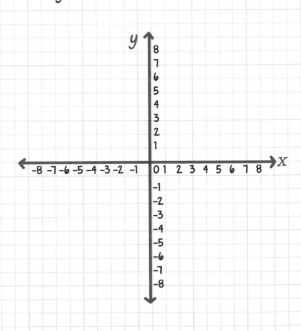

5. Graph a polygon with the following points: T (0, 8), E (4, –6), and N (–4, –6). Then dilate it by a scale factor of $\frac{1}{2}$.

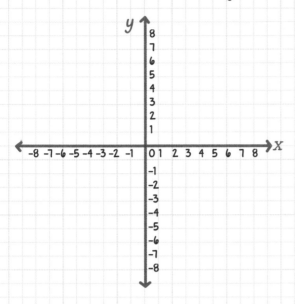

6. Graph a polygon with the following points: F (–2, 0), G (2, 0), P (2, 3), and N (–2, 3). Then dilate it by a scale factor of 3.

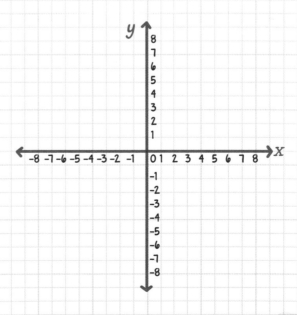

7. Graph a polygon with the following points: L (1, -3), K (1, -6), J (4, -6), and O (4, -2). Then rotate it 270° clockwise around the origin (the center of rotation).

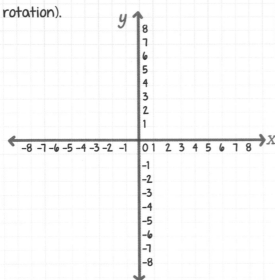

8. Graph a polygon with the following points: W (-2, 5), S (-2, 1), and Z (-5, 1). Then rotate it 180° clockwise around the origin (the center of rotation).

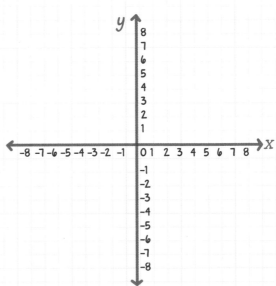

PROPORTIONAL RELATIONSHIPS AND GRAPHS

A **PROPORTION** is a number sentence where two ratios are equivalent. Example: $\frac{4}{5} = \frac{8}{10}$.

A **PROPORTIONAL RELATIONSHIP** between two quantities is a series of equivalent ratios related to one another by a constant value.

EXAMPLE:

$\frac{4}{5} = \frac{8}{10} = \frac{12}{15} = \frac{16}{20} = \frac{20}{25}$ Notice each ratio changes at the same rate. Each of the listed fractions can be reduced to $\frac{4}{5}$.

A table or graph can be used to show a proportional relationship and find the unit rate.

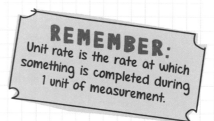

REMEMBER:
Unit rate is the rate at which something is completed during 1 unit of measurement.

The graph of a proportional relationship is a straight line that goes through the origin (0, 0).

On Friday, a bakery uses 4 gallons of milk for 12 batches of muffins. On Saturday, the bakery uses 24 gallons of milk for 72 batches of muffins.

Use this information to answer questions A through D.

A. On Sunday the bakery uses 36 gallons of milk. How many batches of muffins did the bakery make?

Complete the table below.

Gallons of Milk	Batches of Muffins
4	12
24	72
36	?

Make a proportion to find the missing number.

Let x represent the number of muffin batches made from 36 gallons of milk.

$$\frac{24}{72} = \frac{36}{x}$$

$24x = 2{,}592$

$x = 108$

So, since the bakery used 36 gallons of milk, it made 108 batches of muffins.

B. Use the table to plot points on a graph.

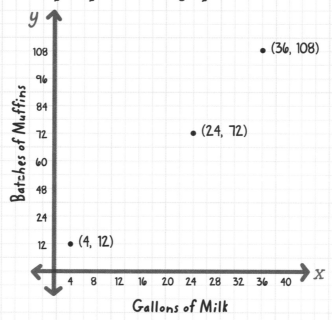

C. Based on the graph, is this a proportional relationship?

Yes. The data graphed forms a straight line that goes through the origin (0, 0).

D. Find the unit rate for this proportional relationship. What coordinates would show the unit rate?

Let the x-axis represent: Gallons of Milk.

Let the y-axis represent: Batches of Muffins.

1 gallon of milk makes 3 batches of muffins. The coordinates (1, 3) would show the unit rate: 1:3.

ANSWER THE QUESTIONS. USE WHAT YOU KNOW ABOUT PROPORTIONAL RELATIONSHIPS AND GRAPHS.

The admissions department at a specialized high school created a table to show the number of student applicants and the number of students accepted.

1. Complete the missing parts of the table. Show your work.

Number of Student Applicants	Number of Students Accepted
3	2
6	4
9	6
12	?
15	?

2. Use the table to plot the points on a graph.

3. Based on your table or graph, is this a proportional relationship?

4. Ms. Ronen's homeroom is raising money for the community food bank. The table below shows the amount of money the class raises each week. Does the weekly fundraising table show a proportional relationship? Use the table and a graph to justify your answer.

Week	Dollar Amount Collected
1	$16
2	$18
3	$22
4	$25

5. Eric's online electronics store sells 8 wireless headphones every 20 minutes and 6 tablets every 15 minutes. Is this a proportional relationship? How do you know?

6. For every 5 hours of volunteer work, Pascal Middle School students earn 20 points of community service credit. Use a graph to find the unit rate.

SOLUTIONS

Answer Key

UNIT 1
The Number System
CHAPTER 1

TYPES OF NUMBERS AND THE NUMBER LINE

1. 4 is a natural number, whole number, integer, rational, and real.

2. –6.5 is a rational number because it can also be written as a fraction or ratio and can be found to the left of the zero on the number line. It is also real.

3. 4.2222…is a rational number because it is a repeating decimal, and it is real.

4. 1.41213562…is irrational because the decimal goes on forever without repeating, and it is real.

5. $3\frac{1}{5}$ is a rational number because it can be written as a fraction or ratio and can be found to the right of zero on the number line, and it is real.

6. –9.353535…is a repeating decimal because 35 repeats. It is rational because it can be written as a fraction or ratio, and it is real.

7. False; a repeating decimal, such as .555…,is a rational number.

8. False; it is a rational number but not an integer. Integers cannot be fractions.

9. True; –3.56 is a rational number but not an integer. Integers cannot be fractions or decimals.

10. False; it is less than zero and to the left of zero.

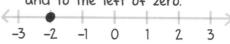

11. True.

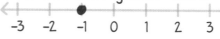

12. True; negative numbers closer to zero have greater value.

13. Kelly is correct. Integers cannot include fractions or decimals.

14. Hailey is correct because $2\frac{1}{3}$ is rational and real.

15. Gia is correct. All integers are rational numbers, but not all rational numbers are integers.

CHAPTER 2

POSITIVE AND NEGATIVE NUMBERS

1. +12

2. −500

3. +25

4. −950

5. −365

6. +12,000

7. 100 feet below sea level

8. −35 degrees

9. Losing 6% of the stock revenue

10. 75 feet

11. −3
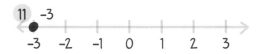

12. 0
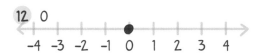

CHAPTER 3

ABSOLUTE VALUE

1. 98

2. 6.35

3. $-7\frac{3}{5}$

4. $1\frac{1}{5}$

5. 6

6. 21

7. 22

8. −1

9. 6

10. $22

11. −68

12. 118 feet

CHAPTER 4

FACTORS AND GREATEST COMMON FACTOR

1. The factors of 64 are 1, 2, 4, 8, 16, 32, 64.
   $1 \bullet 64 = 64$
   $2 \bullet 32 = 64$
   $4 \bullet 16 = 64$
   $8 \bullet 8 = 64$

2. The factors of 49 are 1, 7, 49.
   $1 \bullet 49 = 49$
   $7 \bullet 7 = 49$

3. The factors of 55 are 1, 5, 11, 55.
   $1 \bullet 55 = 55$
   $5 \bullet 11 = 55$

4. The different ways the grocer can arrange rows of soup:

1 • 60 = 60 (1 can in 60 rows)
2 • 30 = 60 (2 cans in 30 rows)
3 • 20 = 60 (3 cans in 20 rows)
4 • 15 = 60 (4 cans in 15 rows)
5 • 12 = 60 (5 cans in 12 rows)
6 • 10 = 60 (6 cans in 10 rows)

Each of these can also be reversed:
60 cans in 1 row
30 cans in 2 rows
20 cans in 3 rows
15 cans in 4 rows
12 cans in 5 rows
10 cans in 6 rows

5 The numbers 21, 36, and 54 are not prime because they have additional factors other than 1 and the number itself.

6 The number 528 is divisible by 2 because the last digit of the number is 8, which is an even number and divisible by 2.

7 The number 105 is divisible by 3 because the sum of its digits is 6, which is divisible by 3.

8 The number 693 is divisible by 9 because the sum of its digits is 18, which is divisible by 9.

9 The number 260 is divisible by both 5 and 10 because it ends in zero.

10 The GCF of 45 and 75 is 15. Factors of 45 are 1, 3, 5, 9, 15, 45. Factors of 75 are 1, 3, 5, 15, 25, 75.

11 The GCF of 56 and 96 is 8. Factors of 56 are 1, 2, 4, 7, 8, 14, 28, 56. Factors of 96 are 1, 2, 3, 4, 6, 8, 12, 16, 24, 32, 48, 96.

12 The GCF of 39 and 104 is 13. Factors of 39 are 1, 3, 13, 39. Factors of 104 are 1, 2, 4, 8, 13, 26, 52, 104.

13 The greatest number of bouquets that can be made is 18 because the GCF of 72 and 90 is 18. Factors of 72 are 1, 2, 3, 4, 6, 8, 9, 12, 18, 24, 36, 72. Factors of 90 are 1, 2, 3, 5, 6, 9, 10, 15, 18, 30, 45, 90. Each bouquet has 5 yellow roses (5 • 18 = 90) and 4 white orchids (4 • 18 = 72).

14 The greatest amount of emergency kits that can be made is 6 because the GCF of 42 and 54 is 6. Factors of 42 are 1, 2, 3, 6, 7, 14, 21, 42. Factors of 54 are 1, 2, 3, 6, 9, 18, 27, 54.

Each emergency kit has 7 bandages (7•6 = 42) and 9 water bottles (9•6 = 54).

CHAPTER 5

MULTIPLES AND LEAST COMMON MULTIPLE

1 The first five multiples of 7 are 7, 14, 21, 28, 35.
$1•7 = 7$
$2•7 = 14$
$3•7 = 21$
$4•7 = 28$
$5•7 = 35$

2 The first five multiples of 15 are 15, 30, 45, 60, 75.
$1•15 = 15$
$2•15 = 30$
$3•15 = 45$
$4•15 = 60$
$5•15 = 75$

3 The LCM of 3 and 11 is 33.
Multiples of 3 are 3, 6, 9, 12, 15, 18, 21, 24, 27, 30, 33.
Multiples of 11 are 11, 22, 33.

4 The LCM of 12 and 18 is 36.
Multiples of 12 are 12, 24, 36.
Multiples of 18 are 18, 36.

5 The LCM of 4 and 13 is 52.
Multiples of 4 are 4, 8, 12, 16, 20, 24, 28, 32, 36, 40, 44, 48, 52.
Multiples of 13 are 13, 26, 39, 52.

6 The LCM of 2, 5, and 12 is 60.
Multiples of 2 are 2, 4, 6, 8, 10, 12, 14, 16, 18, 20, 22, 24, 26, 28, 30, 32, 34, 36, 38, 40, 42, 44, 46, 48, 50, 52, 54, 56, 58, 60.
Multiples of 5 are 5, 10, 15, 20, 25, 30, 35, 40, 45, 50, 55, 60.
Multiples of 12 are 12, 24, 36, 48, 60.

7 The next day Brad will have both piano and guitar lessons is June 20 because the LCM of 4 and 5 is 20.
Multiples of 4 are 4, 8, 12, 16, 20.
Multiples of 5 are 5, 10, 15, 20.

8 The next time the trains will leave the station together is at 6:24 because the LCM of 6 and 8 is 24.
Multiples of 6 are 6, 12, 18, 24.
Multiples of 8 are 8, 16, 24.

9 Martin will save $36 first, after 3 weeks. It will take Patricia 2 weeks to save that much.

10 The GCF is the largest factor that both numbers share.
The factors of 6 are 1, 2, 3, 6.
The factors of 8 are 1, 2, 4, 8.
The GCF of 6 and 8 is 2.

The LCM is the smallest multiple that both numbers have in common.

The multiples of 6 are 6, 12, 18, 24.
The multiples of 8 are 8, 16, 24.
The LCM of 6 and 8 is 24.

CHAPTER 6

FRACTION BASICS: TYPES OF FRACTIONS, AND ADDING AND SUBTRACTING FRACTIONS

1. $\frac{1}{4} + \frac{1}{6} = \frac{1 \times 3}{4 \times 3} + \frac{1 \times 2}{6 \times 2} = \frac{3}{12} + \frac{2}{12} = \frac{5}{12}$

2. $\frac{1}{3} + \frac{5}{7} = \frac{1 \times 7}{3 \times 7} + \frac{5 \times 3}{7 \times 3} = \frac{7}{21} + \frac{15}{21} = \frac{22}{21}$
   or $1\frac{1}{21}$

3. $\frac{5}{16} + \frac{13}{16} = \frac{18}{16}$ or $1\frac{1}{8}$

4. $\frac{5}{12} + \frac{7}{10} = \frac{5 \times 5}{12 \times 5} + \frac{7 \times 6}{10 \times 6} = \frac{25}{60} + \frac{42}{60} = \frac{67}{60}$ or $1\frac{7}{60}$

5. $\frac{11}{12} - \frac{5}{12} = \frac{6}{12} = \frac{1}{2}$

6. $\frac{14}{15} - \frac{2}{3} = \frac{14 \times 1}{15 \times 1} - \frac{2 \times 5}{3 \times 5} = \frac{14}{15} - \frac{10}{15} = \frac{4}{15}$

7. $\frac{7}{9} - \frac{5}{6} = \frac{7 \times 2}{9 \times 2} - \frac{5 \times 3}{6 \times 3} = \frac{14}{18} - \frac{15}{18} = -\frac{1}{18}$

8. $\frac{13}{12} - \frac{13}{16} = \frac{13 \times 4}{12 \times 4} - \frac{13 \times 3}{16 \times 3} = \frac{52}{48} - \frac{39}{48} = \frac{13}{48}$

9. Stephanie worked on her science project for 1 and $\frac{7}{10}$ of an hour.
   $\frac{4}{5} + \frac{9}{10} = \frac{4 \times 2}{5 \times 2} + \frac{9 \times 1}{10 \times 1} = \frac{8}{10} + \frac{9}{10} = \frac{17}{10}$
   or $1\frac{7}{10}$

10. Jack has $2\frac{3}{8}$ yards of material left.

    $\frac{3}{1} - \frac{5}{8} = \frac{3 \times 8}{1 \times 8} - \frac{5 \times 1}{8 \times 1} = \frac{24}{8} - \frac{5}{8} = \frac{19}{8}$
    or $2\frac{3}{8}$

CHAPTER 7

MULTIPLYING AND DIVIDING FRACTIONS

1. $\frac{5}{6} \div \frac{3}{4} = \frac{5}{6} \cdot \frac{4}{3} = \frac{5}{\cancel{6}\,3} \cdot \cancel{4}\frac{2}{3} = \frac{5}{3} \cdot \frac{2}{3} = \frac{10}{9}$
   or $1\frac{1}{9}$

2. $\frac{15}{28} \cdot \frac{14}{9} = \frac{\cancel{15}\,5}{\cancel{28}\,2} \cdot \frac{\cancel{14}\,1}{\cancel{9}\,3} = \frac{5}{2} \cdot \frac{1}{3} = \frac{5}{6}$

3. $\frac{\cancel{7}\,1}{\cancel{10}\,2} \cdot \frac{\cancel{5}\,1}{\cancel{42}\,6} = \frac{1}{12}$

4. $1\frac{1}{7} \div 1\frac{13}{22} = \frac{8}{7} \cdot \frac{22}{35} = \frac{176}{245}$

5. $2\frac{1}{3} \cdot \frac{6}{8} = \frac{7}{\cancel{3}\,1} \cdot \frac{\cancel{6}\,2}{8} = \frac{\cancel{14}\,7}{\cancel{8}\,4}$ or $1\frac{3}{4}$

6. $8\frac{2}{3} \div \frac{4}{3} = \frac{\cancel{26}\,13}{\cancel{3}\,1} \cdot \frac{\cancel{3}\,1}{\cancel{4}\,2} = \frac{13}{2}$ or $6\frac{1}{2}$

7. $6\frac{1}{2} \cdot 4\frac{4}{7} = \frac{13}{\cancel{2}\,1} \cdot \frac{\cancel{32}\,16}{7} = \frac{208}{7}$ or $29\frac{5}{7}$

8. Each baker will get $\frac{3}{8}$ of a cup of flour.
   $1\frac{1}{2} \div \frac{4}{1} = \frac{3}{2} \cdot \frac{1}{4} = \frac{3}{8}$

9. There are $14\frac{1}{4}$ $\frac{1}{3}$-ounce spoonfuls of salt in a saltshaker.
   $4\frac{3}{4} \div \frac{1}{3} = \frac{19}{4} \cdot \frac{3}{1} = \frac{57}{4}$ or $14\frac{1}{4}$

10. Jason needs $1\frac{1}{4}$ cups of milk.
    $\frac{5}{\cancel{8}\,4} \cdot \frac{\cancel{2}\,1}{1} = \frac{5}{4}$ or $1\frac{1}{4}$

11 The system will use $20\frac{7}{10}$ gallons of water.

$$5\frac{9}{12} \cdot 3\frac{3}{5} = \frac{69}{12}\cancel{2} \cdot \frac{\cancel{18}\,3}{5} = \frac{207}{10} \text{ or } 20\frac{7}{10}$$

12 Tasha can run $4\frac{3}{16}$ miles in 1.25 seconds.

$$7\frac{7}{10} \div 1\frac{1}{4} = \frac{77}{\cancel{10}\,5} \cdot \frac{\cancel{4}\,2}{5} = \frac{154}{25} \text{ or } 6\frac{4}{25}$$

CHAPTER 8

ADDING AND SUBTRACTING DECIMALS

1
```
     1
   6.29
 + 3.48
   9.77
```

2
```
    1  1
  $43.26
+ $98.06
  141.32
```

3
```
  15.000
+  0.074
  15.074
```

4
```
  1 12.1
  6,789.020
    456.235
+ 1,406.910
  8,652.165
```

5
```
  01113
  7̶7̶.̶2̶3̶
 - 0.98
  70.25
```

6
```
  8 16 14 12
  1,9̶7̶5̶.̶2̶3̶
 -   88.52
  1,886.71
```

7
```
  2 9 9 9 10
  3̶0̶0̶.̶0̶0̶
 -  65.11
  2 34.89
```

8 Allen cycled 23.7 miles.
```
    11 1
    7.25
    5.80
 + 10.65
   23.70
```

9 There are 7.7 feet of wooden board left.
```
   13 15
   1̶4̶.̶5̶
 -  6.8
    7.7
```

10 The band has $30.02 remaining.
```
     11 1
   $119.99
 + $349.99
   $469.98
```

Now subtract $469.98 from the original $500 to get the answer.
```
   4 9 9 9 10
   $̶5̶0̶0̶.̶0̶0̶
 - $469.98
    $30.02
```

CHAPTER 9

MULTIPLYING DECIMALS

1
```
    8.7
  × 6.2
   174
  522
  53.94
```

2
```
   53.526
   × 7.41
   53526
  214104
  374682
  396.62766
```

3
```
    9.96
  × 3.74
   3984
  6972
  2988
  37.2504
```

4
```
    0.35
  × 0.88
   280
  280
  0.3080
```

5
```
     750
  × 0.0003
   0.2250
```

6
```
   9.6102
   × 3.44
   384408
   384408
   288306
   33.059088
```

7 The total sale of the fencing is $522.45.
```
    32.25
  × 16.20
   0000
  6450
  19350
  3225
  $522.45
```

8 Ms. Jessa paid $592.25 for the tickets.
```
   $25.75
    × 23
   7725
  5150
  $592.25
```

9 The total value of Mia's shares of stock is $85,212.
```
    2700
  × $31.56
   16200
  13500
  2700
  8100
  $85,212.00
```

10 Daren will run more kilometers because he will run 29.925 kilometers, and Umberto will run 28.5 kilometers.

Daren

$$\begin{array}{r} 8.55 \\ \times\ 3.5 \\ \hline 4275 \\ 2565 \\ \hline 29.925 \end{array}$$

Umberto

$$\begin{array}{r} 9.5 \\ \times\ 3 \\ \hline 28.5 \end{array}$$

CHAPTER 10

DIVIDING DECIMALS

1 $6.24 \div 2.4 = 2.6$

$2.4\overline{)6.24}$

$$\begin{array}{r} 2.6 \\ 24\overline{)62.4} \\ -48 \\ \hline 144 \\ -144 \\ \hline 0 \end{array}$$

2 $52.17 \div 14.1 = 3.7$

$14.1\overline{)52.17}$

$$\begin{array}{r} 3.7 \\ 141\overline{)521.7} \\ -423 \\ \hline 987 \\ -987 \\ \hline 0 \end{array}$$

3 $254.01 \div 0.2 = 1270.05$

$0.2\overline{)254.01}$

$$\begin{array}{r} 1270.05 \\ 2\overline{)2540.10} \\ -2 \\ \hline 5 \\ -4 \\ \hline 14 \\ -14 \\ \hline 10 \\ -10 \\ \hline 0 \end{array}$$

4 $3{,}250 \div 0.0005 = 6{,}500{,}000$

$0.0005\overline{)3250}$

$$\begin{array}{r} 6{,}500{,}000 \\ 5\overline{)32500000} \\ -30 \\ \hline 25 \\ -25 \\ \hline 0 \end{array}$$

5 $\dfrac{7.5}{0.24} = 31.25$

6 $\dfrac{2.6}{0.4} = 6.5$

7 $\dfrac{1.066}{0.02} = 53.3$

8 Stephen can bike 7.8 miles in one hour.

$\dfrac{27.3}{3.5} = 7.8$

9 Felicia earns $9.36 per hour.

$\dfrac{175.50}{18.75} = 9.36$

10 They can make 19 items.

$$\frac{14.25}{0.75} = 19$$

CHAPTER 11

ADDING POSITIVE AND NEGATIVE NUMBERS

1 $-4 + 6 = 2$

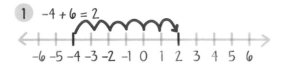

2 $-7 + (-1) = -8$

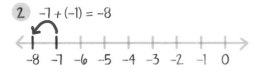

3 $8 + (-5) = 3$

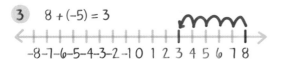

4 $-62 + (-108) = -170$
(If the signs are the same, add the numbers and keep the sign.)

5 $-245 + 691 = 446$
(The signs are different, so we subtract. 691 has the greater absolute value, so the answer is positive.)

6 $48 + (-79) = -31$
(The signs are different, so subtract. 79 has the greater absolute value, so the answer is negative.)

7 $-1252 + 864 = -388$
(The signs are different, so subtract. -1252 has the greater absolute value, so the answer is negative.)

8 Jake still owes $19.
$-35 + 16 = -19$

9 The temperature at 2 p.m. has risen to 26 degrees Fahrenheit.
$-4 + 30 = 26$

10 The total account balance is $57.
$75 - 18 = 57$

11 The submarine is 525 feet below sea level.
$-310 + -215 = -525$

12 Bill's savings account had $360.
$265 + 95 = 360$

13 Tara is correct, 715 years.
$510 + 205 = 715$

CHAPTER 12

SUBTRACTING POSITIVE AND NEGATIVE NUMBERS

1 $6 - (-2) = 6 + (+2) = 8$

2 $-15 - (-4) = -15 + (+4) = -11$

3 $-7 - 10 = -7 + -10 = -17$

4 $-9 - (-25) = -9 + (+25) = 16$

5 $-141 - 107 = -141 + (-107) = -248$

6 $15 - 132 = 15 + (-132) = -117$

7 $-10 - (2) + (-16) = -10 + (-2) + (-16) = -28$

8 Bea's total points after the second round are -22.
$+56 - 78 = +56 + (-78) = -22$

9 The submarine's new position is 266 feet below sea level.
$-560 + 294 = -266$

10 The debt acquired is $2,420.
$$\begin{array}{r} -1750 \\ -335 \\ +\ -335 \\ \hline -2420 \end{array}$$
$-1750 + (-335) + (-335) = -2420$

CHAPTER 13

MULTIPLYING AND DIVIDING POSITIVE AND NEGATIVE NUMBERS

1 $-7(-7) = 49$

2 $-40 \cdot 22 = -880$

3 $300 \cdot -10 = -3,000$

4 $96 \div -12 = -8$

5 $-110 \div -110 = 1$

6 $\frac{-48}{6} = -8$

7 $\frac{108}{-9} = -12$

8 Aaron borrowed money for 8 days.
$\frac{-56}{-7} = 8$

9 The temperature at 9 p.m. is -39 degrees Celsius.
Step 1: $-4 \cdot 3 = -12$
Step 2: $-27 + -12 = -39$

10 Tina is correct because when you multiply an even number of negative numbers, the product is positive.

CHAPTER 14

INEQUALITIES

1 $-7 < 2$

2 $4 > -4$

3 $-1.8 < -1.75$

4 $\frac{3}{5} < \frac{2}{3}$

5 $-1\frac{1}{2} < -1\frac{3}{7}$

6 The greater depth below sea level is -48 feet because it is less than -36 feet.
$-48 < -36$

7 Nancy's age is at least 14 years old.
Let n = Nancy's age
$n \geq 14$

8 $x \leq -1\frac{1}{8}$ is false when $x = 0$
because 0 is greater than $-1\frac{1}{8}$.

9 The inequality $y \geq 10$ means that
the value of y can be greater
than or equal to 10.
The inequality $y < 10$ means that the
value of y can be less than 10.

10 Yes, Jan could have sold 85 rolls.
Let $n =$ the number of rolls Jan
has sold.
$n \geq 70$

UNIT 2
Ratios, Proportions, and Percents

CHAPTER 15

RATIOS

1 $\frac{6}{8} = \frac{3}{4}$ Nate's store sells 3
black ink pens for every
4 blue ink pens.

2 $\frac{15}{27} = \frac{5}{9}$ 5 out of every 9
students participate in
the school talent show.

3 $\frac{21}{14} = \frac{3}{2}$ A baker uses 3
ounces of milk for every
2 cups of cake mix.

4 $\frac{5}{55} = \frac{1}{11}$ Nancy earns $11 a
day for tutoring math.

5 $\frac{27}{39} = \frac{9}{13}$ There are 9
mountain bicycles for every
13 hybrid bicycles.

6 $\frac{68}{34} = \frac{2}{1}$ There are 2 bottles of
water for every participant.

7 110:175 or 22:35

8 52:8 or 13:2

9 50:20 or 5:2

10 15:150 or 1:10

11 2:30 or 1:15

12 thermometers to stethoscopes
45:20 or 9:4
bandages to gloves
105:95 or 21:19

CHAPTER 16

UNIT RATE AND UNIT PRICE

1 $\frac{30}{2} = 30 \div 2 = 15 = \frac{15}{1}$
15 passengers per attendant

2 $\frac{450}{15} = 450 \div 15 = 30 = \frac{30}{1}$
30 muffins per day

3 $\frac{72}{18} = 72 \div 18 = 4 = \frac{4}{1}$
4 bags of trail mix per second

4 $\frac{144}{12} = 144 \div 12 = 12 = \frac{12}{1}$
12 T-shirts per minute

5. $\frac{3}{4} \div \frac{4}{6} = \frac{3}{4} \cdot \frac{6}{4} = \frac{3}{2} \cdot \frac{3}{4} = \frac{9}{8} = 1\frac{1}{8}$

   $1\frac{1}{8}$ cups of milk per minute

6. $4\frac{1}{2} \div 3 = \frac{9}{2} \div \frac{3}{1} = \frac{9}{2} \cdot \frac{1}{3} = \frac{3}{2} = 1\frac{1}{2}$

   $1\frac{1}{2}$ miles per day

7. $\frac{792}{12} = 792 \div 12 = 66 = \frac{66}{1}$

   66 therms per month

8. $\frac{902.60}{4} = 902.60 \div 4 = 225.65 =$

   $\frac{225.65}{1} = \$225.65$ per week

9. $\frac{288}{36} = 288 \div 36 = 8 = \frac{8}{1}$

   $8 per bottle

10. $\frac{1,988}{7} = 1,988 \div 7 = 284 = \frac{284}{1}$

    284 visitors per day

CHAPTER 17

PROPORTIONS

1. The cross products are equal, so the ratios form a proportion.
   $10 \cdot 3 = 30, \ 6 \cdot 5 = 30$

2. The cross products are not equal, so the ratios do not form a proportion.
   $8 \cdot 8 = 64, \ 9 \cdot 7 = 63$

3. $\frac{3}{5} \neq \frac{7}{12}$ The cross products are not equal, so the ratios do not form a proportion.
   $3 \cdot 12 = 36, \ 5 \cdot 7 = 35$
   $\frac{3}{5} = \frac{9}{15}$ The cross products

are equal, so the ratios form a proportion.
$3 \cdot 15 = 45, \ 5 \cdot 9 = 45$
$\frac{7}{12} \neq \frac{9}{15}$ The cross products are not equal, so the ratios do not form a proportion.
$7 \cdot 15 = 105, \ 12 \cdot 9 = 108$

4. $\frac{20}{32} = \frac{5}{8}$ The cross products are equal, so the ratios form a proportion.
   $20 \cdot 8 = 160, \ 32 \cdot 5 = 160$
   $\frac{20}{32} \neq \frac{4}{14}$ The cross products are not equal, so the ratios do not form a proportion.
   $20 \cdot 14 = 280, \ 32 \cdot 4 = 128$
   $\frac{5}{8} \neq \frac{4}{14}$ The cross products are not equal, so the ratios do not form a proportion.
   $5 \cdot 14 = 70, \ 8 \cdot 4 = 32$

5. $\frac{4}{x} = \frac{16}{36}$
   $16x = 4 \cdot 36$
   $16x = 144$
   $x = 9$

6. $\frac{7}{11} = \frac{y}{22}$
   $11y = 7 \cdot 22$
   $11y = 154$
   $y = 14$

7. $\frac{n}{3.10} = \frac{2.5}{5}$
   $5n = 3.10 \cdot 2.5$
   $5n = 7.75$
   $n = 1.55$

8 $\dfrac{3}{1.25} = \dfrac{x}{8.75}$

$1.25x = 3 \cdot 8.75$

$1.25x = 26.25$

$x = 21$

Kalvin can purchase 21 oranges.

9 $\dfrac{2}{12} = \dfrac{x}{60}$

$12x = 2 \cdot 60$

$12x = 120$

$x = 10$

The class spends 10 minutes stretching.

10 $\dfrac{7}{35} = \dfrac{8}{x}$

$7x = 35 \cdot 8$

$7x = 280$

$x = 40$

The cost of paint for 1 week is $40. The cost of paint for 10 weeks is $400.

$40 \cdot 10 = 400$

CHAPTER 18

CONVERTING MEASUREMENTS

1 $\dfrac{1\ \text{ton}}{2{,}000\ \text{pounds}} = \dfrac{2.5\ \text{tons}}{x}$

$x = 2{,}000 \cdot 2.5$

$x = 5{,}000$

2.5 tons = 5,000 pounds

2 $\dfrac{16\ \text{cups}}{1\ \text{gallon}} = \dfrac{48\ \text{cups}}{x}$

$16x = 48$

$x = 3$

3 gallons = 48 cups

3 $\dfrac{1\ \text{m}}{100\ \text{cm}} = \dfrac{x}{9{,}000\ \text{cm}}$

$100x = 9{,}000$

$x = 90$

9,000 centimeters = 90 meters

4 $\dfrac{16\ \text{ounces}}{1\ \text{pound}} = \dfrac{x}{4.75\ \text{pounds}}$

$x = 16 \cdot 4.75$

$x = 76$

76 ounces = 4.75 pounds

5 $\dfrac{12\ \text{inches}}{1\ \text{foot}} = \dfrac{x}{75.5\ \text{feet}}$

$x = 12 \cdot 75.5$

$x = 906$

75.5 feet = 906 inches

6 $\dfrac{1.609\ \text{km}}{1\ \text{mile}} = \dfrac{38\ \text{km}}{x}$

$1.609x = 38$

$x = 23.6171535$

$x = 24$

38 kilometers = 24 miles

7 $\dfrac{1\ \text{pound}}{.454\ \text{kilograms}} = \dfrac{x}{5\ \text{kilograms}}$

$.454x = 5$

$x = 11.0132159$

$x = 11$

11 pounds = 5 kilograms

8 $\dfrac{1\ \text{meter}}{3.28\ \text{feet}} = \dfrac{19.2\ \text{meters}}{x}$

$x = 3.28 \cdot 19.2$

$x = 62.976$

$x = 63$

The tallest point of the roller coaster is 63 feet in height.

9 $\dfrac{1 \text{ gallon}}{3.785 \text{ liters}} = \dfrac{53 \text{ gallons}}{x}$

$x = 3.785 \cdot 53$

$x = 200.605$

$x = 201$

$201 - 40 = 161$

Zack needs 161 more liters of gas to reach his destination.

10 $\dfrac{x}{50.8 \text{ cm}} = \dfrac{1 \text{ inch}}{2.54 \text{ cm}}$

$2.54x = 50.8$

$x = 20$ inches

$\dfrac{1 \text{ inch}}{2.54 \text{ cm}} = \dfrac{27 \text{ inches}}{x}$

$x = 2.54 \cdot 27$

$x = 68.58$

$x = 69$ centimeters

27 inches is greater than 50.8 centimeters.

CHAPTER 19

PERCENT

1 $\dfrac{32}{100} = \dfrac{8}{25}$

2 $\dfrac{9.2}{100} = \dfrac{2.3}{25}$

3 $\dfrac{48}{100} = \dfrac{12}{25}$

4 $\dfrac{84}{100} = .84$

5 $\dfrac{110.5}{100} = 1.105$

6 $\dfrac{.016}{100} = .00016$

7 $\dfrac{42}{60} = 42 \div 60 = .7$

$.7 \cdot 100 = 70\%$

8 $\dfrac{230}{100} = 230 \div 100 = 2.3$

$2.3 \cdot 100 = 230\%$

9 $\dfrac{5}{9} = \dfrac{x}{100}$

$9x = 500$

$x = 55.5555556$

$x = 56\%$

10 $145 - 110 = 35$

$\dfrac{35}{145} = \dfrac{x}{100}$

$145x = 3500$

$x = 24.137931$

$x = 24$

24% of visitors do not buy ice cream.

11 People who own cats:
$\dfrac{4}{10} = \dfrac{x}{100}$

$10x = 400$

$x = 40$

People who own dogs:
$\dfrac{3}{5} = \dfrac{x}{100}$

$5x = 300$

$x = 60$

40% of the town owns cats.
60% of the town owns dogs.
More people own dogs than cats.

12 $\dfrac{39}{50} = \dfrac{x}{100}$

$50x = 3900$

$x = 78$

The barista is incorrect because 78% of people prefer coffee to tea.

CHAPTER 20

PERCENT WORD PROBLEMS

1. 19% of 300 is 57.
$0.19 \cdot 300 = x$
$x = 57$

2. 32% of 50 is 16.
$0.32 \cdot 50 = x$
$x = 16$

3. 15% of 66 is 9.9.
$0.15 \cdot 66 = x$
$x = 9.9$

4. 147 is 70% of 210.
$147 = x \cdot 210$
$x = .7$
$.7 \cdot 100 = 70\%$

5. 48 is 50% of 96.
$48 = x \cdot 96$
$x = .5$
$.5 \cdot 100 = 50\%$

6. 7 is 20% of 35.
$7 = x \cdot 35$
$x = .2$
$.2 \cdot 100 = 20\%$

7. 1.8 is 75% of 2.40.
$1.8 = x \cdot 2.40$
$x = .75$
$.75 \cdot 100 = 75\%$

8. 75% of $x = 24$
$.75x = 24$
$x = 32$
There were 32 questions on the science test.

9. 30% of $x = 12$
$.30x = 12$
$x = 40$
The pantry still needs 40 boxes of rice.

10. $600 - 520 = 80$
80 is $x\%$ of 600
$80 = x \cdot 600$
$x = .13333333$
$x = .13$
$.13 \cdot 100 = 13\%$
13% of the seats are still available.

CHAPTER 21

TAXES AND FEES

1. $125.36 \cdot .085 = 10.6556$
Sales tax = $10.66
$125.36 + $10.66 = $136.02
The total cost of the skateboard with tax is $136.02.

2. $55.10 \cdot .05 = 2.755$
Sales tax = $2.76
$55.10 + $2.76 = $57.86
The total cost of the textbook is $57.86.

3   $230.41 \cdot .092 = 21.19772$
Sales tax = $21.20
The total amount of
tax paid is $21.20.

4   $85 \cdot .0225 = 1.9125$
Usage tax = $1.91
The monthly amount of
usage tax is $1.91.

5   $.068 \cdot 35.74 = 2.43032$
$35.74 = 1.068x$
$x = 33.46441948$
The cost of the music downloads
without the sales tax was $33.46.

6   $.15 \cdot 286.78 = 43.017$
$286.78 = 1.15x$
$x = 249.373913$
The cost of the Jet Ski rental
without the late fee was $249.37.

7   $580 \cdot .07 = 40.6$
Sales tax = $40.60
$580 + $40.60 = $620.60
The total cost of painting
the apartment is $620.60.

8   $60 \cdot 4 = $240 Cost for 4 hours
$240 \cdot .065 = 15.6$
Sales tax = $15.60
$240 + $15.60 = $255.60
The cost including tax is $255.60.

9   $55 \cdot .075 = 4.125$
Sales tax = $4.13
$55 + $4.13 + $15 = $74.13
The total cost of Miguel's
purchase was $74.13.

10   $2,000,000 \cdot .36 = 720,000$
Taxes = $720,000
$2,000,000 - $720,000 = $1,280,000
Jake will pay $720,000 in taxes.
He will receive $1,280,000.

CHAPTER 22

DISCOUNTS AND MARKUPS

1   $.35 \cdot 199.99 = 69.9965$
Discount = $70
$199.99 - 70 = $129.99
The discount is $70, and the final
price of the guitar is $129.99.

2   $.55 \cdot 139.99 = 76.9945$
Discount = $77
$139.99 - $77 = $62.99
Sabrina will save $77.
The yearly membership will
cost $62.99 with the discount.

3   $100 - 25 = 75$
78.63 is 75% of x.
$78.63 = .75x$
$x = 104.84$
The original price of the
skates was $104.84.

4 100% − 45% − 10% = 45% = 0.45
   .45 • 410 = 184.50
   Supplies will cost $184.50.

5 First offer
   81.36 • .20 = 16.27
   Discount = $16.27
   $81.36 − $16.27 = $65.09

   Online offer
   .05 • 71.25 = 3.5625
   Discount = $3.56
   $71.25 − $3.56 = $67.69

   The first offer is a
   better deal, $65.09.

6 11 • .82 = 9.02
   Markup = $9.02
   $11 + $9.02 = $20.02
   The markup is $9.02, and
   the new price is $20.02.

7 4 • .95 = 3.80
   Markup = $3.80
   $4 + $3.80 = $7.80
   The markup is $3.80, and the
   new selling price is $7.80.

8 88% of x = 554.60
   1.88 • x = 554.60
   x = 295
   The original cost of the
   chair was $295.

9 Original price
   100 − 25 = 75
   75% of x = $38.65
   .75x = 38.65
   x = 51.5333333
   x = 51.53
   38.65 • .25 = 9.6625
   Discount = $9.66
   $38.65 − $9.66 = $28.99
   The original cost is $51.53.
   The sale price of the
   device is $28.99.

10 Long-sleeve shirt
   12.50 • .55 = 6.875
   Markup = $6.88
   $12.50 + $6.88 = $19.38
   Cost of the long-sleeve
   shirt is $19.38.

   Short-sleeve shirt
   9.85 • .60 = 5.91
   Markup = $5.91
   $9.85 + $5.91 = $15.76
   Cost of the short-sleeve shirt
   is $15.76.

   The long-sleeve shirt
   costs more.

CHAPTER 23

GRATUITY AND COMMISSION

1 Harold M.
$38.56 \bullet .18 = 6.9408$
Gratuity = $6.94
$38.56 + $6.94 = $45.50
Harold M.'s final cost is $45.50.

Maria's family
$66.89 \bullet .20 = 13.378$
Gratuity = $13.38
$66.89 + $13.38 = $80.27
Maria's family's final cost is $80.27.

Chailai S.
$31.91 = .15 \bullet x$
$x = $27.75

Campanella Family
$84.22 \bullet .18 = 15.1596$
Gratuity = $15.16
$84.22 + $15.16 = $99.38
Campanella family's final cost is $99.38.

Duante J.
$50.37 = 1.19 \bullet x$
$x = 42.33$
Duante's pizzeria bill is $42.33.

2 Tiffany
$5,445 \bullet .10 = 544.50$
Commission = $544.50

Johanan
$7,256 \bullet .08 = 580.48$
Commission = $580.48

Diego
$6,523 \bullet .12 = 782.76$
Commission = $782.76

Frida
$10,998 \bullet .12 = 1,319.76$
Commission = $1,319.76

Sharon
$8,235 \bullet .11 = 905.85$
Commission = $905.85

3 $575 \bullet .30 = 172.50$
Tip = 172.50
$575 + $172.50 = $747.50
The tip is $172.50, and the total bill is $747.50.

4 $487.56 = 1.16 \bullet x$
$x = 420.3103448$
The cost of the luncheon without the gratuity is $420.31.

5 Commission Plan
$2,000 \bullet .09 = 180$
The commission plan pays $180 per week.

Salary Plan
$10 \bullet 20 = 200$

The salary plan pays $200 per week.

The salary plan provides better compensation because Carl will make more money.

6 Martin
$307.12 \cdot .22 = x$
$x = 67.5664$
$x = \$67.57$

Athena
$398.26 \cdot .18 = x$
$x = 71.6868$
$x = \$71.69$

Athena receives the greater amount of money.

CHAPTER 24

SIMPLE INTEREST

1 Row 1
$I = 2,158.60 \cdot .065 \cdot 5$
$I = 701.545$
$I = \$701.55$

Row 2
$I = 64,155 \cdot .11 \cdot 8$
$I = 56,456.40$
$I = \$56,456.40$

Row 3
$33,710.40 = 37,456 \cdot .09 \cdot T$

$33,710.40 = 3,371.04 \cdot T$
$T = 10$ years

Row 4
$5,578.20 = 5,165 \cdot .18 \cdot T$
$5,578.20 = 929.70 \cdot T$
$T = 6$ years

2 $I = 37,260 \cdot .045 \cdot 8$
$I = 13,413.60$
$\$37,260 + \$13,413.60 = \$50,673.60$
Allen will pay $13,413.60 in interest. The total cost will be $50,673.60.

3 $I = 54,895 \cdot .0325 \cdot 3$
$I = 5,352.2625$
$I = \$5,352.26$
$\$54,895 + \$5,352.26 = \$60,247.26$
Anika will have $60,247.26 in her account.

4 $I = 45,000 \cdot .055 \cdot 6$
$I = \$14,850$
$\$45,000 + \$14,850 = \$59,850$
The family will pay $14,850 in interest, and $59,850 in full for the loan.

5 $I = 11,798 \cdot .08 \cdot 4$
$I = \$3,775.36$
$\$11,798 + \$3,775.36 = \$15,573.36$
The Young family will pay $15,573.36 if they take longer than 48 months to pay the loan.

6 $1,500 = 6,000 \bullet .05 \bullet T$
   $1,500 = 300 \bullet T$
   $T = 5$ years
   It will take Jan 5 years.

7 Valentina
   $I = 1,350 \bullet .05 \bullet 5$
   $I = \$337.50$

   Neil
   $I = 1,150 \bullet .07 \bullet 5$
   $I = \$402.50$
   $\$402.50 - \$337.50 = \$65$
   Neil earns $65 more
   than Valentina.

8 Salvatore
   $I = 4,800 \bullet .08 \bullet 8$
   $I = \$3,072$

   Riley
   $I = 6,150 \bullet .06 \bullet 8$
   $I = \$2,952$
   $\$3,072 - \$2,952 = \$120$

   Salvatore pays $120 more
   in interest for his loan.

CHAPTER 25

PERCENT RATE OF CHANGE

1 $8,834 - 7,959 = 875$

   $\frac{875}{7,959} = .109938$
   $.11 = 11\%$
   The rate of change is 11%.

2 $56 - 24 = 32$
   $\frac{32}{56} = .57142857$
   $.57 = 57\%$
   The rate of change is 57%.

3 $2,227 - 1,168 = 1,059$
   $\frac{1,059}{1,168} = .90667808$
   $.91 = 91\%$
   The rate of change is a 91%
   increase.

4 $1,275 - 1,050 = 225$
   $\frac{225}{1,050} = .21428571$
   $.21 = 21\%$
   The rate of change is 21%.

5 $4,026 - 2,084 = 1,942$
   $\frac{1,942}{4,026} = .48236463$
   $.48 = 48\%$
   The rate of change is 48%.

6 $16.25 - 8.85 = 7.40$
   $\frac{7.40}{8.85} = .836159$
   $.84 = 84\%$
   The rate of change is 84%.

7 $14.8 - 9.2 = 5.6$
   $\frac{5.6}{14.8} = .37837838$
   $.38 = 38\%$
   The rate of change is 38%.

8 A rate of change that increases
   happens when the original amount
   has gone up. A rate of change
   that decreases happens when the
   original amount has gone down.

CHAPTER 26

TABLES AND RATIOS

1 $\dfrac{1{,}250}{2} = \dfrac{2{,}500}{x}$

$1{,}250x = 2 \cdot 2{,}500$

$x = 4$

2,500 crayons in 4 minutes

$\dfrac{7{,}500}{6} = \dfrac{x}{8}$

$6x = 7{,}500 \cdot 8$

$x = 10{,}000$

10,000 crayons in 8 minutes

2 $\dfrac{3{,}000}{x} = \dfrac{6{,}000}{20}$

$6{,}000x = 3{,}000 \cdot 20$

$x = 10$

3,000 markers in 10 minutes

$\dfrac{12{,}000}{40} = \dfrac{x}{30}$

$40x = 12{,}000 \cdot 30$

$x = 9{,}000$

9,000 markers in 30 minutes

3 $\dfrac{x}{3} = \dfrac{3{,}375}{9}$

$9x = 3 \cdot 3{,}375$

$x = 1{,}125$

1,125 paint pallets in 3 minutes

$\dfrac{2{,}250}{x} = \dfrac{3{,}375}{9}$

$3375x = 9 \cdot 2250$

$x = 6$

2,250 paint pallets in 6 minutes

4 $\dfrac{2{,}130}{6} = \dfrac{4{,}260}{x}$

$2{,}130x = 6 \cdot 4{,}260$

$x = 12$

4,260 pencils in 12 minutes

$\dfrac{6{,}390}{18} = \dfrac{x}{24}$

$18x = 6{,}390 \cdot 24$

$x = 8{,}200$

8,200 pencils in 24 minutes

5

Crayons: Minutes	Markers: Minutes
$\dfrac{1{,}250}{2} = \dfrac{x}{1}$ $x = 625$	$\dfrac{3{,}000}{10} = \dfrac{x}{1}$ $x = 300$
Unit rate: 625 crayons every minute.	Unit rate: 300 markers every minute.
Paint Pallets: Minutes	Drawing Pencils: Minutes
$\dfrac{1{,}125}{3} = \dfrac{x}{1}$ $x = 375$	$\dfrac{2{,}130}{6} = \dfrac{x}{1}$ $x = 355$
Unit rate: 375 paint pallets every minute.	Unit rate: 355 drawing pencils every minute.

So, the manufacturer can produce more crayons per minute than any other art supply.

6 $\dfrac{4}{6} = \dfrac{x}{375}$

$6x = 4 \cdot 375$

$x = 250$

250 raffle tickets cost $375.

7 $\frac{1}{28} = \frac{x}{840}$

$28x = 840$

$x = 30$

The school will need 30 buses.

8 $\frac{4}{270} = \frac{x}{3,510}$

$270x = 4 \cdot 3,510$

$x = 52$

52 muffin batter batches can be made in 3,510 seconds.

UNIT 3
Expressions and Equations

CHAPTER 27

EXPRESSIONS

1 $6w$, 55

2 -75, $98d$

3 $8h$, $\frac{1}{16}$, -18

4 variables: x, c
coefficient: -1.9, 1
constant: 52

5 variables: m, d
coefficient: 8,022, 1
constants: -4, 1.23

6 variables: y, r
coefficients: 3, 2
constant: 4

7 $\frac{2}{3}h + 26$

8 $\frac{w}{.66}$ or $w \div .66$

9 $(r + 5) - 11c$

10 $x =$ Jonathan's sister's age
$x + 5 =$ Jonathan's age

11 $x =$ last year's students
$2x =$ this year's students

12 $x =$ number of people who live in the community
$\frac{1}{2}x =$ number of people who shop at the big box store

13 $x =$ stock of milk containers
$x + 250 =$ stock of increased milk containers

14 $x =$ all children at field day
$\frac{30}{x} =$ juice boxes divided among the children at field day

15 $x =$ computers in stock
$x - 73 =$ computers sold

CHAPTER 28

PROPERTIES

1 $5 + m$
Commutative Property of Addition

2 $6h - dh$
Distributive Property of Multiplication over Subtraction

391

3 $c \cdot 18$
Commutative Property
of Multiplication

4 $n \cdot (2 \cdot 3)$
Associative Property
of Multiplication

5 $9x + 54$
Distributive Property of
Multiplication over Addition

6 $(-y + 8) + 11$
Associative Property of Addition

7 g or $0 + g$
Identity Property or Commutative
Property of Addition

8 ba
Commutative Property
of Multiplication

9 $16x + 28$

10 $4x - 28y + 64$

11 $2m + 16n + \frac{2}{3}r$

12 $8(m + 4)$

13 $7(y - 4x + 2)$

14 $6(a + 2b + 5c)$

15 Sue's store
$6(4x) = 5.50$

$24x = 5.50$
$x = .22916667$
$x = \$.23$

Darleen's store
$4(6x) = 5.50$
$24x = 5.50$
$x = .22916667$
$x = \$.23$

Both stores charge the same price.

CHAPTER 29

LIKE TERMS

1 y^2, $-9y$, 6

2 $5cd$, $-3d$, 11

3 $14mn$, m^2, $-7m$, 8

4 coefficients: 9, 25
constant: -3

5 coefficients: 2, -13
constant: -8

6 coefficients: 1.52, $\frac{2}{3}$
constant: 36

7 $-40h$

8 $-6w - 37$

9 $x^2 - 8x + 22$

10 $2x + 27.2$

11 $5t^2 + 6gh + 9g - 32$

12 $2ab + 15$

CHAPTER 30

EXPONENTS

1 $9^3 = 9 \cdot 9 \cdot 9 = 729$

2 $(\frac{1}{3})^3 \cdot (-10^2) = \frac{1}{27} \cdot -100 -$
$-3.7037037 = -3.7$

3 $(7p)^2 = 49p^2$

4 $-(5^4) = -625$

5 $m^{11} \div m^8 = m^{11-8} = m^3$

6 $-6y^3 \cdot 3y \cdot -y^4 = 18y^8$

7 $(-\frac{3}{4})^3 = \frac{-27}{64} = .421875$

8 $\frac{48h^{12}}{-8h^{-2}} = -6h^{14}$

9 $\frac{16a^9b^7}{3a^4b^2} = \frac{16a^5b^5}{3}$

10 $-(2^4)^3 = -(2^{12}) = -4,096$

11 $(6m^2n^5)^4 = 1,296m^8n^{20}$

12 $\frac{r^{-4}s^6}{r^4s^7} = \frac{1}{r^8s}$

CHAPTER 31

ORDER OF OPERATIONS

1 $5 + 3^3 \cdot 6$
$5 + 27 \cdot 6$
$5 + 162 = 167$

2 $300 \div (11 \cdot 1)^2$
$300 \div 11^2$
$300 \div 121 = 2.479338843$

3 $-2^5 + 3 - 4(8)$
$-2^5 + 3 - 32$
$-32 + 3 - 32 = -61$

4 $6 + 2(9 - 5) \div -2$
$6 + 2 \cdot 4 \div -2$
$6 + 8 \div -2$
$6 + -4 = 2$

5 $10 + (-1)^3 \cdot 3 - 4(12 + 7)$
$10 + -1 \cdot 3 - 4(19)$
$10 - 3 - 76 = -69$

6 $(56 \div 7) \cdot 5 - 18 \div 2$
$8 \cdot 5 - 18 \div 2$
$40 - 18 \div 2$
$40 - 9 = 31$

7 $\frac{4^2 + (59 - 3^3)}{-16}$
$\frac{4^2 + 32}{-16}$
$\frac{16 + 32}{-16} = \frac{48}{-16} = -3$

8 $|24 - 40| - [(8 + 6) \cdot 4]^2$
$|24 - 40| - 56^2$
$16 - 3,136 = -3,120$

9 $6 + (26 - 2) \div 8$
$6 + 24 \div 8$
$6 + 3 = 9$

10 $(36 \div 2^2) \cdot 3 + 10 \cdot 0.5$
    $9 \cdot 3 + 10 \cdot 0.5$
    $27 + 5 = 32$

11 There are 161 bottles of mustard
    remaining in the supply room.
    $11 + (10 \cdot 12) + (8 \cdot 6) - 18$
    $11 + 120 + 48 - 18 = 161$

12 $165 + (36 \cdot 50) - 475$
    $165 + 1,800 - 475$
    $1,965 - 475 = 1,490$
    Stephan's account has $1,490
    after the withdrawal.

13 Brian is correct because he
    followed the Order of Operations.
    $-12 \cdot 8 + 4^2 \cdot (63 \div 7) - 3$
    $-12 \cdot 8 + 4^2 \cdot 9 - 3$
    $-12 \cdot 8 + 16 \cdot 9 - 3$
    $-96 + 144 - 3 = 45$

CHAPTER 32

SCIENTIFIC NOTATION

1 $3.2 \cdot 10^8$

2 $8.061 \cdot 10^7$

3 $1.29 \cdot 10^{-7}$

4 $9,480,000$

5 $.0000000307$

6 $556,000,000,000$

7 $1.25 \cdot 10^4 = 12,500$
   $8.16 \cdot 10^3 = 8,160$

8 $-3.08 \cdot 10^6 = -3,080,000$
   $-7.9 \cdot 10^7 = -79,000,000$

9 $6.31 \cdot 10^{-8} = .0000000631$
   $9.4 \cdot 10^{-5} = .000094$

10 $5.4976 \cdot 10^{10}$

11 $-4.343 \cdot 10^{-4}$

12 $-1.0609 \cdot 10^{-14}$

13 $2 \cdot 10^{13}$

14 $4 \cdot 10^{-6}$

15 $1.5 \cdot 10^{10}$

CHAPTER 33

SQUARE AND CUBE ROOTS

1 ± 7

2 ± 11

3 ± 15

4 $\pm \dfrac{1}{6}$

5 ± 4.5

6 $-.5$

7 117

8 2

9   -8

10   12

11   $\frac{-1}{9}$

12   -4 + 1.85 = -2.15

13   7 • 6 = 42

14   $\frac{-5}{10}$ = -.5

15   Nelson assumed that the square root of all numbers can be found by dividing by 2. This is not true. This method will only work for the number 4.

CHAPTER 34

COMPARING IRRATIONAL NUMBERS

1   $\frac{-2}{3}$ • 3.14 = -2.09

2   $\sqrt{16} + \sqrt{50}$ = 4 + 7.07 = 11.07

3   $-(\sqrt{82}) - \sqrt{38}$ = -9.06 - 6.16 = -15.22

4   $\sqrt{50}$ • π = 7.07 • 3.14 = 22.1998 = 22.20

5   $\frac{\pi}{3}$ = 1.046666667 = 1.05

6   $\sqrt{47} + 3^2 + \sqrt{88}$ = 6.86 + 9 + 9.38 = 25.24

7   $\sqrt{95}$ = 9.75
    2π = 6.28
    $\sqrt{29}$ = 5.39
    Least to greatest: $\sqrt{29}$, 2π, $\sqrt{95}$

8   $-\sqrt{74}$ = -8.60
    -4^3 = -64
    $-\sqrt{68}$ = -8.25
    Greatest to least: $-\sqrt{68}$, $-\sqrt{74}$, -4^3

9   10.49

10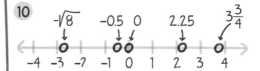

CHAPTER 35

EQUATIONS

1   h - 15
    31 - 15 = 16

2   78 + 3m
    78 + 3(-6)
    78 + (-18) = 60

3   $\frac{5}{8}k + 11$
    $\frac{5}{8}(48) + 11$
    30 + 11 = 41

4 |7mn|
    |7(-1) (32)|
    |-224| = 224

5   $-6s + 4v^2$
    -6(-3) + 4(4²)
    18 + 64 = 82

6   $\frac{2xy - 8}{xy + 15}$
    $\frac{2(-2)(7) - 8}{(-2)(7) + 15}$
    $\frac{-36}{1}$ = -36

7 $d = -c + 11$

$d = -18 + 11$

$d = -7$

Check: $-7 = -18 + 11$

$-7 = -7$

8 $d = 22 - |3p|$

$d = 22 - |3(-5)|$

$d = 22 - 15$

$d = 7$

Check: $7 = 22 - 15$

$7 = 7$

9 $d = 16m^3$

$d = 16 \cdot -3^3$

$d = 16 \cdot -27$

$d = -432$

Check: $-432 = 16 \cdot -27$

$-432 = -432$

10 $125 - z \div 12 = d$

$125 - 60 \div 12 = d$

$125 - 5 = d$

$120 = d$

Check: $120 = 125 - 5$

$120 = 120$

11 $d = \dfrac{5c - a}{b + 21}$

$d = \dfrac{5(-13) - (-4)}{-8 + 21}$

$d = \dfrac{-65 + 4}{13}$

$d = \dfrac{-61}{13}$

Check: $\dfrac{-61}{13} = \dfrac{-65 + 4}{13}$

$\dfrac{-61}{13} = \dfrac{-61}{13}$

12 $7v(4w^2 - 92) = d$

$7(-10)(4 \cdot 5^2 - 92) = d$

$-70 \cdot (100 - 92) = d$

$-70 \cdot 8 = d$

$-560 = d$

Check: $-560 = -70 \cdot 8$

$-560 = -560$

CHAPTER 36

SOLVING FOR VARIABLES

1 $r + 21 = -148$

$-21 \quad\ -21$

$r = -169$

2 $x - 9 = 33$

$+9 \quad +9$

$x = 42$

3 $14n = -70$

$\dfrac{14n}{14} = \dfrac{-70}{14}$

$n = -5$

4 $-62 + s = -218$

$+62 \qquad +62$

$s = -156$

5 $\dfrac{9g}{9} = \dfrac{117}{9}$

$g = 13$

6 $\dfrac{-81}{-3} = \dfrac{-3p}{-3}$

$p = 27$

7 $\dfrac{y}{4} = 196$

$4\left(\dfrac{y}{4}\right) = 196(4)$

$y = 784$

8 $w \div 22 = 60$

$\quad \times 22 \quad \times 22$

$\quad w = 1,320$

9 $\frac{1}{2}d = -52$

$\quad (\frac{2}{1})\frac{1}{2}d = -52(\frac{2}{1})$

$\quad d = -104$

10 $c^2 = 400$

$\quad c = \sqrt{400}$

$\quad c = \pm 20$

11 $216 = b^3$

$\quad b = \sqrt[3]{216}$

$\quad b = 6$

12 $m^2 = 343$

$\quad m = \sqrt{343}$

$\quad m = 18.52$

CHAPTER 37

SOLVING MULTISTEP EQUATIONS

1 $8r + 16 = 96$

$\quad -16 \quad -16$

$\quad 8r = 80$

$\quad r = 10$

2 $-3x - 25 = -100$

$\quad\quad +25 \quad +25$

$\quad -3x = -75$

$\quad x = 25$

3 $11y + 3 - 6y + 28 = 96$

$\quad 5y + 31 = 96$

$\quad\quad -31 \quad -31$

$\quad 5y = 65$

$\quad y = 13$

4 $17n + 8 = 104 + 5n$

$\quad\quad -5n \quad\quad -5n$

$\quad 12n + 8 = 104$

$\quad -8 \quad\quad -8$

$\quad 12n = 96$

$\quad n = 8$

5 $\frac{d}{4} + 17 = -3$

$\quad 4(\frac{d}{4}) + (4)17 = -3(4)$

$\quad d + 68 = -12$

$\quad\quad -68 \quad -68$

$\quad d = -80$

6 $74 - 2m = -5(m - 4)$

$\quad 74 - 2m = -5m + 20$

$\quad\quad +2m \quad +2m$

$\quad 74 = -3m + 20$

$\quad -20 \quad\quad -20$

$\quad 54 = -3m$

$\quad m = -18$

7 $2r - 7 + r = 1 + 4r$

$\quad 3r - 7 = 1 + 4r$

$\quad\quad -1 \quad -1$

$\quad 3r - 8 = 4r$

$\quad -3r \quad\quad -3r$

$\quad -8 = r$

8 $(b+7)(-12) = 48$

$-12b - 84 = 48$

$+84\ +84$

$-12b = 132$

$b = -11$

9 $12 = -(a+14) + 8$

$12 = -a - 14 + 8$

$12 = -a - 6$

$+6 +6$

$18 = -a$

$a = -18$

10 $\frac{2}{3}(4x - 16) = -8$

$\frac{3}{2} \cdot \frac{2}{3}(4x - 16) = -8 \cdot \frac{3}{2}$

$4x - 16 = -12$

$+16 +16$

$4x = 4$

$x = 1$

CHAPTER 38

SOLVING AND GRAPHING INEQUALITIES

1

2

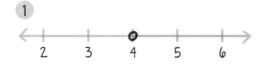

3

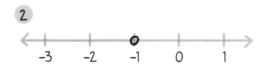

4 $n > -10$

5 $n \leq 6$

6 $n \leq 0$

7 $3a - 2 \geq a + 4$

$+2 +2$

$3a \geq a + 6$

$-a -a$

$\frac{2a}{2} \geq \frac{6}{2}$

$a \geq 3$

8 $-\frac{1}{6}(m + 12) \leq 8$

$-\frac{1}{6}m - 2 \leq 8$

$+2 +2$

$-\frac{6}{1}\left(-\frac{1}{6}m\right) \leq 10 \cdot \frac{-6}{1}$

$m \geq -60$

9 $-17 + 6b \geq -4b + 11$

$+17 +17$

$6b \geq -4b + 28$

$+4b +4b$

$10b \geq 28$

$b \geq 2.8 \text{ or } 2\frac{8}{10} \text{ or } 2\frac{4}{5}$

10 $-3(x-1) < -39$

$$\frac{-3(x-1)}{-3} > \frac{-39}{-3}$$

$x - 1 > 13$

$x > 14$

Sasha did not reverse the inequality sign when she divided by 3.

CHAPTER 39

WORD PROBLEMS WITH EQUATIONS AND INEQUALITIES

1 x = students enrolled in the traditional program

$319 + 168 + x = 652$

$487 + x = 652$

$x = 165$

165 students will be enrolled in the traditional program.

Check: $319 + 168 + 165 = 652$

2 x = a withdrawal

$956 - 4x = 656$

$-956 \qquad -956$

$-4x = -300$

$x = 75$

The amount of each withdrawal was $75.

Check: $956 - 4(75) = 656$

$656 = 656$

3 x = monthly fee

$(12x - 5) + 20 = 399$

$12x + 15 = 399$

$\qquad -15 \quad -15$

$12x = 384$

$x = 32$

Simon will pay $32 monthly.

Check: $12(32) - 5 + 20 = 399$

$399 = 399$

4 x = the number of flyers in each stack

$18x = 4{,}500$

$x = 250$

There are 250 flyers in each stack.

Check: $18(250) = 4{,}500$

$4{,}500 = 4{,}500$

5 x = least amount of weeks Tamera must babysit

$14x(12) \geq 1{,}008$

$168x \geq 1{,}008$

$x \geq 6$

The least amount of weeks Tamera must babysit is 6.

Check: $(14 \bullet 12) \bullet 6 \geq 1{,}008$

$1{,}008 \geq 1{,}008$

6 x = amount of T-shirts Adrian can purchase

$16x - 10 \leq 86$

$+10 \quad +10$

$16x \geq 96$

$x \geq 6$

Adrian can purchase at least 6 T-shirts.

Check: $16(6) - 10 \leq 86$

$86 \leq 86$

7 x = greatest number of people Marla can invite

$16x \leq 1,620$

$x \leq 101.25$

The greatest amount of people that Marla can invite is 101.

Check: $16(101.25) \leq 1,620$

$1,620 \leq 1,620$

8 x = cost of child's ticket

$x + x + 5 = 23$

$2x + 5 = 23$

$-5 \quad -5$

$2x = 18$

$x = 9$

The cost of a child's ticket is $9.

Check: $9 + 9 + 5 = 23$

$23 = 23$

9 x = number of hours rented

$5x + 15 = 45$

$-15 \quad -15$

$5x = 30$

$x = 6$

Maron used the bike for 6 hours.

Check: $5(6) + 15 = 45$

$45 = 45$

10 x = hours Christy could work

$12x + 350 \leq 890$

$-350 \quad -350$

$12x \leq 540$

$x \leq 45$

Christy possibly worked 45 hours.

Check: $12(45) + 350 \leq 890$

$890 \leq 890$

UNIT 4
Geometry

CHAPTER 40

INTRODUCTION TO GEOMETRY

1. Vertex: ∠B or ∠ABC or ∠CBA
   Ray: BA
   Ray: BC

2. line segment, ray, line

3. Obtuse: ∠XYZ or ∠ZYX or ∠Y
   Acute: ∠RST or ∠TSR or ∠S

4. Pyramid: three-dimensional figure
   Heptagon: two-dimensional figure

5.

   8 cm

   _____

   5 in.

6.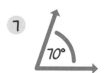
   125°

7. 70°

8.

9.

10. ⟨angle figures⟩

CHAPTER 41

ANGLES

1. **Obtuse angles** are greater than 90° but less than 180°.

2. **Complementary** angles are two angles that add up to 90°.

3. **Adjacent** angles are two angles that share a vertex and common side.

4. ∠C = 136°
   ∠D = 44°

5. ∠x = 25°

6. ∠JHI = 55°

7. ∠H = 140°

8. Adjacent angles = ∠A and ∠B, ∠B and ∠C, ∠C and ∠D, ∠D and ∠E, ∠A and ∠E

9. ∠C, ∠D and ∠E form a straight angle; ∠B, ∠C, and ∠D form a straight angle

10. ∠B = 35°

CHAPTER 42

QUADRILATERALS AND AREA

1. $A = b \cdot h$
   $A = 3 \cdot 8$
   $A = 24 \, cm^2$

2. $A = b \cdot h$
   $A = 12 \cdot 7$
   $A = 84 \, in.^2$

3. $A = b \cdot h$
   $A = 16 \cdot 9$
   $A = 144 \, ft.^2$

4. $A = b \cdot h$
   $A = 10.5 \cdot 10.5$
   $A = 110.25 \, m^2$

5. $A = \dfrac{b1 + b2}{2} \cdot h$
   $A = \dfrac{8 + 16}{2} \cdot 5$
   $A = 60 \, cm^2$

6. Area of the rectangle $= b \cdot h$
   $A = 32 \cdot 16$
   $A = 512 \, ft.^2$

   Area of the square $= b \cdot h$
   $A = 14 \cdot 14$
   $A = 196 \, ft.^2$
   $512 + 196 = 708 \, ft.^2$
   The area of Pedro's living space is 708 ft.²

7. $P = b + h + b + h$
   $P = 18.288 + 15.24 + 18.288 + 15.24$
   $P = 67.056$
   $P = 67 \, m$
   The perimeter of the property is 67 m.

8. $A = l \cdot w$
   $A = 360 \cdot 160$
   $A = 57,600 \, ft.^2$
   The square footage of the football field is 57,600 ft.²

9. $A = \dfrac{b1 + b2}{2} \cdot h$
   $A = \dfrac{9 + 6}{2} \cdot 8$
   $A = 7.5 \cdot 8$
   The new playground sandbox is 60 ft.²

10. Perimeter of trapezoid
    $20 + 17 + 36 + 17$
    $P = 90 \, cm$

    Perimeter of the other trapezoid
    $33 + 17 + 25 + 15$
    $P = 90 \, cm$

    Area of the trapezoid $= \dfrac{b_1 + b_2}{2} \cdot h$
    $A = \dfrac{20 + 36}{2} \cdot 15$
    $A = 42 \, cm^2$

    Area of the other
    trapezoid $= \dfrac{b_1 + b_2}{2} \cdot h$

$A = \dfrac{33 + 25}{2} \cdot 15$

$A = 435 \text{ cm}^2$

Cheryl is correct. The perimeters are the same but the areas are different.

CHAPTER 43

TRIANGLES AND AREA

1 $A = \dfrac{1}{2}bh$

$A = \dfrac{1}{2}(14)(9)$

$A = 63 \text{ yd.}^2$

2 $A = \dfrac{1}{2}(5)(8)$

$A = 20 \text{ mm}^2$

3 $A = \dfrac{1}{2}(14)(2)$

$A = 14 \text{ yd.}^2$

4 $A = \dfrac{1}{2}(14)(2)$

$A = 14 \text{ yd.}^2$

5 $A = \dfrac{1}{2}(18)(10)$

$A = 90 \text{ ft.}^2$

6 $A = \dfrac{1}{2}(32)(9.5)$

$A = 152 \text{ ft.}^2$

7 Area of left triangle $= \dfrac{1}{2}bh$

$A = \dfrac{1}{2}(15)(20)$

$A = 150 \text{ ft.}^2$

Area of right triangle $= \dfrac{1}{2}bh$

$A = \dfrac{1}{2}(38)(42)$

$A = 798 \text{ ft.}^2$

$150 + 798 = 948 \text{ ft.}^2$

The area of Emily's patio is 948 ft.^2

8 $A = \dfrac{1}{2}(8)(16.25)$

$A = 65 \text{ ft.}^2$

The area of the sail is 65 ft.^2

9 $A = \dfrac{1}{2}(45)(25)$

$A = 562.5 \text{ ft.}^2$

The area of the space is 562.5 ft.^2

10 Both Bella and Robert are correct. They just have different approaches. The area of triangle ABC is the same as the combined area of triangles ABD and CBD.

CHAPTER 44

THE PYTHAGOREAN THEOREM

1 $a^2 + b^2 = c^2$

$16^2 + 12^2 = c^2$

$c^2 = 400$

$c = \sqrt{400}$

$c = 20 \text{ mm}$

2 $5^2 + b^2 = 13^2$

$25 + b^2 = 169$

$-25 \qquad -25$

$b^2 = 144$

$b = \sqrt{144}$

$b = 12 \text{ ft.}$

3 $7^2 + 6^2 = c^2$

$c^2 = 85$

$c = \sqrt{85} \text{ cm}$

4 $24^2 + b^2 = 25^2$

$576 + b^2 = 625$

$-576 \qquad -576$

$b^2 = 49$
$b = \sqrt{49}$
$b = 7$ in.

5 $4.8^2 + b^2 = 6.4^2$
$b^2 = 17.92$
$b = \sqrt{17.92}$ m

6 $a^2 + b^2 = c^2$
$a^2 + 5^2 = 13^2$
$a^2 = 144$
$a = \sqrt{144}$
$a = 12$ ft.
The roof of the home is 20 feet above the ground, and the ladder will only reach 12 feet.

7 $40^2 + 9^2 = c^2$
$c^2 = 1681$
$c = \sqrt{1681}$ ft.
$c^2 = 41$ ft.
The wire is 41 feet long.

8 $a^2 + 4^2 = 10^2$
$a^2 = 84$
$a = \sqrt{84}$ ft.
The oak tree is $\sqrt{84}$ feet tall.

9 $3^2 + b^2 = 35^2$
$b^2 = 1081$
$b = \sqrt{1215}$ ft.
The distance between the base of the ramp and the building is $\sqrt{1215}$ feet.

10 $14^2 + 15^2 ? 16^2$
$421 \neq 256$
Paul is incorrect because $a^2 + b^2 \neq c^2$.

CHAPTER 45

CIRCLES, CIRCUMFERENCE, AND AREA

1

2 $C = \pi d$
$C = 3.14 \cdot 8$
$C = 25.12$ cm

3 $C = 2\pi r$
$C = (2)(\frac{22}{7})(7)$
$C = 44$ in.

4 $C = \pi d$
$C = 3.14 \cdot 4.25$
$C = 13.345$
$C = 13.35$ cm

5 $A = \pi r^2$
$A = (3.14)(6.5)^2$
$A = 132.665$
$A = 132.67$ cm^2

6 $A = \pi r^2$
$A = \frac{22}{7} \cdot 3^2$
$A = 28.29$ in.^{2}

7 $A = \pi r^2$
   $A = 3.14 \cdot 8^2$
   $A = 200.96 \, cm^2$

8 $A = \pi r^2$
   $A = 3.14 \cdot 6^2$
   $A = 113.04 \, yd.^2$

9 $C = \pi d$
   $C = 3.14 \cdot 6$
   $C = 18.84 \, ft.$
   The circumference of the
   circle to be cut is 18.84 ft.

10 $C = \pi d$
    $C = (\frac{22}{7})(7)$
    $C = 22 \, cm$
    The circumference of the
    cupcake is 22 cm.

11 $A = \pi r^2$
    $A = 3.14 \cdot 9^2$
    $A = 254.34 \, in.^2$
    The area of the plant is 254.34 in.²

    $C = \pi d$
    $C = 3.14 \cdot 18$
    $C = 56.52 \, in.$
    The circumference of the
    plant is 56.52 inches.

12 $A = \pi r^2$
    $A = 3.14 \cdot 10^2$
    $A = 314 \, in.^2$
    The area that must be
    marked is 314 in².

CHAPTER 46

THREE-DIMENSIONAL FIGURES

1 Sphere: D

2 Triangular prism: A

3 Regular polyhedron: F

4 3-D figure: C

5 Polyhedron: E

6 Octahedron: G

7 Rectangular pyramid: H

8 3-D figure: B

9 The vertical cross section of a
   rectangular prism is a rectangle.
   The diagonal cross section
   of a rectangular prism
   is a parallelogram.

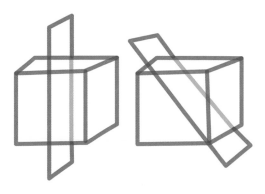

10 You can cut a cone vertically to get a triangle. You can cut a rectangular pyramid horizontally to get a rectangle.

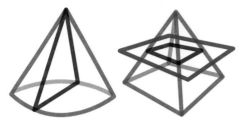

11 Pyramids and prisms are both polyhedra. A prism has two bases, while a pyramid has only one base. The sides of a prism are rectangles or parallelograms, while the sides of a pyramid are triangles.

12 Regular polyhedron: All faces are identical polygons, such as a cube (all squares). A cylinder and a cone are not regular polyhedra. All their faces are not identical polygons.

CHAPTER 47

VOLUME

1 $V = (lw) \cdot \text{height of prism}$
$V = (7)(3)(11)$
$V = 231 \, cm^3$

2 $V = (\frac{1}{3}bh) \cdot \text{height of prism}$
$V = (\frac{1}{3} \cdot 6 \cdot 10) \cdot 14$
$V = 280 \, in.^3$

3 $V = \frac{1}{3}(\pi r^2) \cdot \text{height of cone}$
$V = \frac{1}{3}(3.14 \cdot 4^2) \cdot 12$
$V = 200.96 \, ft.^3$

4 $V = (lw) \cdot \text{height of prism}$
$V = (9)(9)(9)$
$V = 729 \, cm^3$

5 $V = \frac{1}{3}(\pi r^2) \cdot \text{height of cone}$
$V = \frac{1}{3}(3.14 \cdot 8^2) \cdot 16$
$V = 1,071.79 \, mm^3$

6 $V = \frac{4}{3}\pi r^3$
$V = \frac{4}{3}(3.14 \cdot 30^3)$
$V = 113,040 \, cm^3$

7 $V = (\frac{1}{2}bh) \cdot \text{height of prism}$
$V = (\frac{1}{2} \cdot 12 \cdot 6) \cdot 14$
$V = 504 \, yd.^3$

8 Yum Treats
$V = (lw) \cdot \text{height of prism}$
$V = 4 \cdot 4 \cdot 6$
$V = 96 \, in.^3$

Tasty Treats
$V = (\pi r^2) \cdot \text{height of cylinder}$

$V = 3.14 \bullet 3^2 \bullet 4$

$V = 113.04$ in.^{3}

Tasty Treats are a better buy because the volume of their container is greater.

9 $V = (lw) \bullet$ height of prism

$V = 20 \bullet 10 \bullet 5$

$V = 1,000$ ft.^{3}

The pool will hold 1,000 ft.^{3}

CHAPTER 48

SURFACE AREA

1 Surface area of cube =
$(7 \bullet 7) \bullet 6$ sides = 294 ft.^{2}

2 Surface area of rectangular prism = Base1 + Base2 + Side1 + Side2 + Side3 + Side4

Surface area = $(16 \bullet 8) + (16 \bullet 8) + (16 \bullet 3) + (16 \bullet 3) + (8 \bullet 3) + (8 \bullet 3)$

Surface area = 128 m^2 + 128 m^2 + 48 m^2 + 48 m^2 + 24 m^2 + 24 m^2 = 400 m^2

3 Surface area of cylinder = Base1 + Base2 + Lateral Area

First, find the circumference of the base. The formula is C = πd.

$C = (3.14)(6)$

$C = 18.84$ cm

Then, find the area of the rectangular lateral area.

$A = l \bullet w$

$A = 16 \bullet 18.84$

$A = 301.44$ cm^2

Then, find the area of the bases.

$A = \pi r^2$

$A = 3.14(3^2)$

$A = 28.26$ cm^2

Add up all the surface areas:

Base1 + Base2 + Lateral Area = 28.26 cm^2 + 28.26 cm^2 + 301.44 cm^2 = 357.96 cm^2

Surface area of cylinder = 357.96 cm^2

4 Surface area of triangular prism = Base1 + Base2 + Side1 + Side2 + Side3

Surface area = $\frac{1}{2}(12)(5) + \frac{1}{2}(12)(5) + 12(16) + 5(16) + 13(16)$

Surface area = 30 ft.^{2} + 30 ft.^{2} + 192 ft.^{2} + 80 ft.^{2} + 208 ft.^{2} = 540 ft.^{2}

5 Surface area of sphere = $4\pi r^2$

Surface area = $4(3.14)(8)^2$ = 803.84 in.^{2}

6 Surface area of rectangular chest = Base1 + Base2 + Side1 + Side2 + Side3 + Side4

Surface area = $(4 \bullet 3) + (4 \bullet 3) + (6 \bullet 4) + (6 \bullet 4) + (6 \bullet 3) + (6 \bullet 3)$

Surface area = 12 ft.^{2} + 12 ft.^{2} + 24 ft.^{2} + 24 ft.^{2} + 18 ft.^{2} + 18 ft.^{2} = 108 ft.^{2}

7 Surface area of cylinder container = Base1 + Base2 + Lateral area (Length)

Surface area = $3.14(3)^2 + 3.14(3)^2 + \{[(2)\,(3.14)\,(3)] \bullet 16\} = 357.96$

8 Surface area of triangular prism sculpture = Base1 + Base2 + Side1 + Side2 + Side3

Surface area = $\frac{1}{2}(28)(21) + \frac{1}{2}(28)(21) + 21(33) + 35(33) + 28(33)$

Surface area = 294 in.^{2} + 294 in.^{2} + 693 in.^{2} + 1,155 in.^{2} + 924 in.^{2} = 3,360 in.^{2} of fabric

9 Surface area of cube = (5.5 • 5.5) • 6 sides = 181.5 in.^{2}

10 boxes • 181.5 in.^{2} of wrapping paper *per* box = 1,815 in.^{2} of wrapping paper

10 Surface area of sphere = $4\pi r^2$ = $4(3.14)(7)^2$ = 615.44 in.^{2} of glass is needed.

CHAPTER 49

ANGLES, TRIANGLES, AND TRANSVERSAL LINES

1 $\angle A = 41°$
   $\angle T = 104°$

2 $\angle Y = 105°$
   $\angle Z = 75°$

3 $\angle S = 37°$

4 $\angle 2 = 118°$
   $\angle 3 = 62°$
   $\angle 4 = 118°$
   $\angle 5 = 62°$

$\angle 6 = 118°$
$\angle 7 = 62°$
$\angle 8 = 118°$

5 $\angle H = 127°$
   $\angle I = 53°$
   $\angle J = 127°$
   $\angle K = 53°$
   $\angle L = 53°$
   $\angle M = 127°$
   $\angle N = 53°$

CHAPTER 50

SIMILAR FIGURES AND SCALE DRAWINGS

1 $\frac{x}{8} = \frac{2}{4}$
   $4x = 16$
   $x = 4$

2 $\frac{8}{24} = \frac{4}{y}$
   $8y = 96$
   $y = 12$

3 $77 + 36 = 113,\ 180 - 113 = 67$
   $\angle Q = 67°$

4 $\frac{m}{18} = \frac{5}{6}$
   $6m = 90$
   $m = 15$

5 $\frac{18}{21} = \frac{6}{n}$
   $18n = 126$
   $n = 7$

6 $\frac{2}{12} = \frac{16}{x}$

$2x = 192$

$x = 96$

Jacob and his family will travel 96 miles.

7 $\frac{4}{2} = \frac{36}{x}$

$4x = 72$

$x = 18$

Veronica can ride 18 miles.

8 $\frac{3}{36} = \frac{39}{x}$

$3x = 1{,}404$

$x = 468$

$\frac{3}{36} = \frac{48}{x}$

$3x = 1{,}728$

$x = 576$

$468 + 468 + 576 + 576 = 2{,}088$

The perimeter of the property is 2,088 feet.

9 $\frac{2}{4} = \frac{x}{32}$

$4x = 64$

$x = 16$

The drawing of the den is 16 inches long.

10 $\frac{2}{4} = \frac{x}{376}$

$4x = 752$

$x = 188$

The drawing of the route between Bart's house and his grandparents' house is 188 centimeters long.

UNIT 5
Statistics and Probability
CHAPTER 51
INTRODUCTION TO STATISTICS

1   A. Statistical
B. Statistical
C. Not statistical
D. Statistical
E. Not statistical

2   A. Qualitative
B. Quantitative
C. Quantitative
D. Qualitative
E. Quantitative

3   A. High variability
B. Low variability
C. Low variability
D. Low variability
E. High variability

4 $\frac{14}{34} \bullet 895 = 368.53 = 369$
369 actors are actively performing.

5 $\frac{6}{45} \bullet 315 = 42$
Carol can expect to send back 42 jump ropes.

6 $\frac{27}{1} \bullet 9 = 243$
The car wash will clean 243 cars.

7 $\frac{8}{1} \cdot 9 = 72$

There are about 72 blueberry mini-muffins in the box.

8 $\frac{19}{100} \cdot 1{,}881 = 357.39$

About 357 visitors were dressed as their favorite cartoon characters.

CHAPTER 52

MEASURES OF CENTRAL TENDENCY AND VARIATION

1 A. Mean

$$\frac{\begin{array}{c}40{,}000 + 74{,}250 + 78{,}000 + 74{,}250 \\ + \ 95{,}000 + 64{,}500 + 68{,}000 + \\ 72{,}000 + 62{,}050 + 58{,}950\end{array}}{10}$$

$= \$68{,}700$

B. Median

40,000, 58,950, 62,050, 64,500, 68,000, 72,000, 74,250, 74,250, 78,000, 95,000

68,000 + 72,000 = 140,000

÷ 2 = $70,000

C. The mode is $74,250.

D. Minimum: $40,000

Maximum: $95,000

E. Range

95,000 – 40,000 = $55,000

F. $40,000 is the lower outlier. $95,000 is the higher outlier. Outliers throw off the mean and give a skewed portrayal of the data.

2 A. Mean

$$\frac{\begin{array}{c}558 + 351 + 316 + 486 + 510 + \\ 398 + 600 + 545 + 510 + 815\end{array}}{10}$$

$= 508.9$

B. Median

316, 351, 398, 486, 510, 510, 545, 558, 600, 815

$\frac{510 + 510}{2} = 510$

C. The mode is 510.

D. Minimum: 316

Maximum: 815

E. Range

815 – 316 = 499

F. 815 is the higher outlier. Outliers throw off the mean and give a skewed portrayal of the data.

CHAPTER 53

DISPLAYING DATA

1 A. 9

B. 11

C. 25

D. 6

2

```
                    x
                    x
                    x        x
                    x   x    x
                    x   x    x
        x   x   x   x   x   x       x
        x   x   x   x   x   x   x   x   x   x
    ←───┼───┼───┼───┼───┼───┼───┼───┼───┼───┼──→
        1   2   3   4   5   6   7   8   9   10
```

Daily Intake of Fruits and Vegetables

3

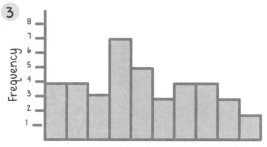

Daily Rainfall, March - May
(in millimeters)

4 1st Quartile = 22, Median = 41, 3rd
Quartile = 65

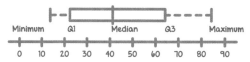

5 1st Quartile = 4.5, Median = 7, 3rd
Quartile = 8.5

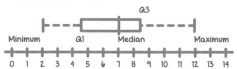

6 A.

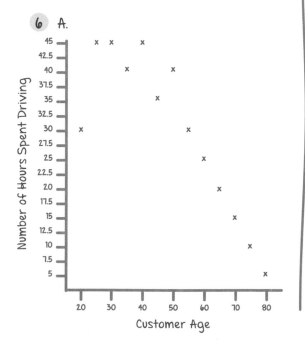

B. The scatter plot illustrates
a negative correlation since
the customer's age increases
as the number of hours
spent driving decreases.

CHAPTER 54

PROBABILITY

1 $\frac{1}{4} = 25\%$

2 red red, red blue, blue
red, blue blue $\frac{1}{4} = 25\%$

3 A. $\frac{4}{20} = \frac{1}{5} = 20\%$

B. $\frac{5}{20} = \frac{1}{4} = 25\%$

C. $\frac{6}{20} = \frac{3}{10} = 30\%$

D. $\frac{15}{20} = \frac{3}{4} = 75\%$

E. $\frac{16}{20} = \frac{4}{5} = 80\%$

4 A. $\frac{3}{6} = \frac{1}{2} = 50\%$

B. $\frac{(3, 4, 5, 6)}{6} = \frac{4}{6}$ or $\frac{2}{3}$ or 66%

C. $\frac{3}{6} = \frac{1}{2} = 50\%$

UNIT 6

The Coordinate Plane and Functions

CHAPTER 55

THE COORDINATE PLANE

1

	Ordered Pair	Location on the Coordinate Plane
A	(0, 6)	y-axis
B	(4, 0)	x-axis
C	(-7, 6)	Quadrant II
D	(-4, -3)	Quadrant III
E	(3, -4)	Quadrant IV
F	(5, 5)	Quadrant I
G	(-4, 1)	Quadrant II
H	(0, -6)	y-axis
I	(7, -6)	Quadrant IV
J	(-8, -6)	Quadrant III

2

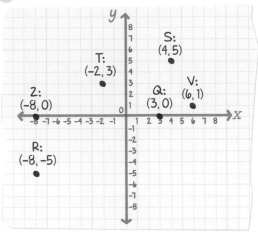

3 M:(-2, -5), N:(7, -5)

The points share the same y-coordinate.

$-2 - 7 = |-9|$

These points are 9 units apart.

4 $x_1 = -3, \quad y_1 = 2 \qquad x_2 = 12, \quad y_2 = 10$

Substitute these values into the Distance Formula. Use the Order of Operations to evaluate.

$d = \sqrt{(x_2 - x_1)^2 + (y_2 - y_1)^2}$

$d = \sqrt{(12 - (-3))^2 + (10 - 2)^2}$

$d = \sqrt{(15)^2 + (8)^2}$

$d = 17$

These points are 17 units apart.

CHAPTER 56

RELATIONS, LINES, AND FUNCTIONS

1 The numbers that make up the domain of the relation are:
0, 3, 5, −4

2 The numbers that make up the range of the relation are:
5, 1, 0, −3, −5

3 The relation is not a function because there are values in the domain that repeat.

4

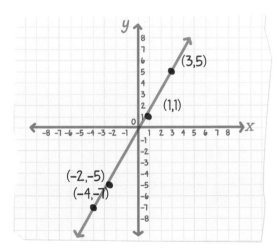

Yes, it is a function because when it's graphed, it passes the vertical line test.

5

Input (x)	Function: y = x − 6	Output (y)	Ordered Pair (x, y)
-1	y = -1 - 6	-7	(-1, -7)
0	y = 0 - 6	-6	(0, -6)
8	y = 8 - 6	2	(8, 2)
10	y = 10 - 6	4	(10, 4)

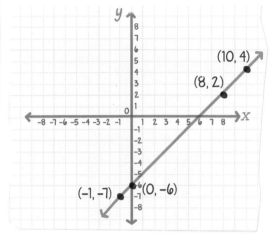

6

Input (x)	Function: $y = \frac{1}{2}x - 1$	Output (y)	Ordered Pair (x, y)
-2	$y = \frac{1}{2}(-2) - 1$	-2	(-2, -2)
0	$y = \frac{1}{2}(0) - 1$	-1	(0, -1)
2	$y = \frac{1}{2}(2) - 1$	0	(2, 0)
4	$y = \frac{1}{2}(4) - 1$	1	(4, 1)

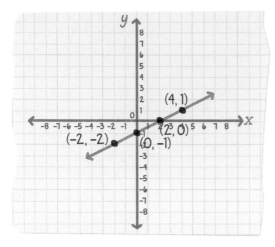

8

Input (x)	Function: y = -3 - 3x	Output (y)	Ordered Pair (x, y)
-3	y = -3 - 3(-3)	6	(-3, 6)
-2	y = -3 - 3(-2)	3	(-2, 3)
0	y = -3 - 3 (0)	-3	(0, -3)
2	y = -3 - 3(2)	-9	(2, -9)

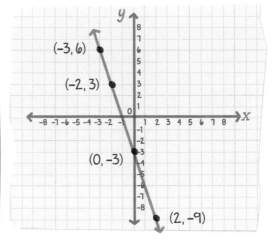

7

Input (x)	Function: y = -4x	Output (y)	Ordered Pair (x, y)
-2	y = -4(-2)	8	(-2, 8)
-1	y = -4(-1)	4	(-1, 4)
1	y = -4(1)	-4	(1, -4)
2	y = -4(2)	-8	(2, -8)

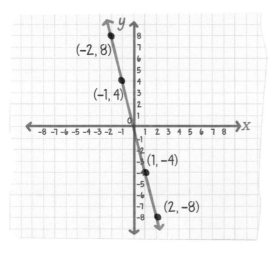

CHAPTER 57

SLOPE

1 B

2 A

3 C

4 D

5 Slope = $\frac{\text{Rise}}{\text{Run}} = \frac{8}{4} = 2$

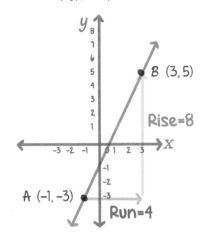

6 Slope = $\frac{\text{Rise}}{\text{Run}} = \frac{-6}{9} = \frac{-2}{3}$

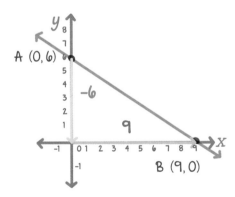

7 The slope of the line that passes through the points (4, –1) and (–2, –3) is $\frac{1}{3}$.

Slope $(m) = \frac{y_2 - y_1}{x_2 - x_1} =$
$\frac{-3 - (-1)}{-2 - 4} = \frac{-2}{-6} = \frac{2}{6} = \frac{1}{3}$

8 The slope of the line that passes through the points (12, –9) and (–6, 11) is $\frac{-10}{9}$.

Slope $(m) =$
$\frac{y_2 - y_1}{x_2 - x_1} = \frac{11 - (-9)}{-6 - 12} = \frac{20}{-18} = \frac{10}{-9}$

9 Slope = $\frac{\text{Rise}}{\text{Run}} = -\frac{1}{4}$

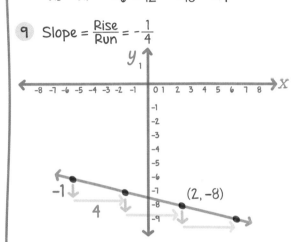

10 Slope = $\frac{\text{Rise}}{\text{Run}} = \frac{3}{1}$

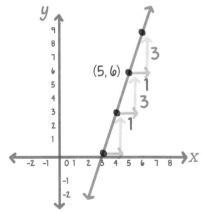

CHAPTER 58

LINEAR EQUATIONS AND FUNCTIONS

1 $y = -\frac{3}{5}x - 8$: slope $(m) = -\frac{3}{5}$ and y-intercept = (0, –8)

2 $y = 5x + 7$: slope $(m) = 5$
and y-intercept $= (0, 7)$

3 $\frac{1}{4}x = y$

$y = \frac{1}{4}x$: slope $(m) = \frac{1}{4}$ and

y-intercept $= (0, 0)$

4 $5x = 3y + 6$

$5x - 6 = 3y$

$\frac{5}{3}x - \frac{6}{3} = y$

$y = \frac{5}{3}x - 2$: slope $(m) = \frac{5}{3}$

and y-intercept $= (0, -2)$

5 $-x + 3 = \frac{y}{2}$

$y = -2x + 6$: slope $(m) = -2$
and y-intercept $= (0, 6)$

6 Graph of $y = -\frac{1}{3}x + 2$:

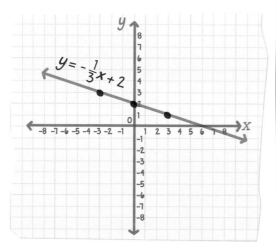

7 Graph of $y = \frac{3}{5}x - 1$:

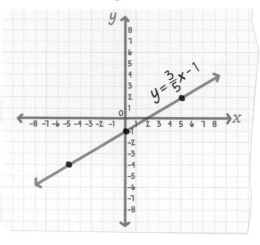

8 Graph of $2x + 2y = 6$ or $y = -x + 3$:

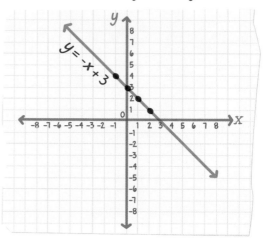

9 Graph of $y + 3 = -1$ or $y = -4$:

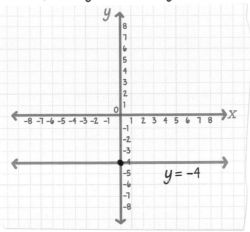

$y = -4$

10 Graph of $-6 + x = -4$ or $x = 2$:

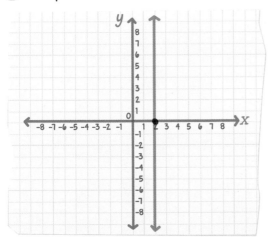

CHAPTER 59

SIMULTANEOUS LINEAR EQUATIONS AND FUNCTIONS

1 $x - y = -4$ or $y = x + 4$
$x + y = 2$ or $y = -x + 2$
Solution: $(-1, 3)$

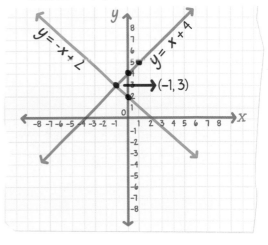

$y = -x + 2$
$y = x + 4$
$(-1, 3)$

2 $-3x + y = -1$ or $y = 3x - 1$
$-2x + y = 1$ or $y = 2x + 1$
Solution: $(2, 5)$

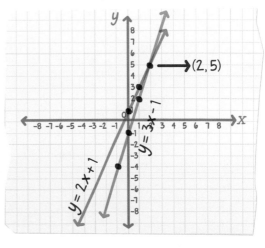

$(2, 5)$
$y = 3x - 1$
$y = 2x + 1$

3 $-\frac{1}{4}x - y = -2$ or $y = -\frac{1}{4}x + 2$

$-\frac{1}{4}x - y = -1$ or $y = -\frac{1}{4}x + 1$

Since these lines are parallel and do not intersect, there is no solution,

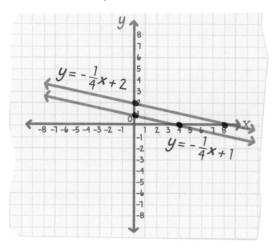

4 $\frac{1}{2}x + y = 0$ or $y = -\frac{1}{2}x$

$-3x - 2y = 4$ or $y = -\frac{3}{2}x - 2$

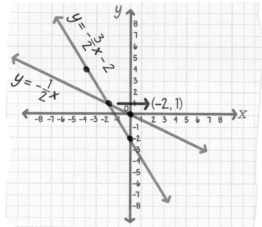

5 Addition Method

$2x - y = 2$

$-3x - 2y = -10$

Multiply each term in the first equation by –2. Add the rewritten equation one and equation two together.

$-4x + 2y = -4$

$-3x - 2y = -10$

_____

$-7x + 0 = -14$

$-7x = -14$

$x = 2$

Substitute $x = 2$ into one of the equations to find the y-coordinate.

$2x - y = 2$

$2(2) - y = 2$

$4 - y = 2$

$-y = -2$

$y = 2$

Solution: (2, 2)

6 Addition Method

$-3x + 3y = 6$

$-4x + y = -4$

Multiply each term in the second equation by –3. Add equation one and the rewritten equation two together.

$-3x + 3y = 6$
$12x - 3y = 12$
_____
$9x + 0 = 18$
$9x = 18$
$x = 2$

Substitute $x = 2$ into one of the equations to find the y-coordinate.

$-3x + 3y = 6$
$-3(2) + 3y = 6$
$-6 + 3y = 6$
$3y = 12$
$y = 4$

Solution: $(2, 4)$

7 Substitution Method
$4x + 2y = 26$
$x - y = -4$

Rewrite the second equation to isolate the y-variable.
$x - y = -4$
$-y = -x - 4$
$y = x + 4$

Substitute $y = x + 4$ into the first equation.
$4x + 2(x + 4) = 26$
$4x + 2x + 8 = 26$
$6x + 8 = 26$
$6x = 18$
$x = 3$

Substitute $x = 3$ into one of the equations to find the y-coordinate.

$x - y = -4$
$3 - y = -4$
$-y = -7$
$y = 7$

Solution: $(3, 7)$

8 Substitution Method
$-2x - y = -7$
$-4x + 4y = -8$

Rewrite the first equation to isolate the y-variable.

$-2x - y = -7$
$-y = 2x - 7$
$y = -2x + 7$

Substitute $y = -2x + 7$ into the second equation.

$-4x + 4(-2x + 7) = -8$
$-4x - 8x + 28 = -8$
$-12x + 28 = -8$
$-12x = -36$
$x = 3$

Substitute $x = 3$ into one of the equations to find the y-coordinate.

$-2x - y = -7$
$-2(3) - y = -7$
$-6 - y = -7$
$-y = -1$
$y = 1$

Solution: $(3, 1)$

CHAPTER 60

NONLINEAR FUNCTIONS

1

Input (x)	Function y = 4x²	Output (y)	Coordinate Points (x, y)
-2	y = 4(-2)²	16	(-2, 16)
-1	y = 4(-1)²	4	(-1, 4)
0	y = 4(0)²	0	(0, 0)
1	y = 4(1)²	4	(1, 4)
2	y = 4(2)²	16	(2, 16)

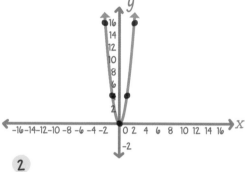

2

Input (x)	Function y = -3x² - 1	Output (y)	Coordinate Points (x, y)
-2	y = -3(-2)² - 1	-13	(-2, -13)
-1	y = -3(-1)² - 1	-4	(-1, -4)
0	y = -3(0)² - 1	-1	(0, -1)
1	y = -3(1)² - 1	-4	(1, -4)
2	y = -3(2)² - 1	-13	(2, -13)

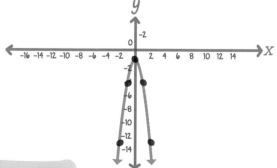

3

Input (x)	Function y = -|2x|	Output (y)	Coordinate Points (x, y)
-4	y = - |2(-4)|	-8	(-4, -8)
-2	y = - |2(-2)|	-4	(-2, -4)
0	y = - |2(0)|	0	(0, 0)
2	y = - |2(2)|	-4	(2, -4)
4	y = - |2(4)|	-8	(4, -8)

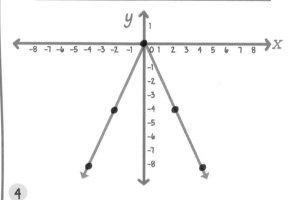

4

Input (x)	Function y = -|3x| - 4	Output (y)	Coordinate Points (x, y)
-4	y = -|3(-4)| - 4	-16	(-4, -16)
-2	y = -|3(-2)| - 4	-10	(-2, -10)
0	y = -|3(0)| - 4	-4	(0, -4)
2	y = -|3(2)| - 4	-10	(2, -10)
4	y = -|3(4)| - 4	-16	(4, -16)

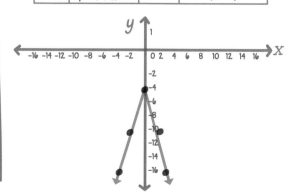

CHAPTER 61

POLYGONS AND THE COORDINATE PLANE

1 The shape formed by the points is a trapezoid.

2 The shape formed by the points is a square.

3 The shape formed by the points is a trapezoid.

4 The shape formed by the points is a pentagon.

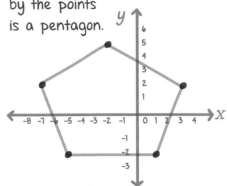

5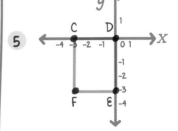

The coordinates of Point F, the 4th vertex, are (–3, –3).

6 The coordinates of Point T, the 4th vertex, are (6, –3).

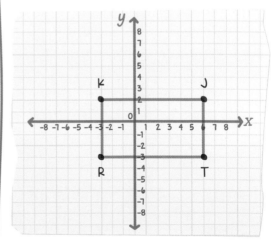

7 The coordinates of Point P, the 4th vertex, are (–2, 4).

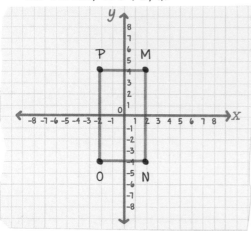

8 The coordinates of Point D, the 4th vertex, are (3, 0).

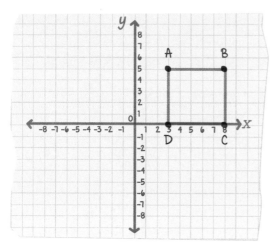

CHAPTER 62

TRANSFORMATIONS

1

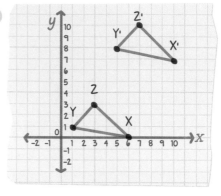

Original	Translation: (x + 4, y + 7)	Image
X (6, 0)	(6 + 4, 0 + 7)	X' (10, 7)
Y (1, 1)	(1 + 4, 1 + 7)	Y' (5, 8)
Z (3, 3)	(3 + 4, 3 + 7)	Z' (7, 10)

2

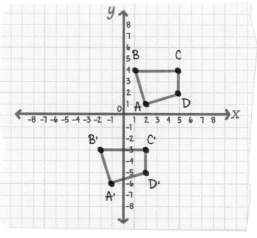

Original	Translation: (x – 3, y – 7)	Image
A (2, 1)	(2 – 3, 1 – 7)	A' (-1, -6)
B (1, 4)	(1 – 3, 4 – 7)	B' (-2, -3)
C (5, 4)	(5 – 3, 4 – 7)	C' (2, -3)
D (5, 2)	(5 – 3, 2 – 7)	D' (2, -5)

3

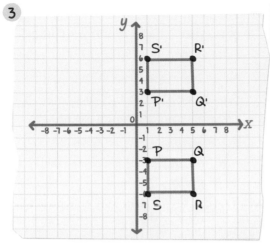

Original	Reflection over the x-axis	Image
P (1, -3)	3 units from x-axis	P' (1, 3)
Q (5, -3)	3 units from x-axis	Q' (5, 3)
R (5, -6)	6 units from x-axis	R' (5, 6)
S (1, -6)	6 units from x-axis	S' (1, 6)

4

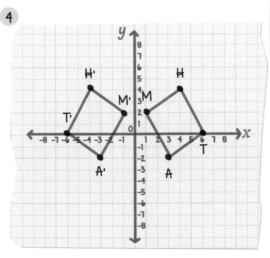

Original	Reflection over the y-axis	Image
M (1, 2)	1 unit from y-axis	M' (-1, 2)
A (3, -2)	3 units from y-axis	A' (-3, -2)
T (6, 0)	6 units from y-axis	T' (-6, 0)
H (4, 4)	4 units from y-axis	H' (-4, 4)

5

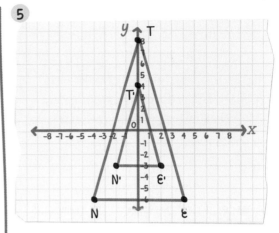

Original	Dilation $\frac{1}{2}$	Image
T (0, 8)	$(0 \cdot \frac{1}{2}, 8 \cdot \frac{1}{2})$	T' (0, 4)
E (4, -6)	$(4 \cdot \frac{1}{2}, -6 \cdot \frac{1}{2})$	E' (2, -3)
N (-4, -6)	$(-4 \cdot \frac{1}{2}, -6 \cdot \frac{1}{2})$	N' (-2, -3)

6

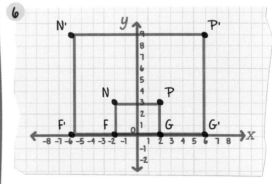

Original	Dilation 3	Image
F (-2, 0)	(-2·3, 0·3)	F' (-6, 0)
G (2, 0)	(2·3, 0·3)	G' (6, 0)
P (2, 3)	(2·3, 3·3)	P' (6, 9)
N (-2, 3)	(-2·3, 3·3)	N' (-6, 9)

7 The polygon is situated in quadrant IV. It is rotated 270° clockwise around the center, which means it rotates three quadrants. So, the *y*-coordinates become positive because the rotation moves the points L'K'J'O' to quadrant 1.

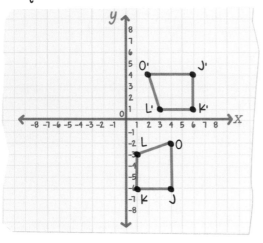

Original	Image
L (1, −3)	L' (3, 1)
K (1, −6)	K' (6, 1)
J (4, −6)	J' (6, 4)
O (4, −2)	O' (2, 4)

8 The polygon is situated in quadrant II. It is rotated 180° clockwise around the center, which means it rotates two quadrants. So, the *x*-coordinates become positive and the *y*-coordinates become negative because the rotation moves the points W'S'Z' to quadrant IV.

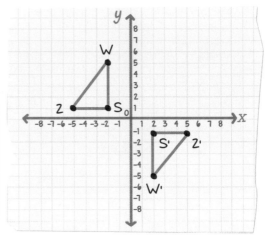

Original	Image
W (−2, 5)	W' (2, −5)
S (−2, 1)	S' (2, −1)
Z (−5, 1)	Z' (5, −1)

CHAPTER 63

PROPORTIONAL RELATIONSHIPS AND GRAPHS

1. $\dfrac{9}{6} = \dfrac{12}{x}$ $\dfrac{12}{8} = \dfrac{15}{x}$

   $9x = 12(6)$ $12x = 15(8)$

   $9x = 72$ $12x = 120$

   $x = 8$ $x = 10$

Number of Student Applicants	Number of Students Accepted
3	2
6	4
9	6
12	8
15	10

2.

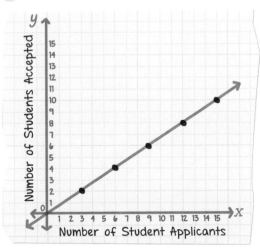

3. This is a proportional relationship because the graph forms a straight line that goes through the origin (0, 0).

4. The weekly fundraising table does not show a proportional relationship because the ratios are not equivalent and the graph does not form a straight line that goes through the origin (0, 0).

Week	Dollar Amount Collected
1	$16
2	$18
3	$22
4	$25

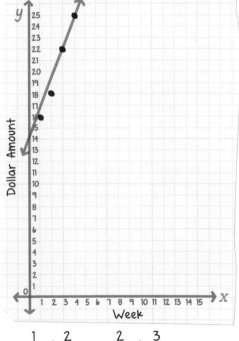

$\dfrac{1}{16} \neq \dfrac{2}{18}$ $\dfrac{2}{18} \neq \dfrac{3}{22}$

5. This is a proportional relationship because the ratios are equivalent.

   $\dfrac{8}{20} = \dfrac{6}{15}$

   $8(15) = 6(20)$

   $120 = 120$

6 For every hour of volunteer work, the students earn 4 points. This is the unit rate.

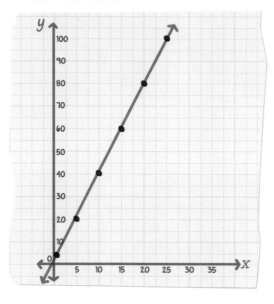

Hours of Volunteer Work	Number of Points Earned
1	4
5	20
10	40
15	60
20	80
25	100

Everything You Need to Ace Math is right here!

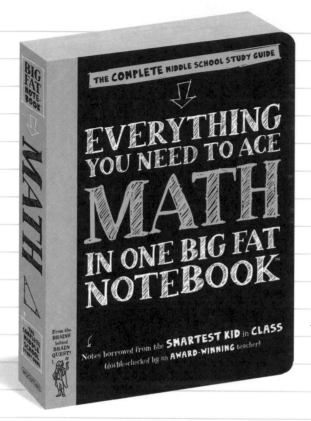

The **Big Fat Notebook** makes all the stuff you need to know sink in with key concepts reinforced through **mnemonic devices, easy-to-understand definitions, doodles, and diagrams.**

ACE ALGEBRA AND GEOMETRY, TOO!

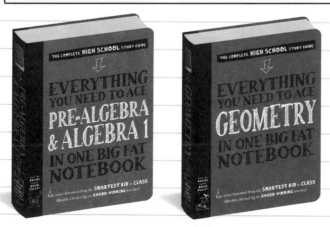

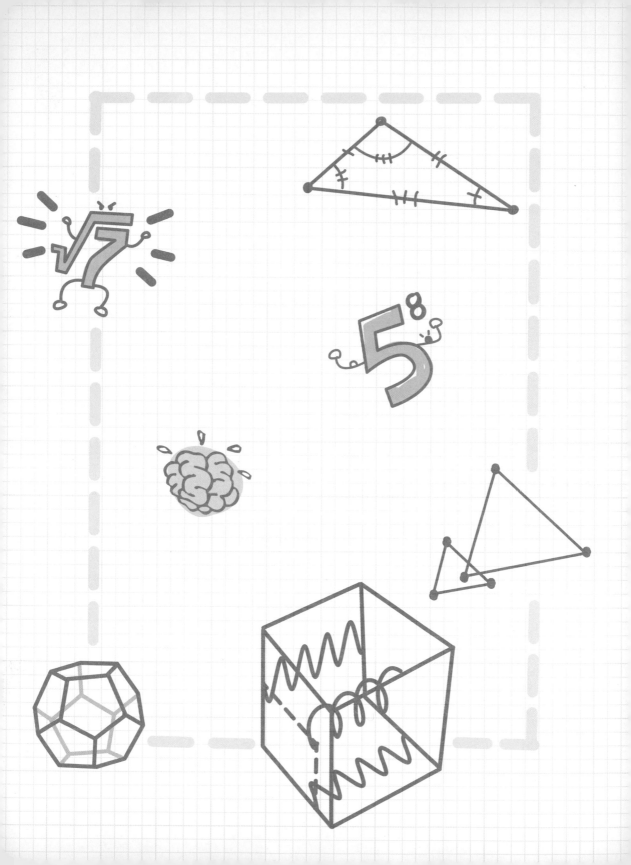